Justice Reinvestment

Rising prison numbers on both sides of the Atlantic are cause for concern. Justice Reinvestment is a major movement in criminal justice reform in the US that is also attracting lots of interest in the UK. Justice Reinvestment is an approach to addressing the penal crisis that uses the best available evidence to re-direct resources to more effective rehabilitation of offenders and better "prehabilitation". It takes a holistic view of criminal justice and is particularly concerned to address the community dimensions of offending and re-offending. The authors highlight competing models of Justice Reinvestment and argue for a more radical version in which criminal justice reform is seen as part of a wider social justice reform programme.

This is the first substantial publication on Justice Reinvestment and shows that the movement has huge potential to re-shape the criminal justice system. It will be essential reading for undergraduate and post-graduate students with an interest in criminal justice reform. Practitioners and policy-makers working in the criminal justice systems of both the US and the UK will also value the fresh perspective it brings to criminal justice reform and its breadth of coverage, including insights into the penal crisis, different models of Justice Reinvestment, the use of criminal justice data and research evidence in redesigning criminal justice services, and new approaches to commissioning.

Chris Fox is Professor of Evaluation at Manchester Metropolitan University and Director of the Policy Evaluation and Research Unit there. He has undertaken numerous research and evaluation projects within the UK criminal justice system, including studies of the effectiveness of community sentences and prisoner resettlement projects.

Kevin Albertson is a researcher in the Policy Evaluation and Research Unit at Manchester Metropolitan University and a Principal Lecturer in the university's Department of Economics, with a focus on quantitative analysis. Kevin has extensive experience of forecasting and quantitative analysis in a commercial and social context, including work with the Ministry of Justice; charities; local government; British Steel (now Corus); Moors for the Future; and Chester Zoo. Kevin is a member of the International Institute of Forecasters and the Home Office's Economics and Resource Analysis Group (ERAG) Advisory Group.

Kevin Wong is Deputy Director of the Hallam Centre for Community Justice at Sheffield Hallam University and has both managed and evaluated a wide range of crime reduction and criminal justice services in the UK.

Routledge frontiers of criminal justice

1 **Sex Offenders: Punish, Help, Change or Control?**
Theory, policy and practice explored
Edited by Jo Brayford, Francis Cowe and John Deering

2 **Building Justice in Post-Transition Europe**
Processes of criminalisation within Central and Eastern European societies
Edited by Kay Goodall, Margaret Malloch and Bill Munro

3 **Technocrime, Policing and Surveillance**
Edited by Stéphane Leman-Langlois

4 **Youth Justice in Context**
Community, compliance and young people
Mairead Seymour

5 **Women, Punishment and Social Justice**
Human rights and penal practices
Margaret Malloch and Gill McIvor

6 **Handbook of Policing, Ethics and Professional Standards**
Edited by Allyson MacVean, Peter Spindler and Charlotte Solf

7 **Contrasts in Punishment**
An explanation of Anglophone excess and Nordic exceptionalism
John Pratt and Anna Eriksson

8 **Victims of Environmental Harm**
Rights, recognition and redress under national and international law
Matthew Hall

9 **Doing Probation Work**
Identity in a criminal justice occupation
Rob C. Mawby and Anne Worrall

10 **Justice Reinvestment**
Can the criminal justice system deliver more for less?
Chris Fox, Kevin Albertson and Kevin Wong

Justice Reinvestment

Can the criminal justice system deliver more for less?

Chris Fox, Kevin Albertson and Kevin Wong

Routledge
Taylor & Francis Group
LONDON AND NEW YORK

First published 2013
by Routledge
2 Park Square, Milton Park, Abingdon, Oxon OX14 4RN

Simultaneously published in the USA and Canada
by Routledge
711 Third Avenue, New York, NY 10017

Routledge is an imprint of the Taylor & Francis Group, an informa business

British Library Cataloguing in Publication Data
A catalogue record for this book is available from the British Library

Library of Congress Cataloging-in-Publication Data
A catalog record has been requested for this book

ISBN: 978-0-415-50034-0 (hbk)
ISBN: 978-0-203-79594-1 (ebk)

Typeset in Times New Roman
by Wearset Ltd, Boldon, Tyne and Wear

Chris Fox dedicates this book to Mum and Tony and to Dad and Julia. Thank you for all your support over the years.

Kevin Albertson would like to thank his supportive colleagues at the Department of Economics, Manchester Metropolitan University. He dedicates this book to his beautiful, supportive and inspiring wife.

Kevin Wong dedicates this book to Catherine, Zahra and Francis.

Contents

Illustrations

Figures

Tables

Acknowledgements

The authors would like to thank all of those who agreed to be interviewed as part of the research for this book. The interviewees are listed in the Appendix.

1 Introduction

> The UK and the USA incarcerate a higher proportion of their populations than other comparable countries. Despite more than a decade of generally decreasing crime rates, incarceration rates have continued to rise. Is incarceration the best way to spend criminal justice resources? We would argue not – nor is it a worthy approach to justice in supposedly free societies.

Introduction

This book aims to capture the birth and early history of a new movement in criminal and social justice in both the USA and the UK: Justice Reinvestment. At its heart, Justice Reinvestment (JR) postulates that it is more economically efficient to prevent criminality in a neighbourhood than it is to try to live with crime and the consequences of crime. This holistic approach locates JR within economic and political debates about criminal justice. However, the breadth of its vision means that it also touches upon broader debates about social justice and the type of society we want to live in.

Where we are

The clink

The citizenry of the United States of America and the United Kingdom – once the "leaders of the free world" – are among the most highly incarcerated on the planet. The growth in incarceration over the last three decades has been unforeseen and unplanned. In the USA of the late 1970s, *A World Without Prisons* was envisaged quite realistically by Dodge (1979), among others (see also Scull 1977, Sommer 1976 and Mitford 1973). The policy of "decarceration", according to Scull (1977), was a product of the social organisation of "advanced capitalism" and the associated rise of welfare.

Notwithstanding, over the last two to three decades the USA prison population has tripled. According to Bureau of Justice Statistics (1999), the total number of inmates in state or federal prisons in mid-1985 was 744,208. This had increased to 1,802,496 by mid-1998 (ibid.). By the beginning of 2008, 2,319,258 adults were incarcerated – 1,596,127 in state or federal prisons and another 723,131 in local jails (Pew Center on the States 2008).

In their 2008 report, the Pew Center also noted that America was the global leader in the rate of incarceration, outpacing South Africa and Iran. The United States incarcerates more people than any country in the world, including the far more populous nation of China. According to the Pew Center, in 2008, the American penal system held more than 2.3 million adults. China was second, with 1.5 million people behind bars, and Russia was a distant third with 890,000 inmates (Pew Center on the States 2008: 5). The UK, like the USA, has seen the prison population rise seemingly inexorably over the same period. In 1991 the prison population in England and Wales was 44,800 (Hicks and Allen 1999); on 22 June 2012, according to the Ministry of Justice (2012a), the prison population in England and Wales was 86,456.

Yet, for all this emphasis on incarceration, there is no evidence that the populations of the USA or the UK feel markedly safer. For example, in the UK, research by Ipsos MORI (reported in Duffy *et al.* 2007) shows that the proportion of the public confident in the government's cracking down on crime fell from 63 per cent in 1997 to 27 per cent in 2007. This occurred despite increases in criminal justice expenditure and decreases in crime rates.

This emphasis on incarceration has occurred despite the lack of evidence that the use of prison discourages criminality (Nagin *et al.* 2009). Indeed, Nagin *et al.* note that incarceration might have a criminogenic, rather than a deterrent effect on some offenders – that is, they emerge from prison more likely to commit crimes than when they were first sentenced.

The think

If the social organisation of "advanced capitalism" and the associated rise of welfare led to the policy of "decarceration" (Scull 1977), has a reversal in this "advance" and a decline in welfare, justified by a social-economic paradigm which emphasises individuality and self-centred behaviour at the expense of society, led to an emphasis on incarceration? This certainly is the conclusion of Beckett and Western (2001), who find high levels of incarceration are associated with weak welfare systems in the USA. They suggest that the rise of an economic paradigm based on individuality and self-interest has seen the state's response to social marginality shift from welfare support to incarceration. See also Cavadino and Dignan (2006) in this context.

As the so-called neo-liberal paradigm came to dominate thinking on social and economic policy, so it became increasingly influential within thinking about crime and criminal justice. Thus, Rational Choice theory, when applied to thinking about crime, began to suggest that all of a nation's citizens (now categorised as economic agents) have the potential for criminality and will commit offences if they can get away with it. This is first set out formally in the analysis of

Becker (1968). Becker's model suggests a system of deterrence through detection and incarceration as the standard state response to crime – though he also emphasises that fines may be imposed for lesser offences, the expected cost of the fine, ideally, being greater than the expected return on criminal behaviour.

On top of this, the public's increasing fear of crime, based in part on the media's portrayal of the problem, has led to "a political arms race in the field of crime and punishment" (Justice Committee 2010: 92), where each party and politician tries to outdo the other. There are major political costs of being seen to be soft on crime (*The Columbus Dispatch* 2008). This fear is compounded by the prevailing paradigm; we have come to believe that our fellow citizens are potential criminals, held in check only through constant vigilance and the threat of sanctions.

There is, however, some justification for the UK's reliance on prisons. Indeed, compared to our European neighbours, we are not especially punitive. In the UK, we lock up a higher proportion of our population because we have a higher rate of crime (Civitas[1] 2010, HEUNI 2010). Paradoxically, it is perhaps promotion of the neo-liberal economic paradigm and the associated decline in community efficacy which has influenced populations to be more criminogenic (Reiner 2005). In other words, the state has arguably undermined social capacity and replaced it with prison capacity.

The brink

Whether or not the rate of incarceration in the UK and the USA is justified, it is apparent that it is no longer affordable. In the UK In 2007, the government spent approximately 2.5 per cent of GDP on public order and safety, the highest of all countries in the Organisation for Economic Co-operation and Development (Duffy *et al.* 2007). Spending has been increasing over recent years. The total budget for the Ministry of Justice for 2009–2010 was just over £10 billion (Ministry of Justice 2009), and the National Offender Management System (NOMS) budget, from which the cost of prisons is met, is approximately £4 billion of this. These costs are likely to rise in the short to medium term (Justice Committee 2010).

Expenditure on corrections in the USA has also increased rapidly over recent decades: total state spending rose from $12 billion in 1987 to $49 billion in 2007 (Pew Center on the States 2008). Henrichson and Delaney (2012) estimate that the average per-inmate cost in the USA is $31,286, although the range was very wide, from $14,603 in Kentucky to $60,076 in New York. In the UK, costs are equally high. According to The American Prospect (2003: unnumbered) it is "neither just nor fiscally possible" to lock up every first-time offender for life.

Back from the brink

If you can't go on the same way, try a different way! In criminal justice, we suggest this way is Justice Reinvestment. The motivating force for the early development of JR was the financial constraint imposed by a burgeoning criminal justice sector in the UK and the USA. Ironically, the same forces which motivated increasing criminal justice budgets have undermined the ability of the state to pay. The current approach to crime is largely ineffective and inefficient, and has little evidence to support it. On the other hand, JR cuts to the heart of the problem by seeking to reduce crime rates and re-offending rates effectively, efficiently and, through evaluation, evidentially.

In this respect, JR isn't a way forward, it is a way out!

In the remainder of this chapter, we briefly summarise the contents of this book, in which we hope to move on the debate about criminal justice and suggest a more effective, more efficient and more just approach to criminal and social justice.

About this book

JR is an approach that can be and has been applied in both the adult and youth justice systems. This book concentrates on the adult criminal justice system. Before we get to JR we need to set out some of the relevant context, and we turn to this in Chapter 2. An essential part of the context for JR is sharply rising prison numbers on both sides of the Atlantic, leading in the USA to the claim that one in a hundred adult Americans is behind bars (Pew Center on the States 2008).

Despite a decade of prosperity in both the USA and the UK, some communities, and some groups within communities, remain relatively disadvantaged and produce a disproportionate number of the people who end up in the criminal justice system. In the current economic crisis, continuing to invest in more prison beds is not an option, and new solutions are needed. However, developments in criminal justice and criminal justice reform must take place within the context of the current structure of the criminal justice system, encompassing the range of organisations and interests responsible for developing criminal justice policy and commissioning and delivering services. These structures in the USA are very different from those in the UK, although in some respects they are becoming more similar.

In Chapter 3 we attempt to answer the question "What is JR?" We begin to examine its development, reflecting the substantial interest that JR has been receiving from policy-makers, practitioners and researchers on both sides of the Atlantic. There is some evidence that JR has been successful in the USA, but relatively little formal evaluation of the USA experience has taken place. Interest in the UK is growing rapidly, but implementation of JR in the more complex policy landscape of the UK presents fresh challenges, and further methodological development will be needed – which will, in turn, be of interest to USA readers.

Arguably, the version of JR dominant in the UK policy dialogue is fairly narrow and focussed primarily on re-offending by individual offenders. This is a departure from the original USA vision, which made stronger links between criminal justice, community safety and wider economic and social justice. To some extent, this may be due to the different context in the USA, where social welfare systems are arguably less developed, and JR represented a means of bringing additional state and federal (criminal justice) resources to bear on social welfare issues. A challenge for the present book is to explore whether this broader vision is relevant to the UK and how it might be further developed to ensure its relevance.

In Chapter 4 we examine some of the existing theories which underpin JR. While JR, with its focus on social justice, is a more universal approach than rehabilitation, it is broadly based on "prehabilitation" and rehabilitation – that is, the reduction of both offending and re-offending. Given that reducing re-offending has been the main policy focus in the UK and an emerging policy aim in the US, we begin to outline our theoretical justification for JR by considering Ward and Maruna's (2007) rehabilitation framework. However, an approach to JR that includes investing in measures to prevent or reduce offending (as opposed to re-offending) may also draw implicitly on developmental criminology and/or the importance of the offender's "life course".

Given that the early underlying principles of JR concentrated on the role of communities and social inclusion, we also examine JR in relation to one of the most influential concepts to emerge from recent sociological theory and research, that of social capacity (Putnam 2000). We complete Chapter 4 with a detailed review of the type of interventions deployed in the USA and the UK which constitute JR, categorising them in relation to their impact on different points in the criminal justice system: arrest, pre-trial, case processing, sentencing, discharge from prison (known as "re-entry" in the US) and community supervision.

JR relies on a detailed understanding of the demands placed on the criminal justice systems and associated social welfare services, with an understanding of the costs and a way of estimating the savings to be derived from investment decisions, both actual savings and averted savings (as noted by La Vigne *et al.* 2010). In Chapter 5, we review the types of data that are required for this understanding, and how they are used, making a distinction between two processes: justice analysis, understanding who is involved in which parts of the criminal justice system, when, for how long, and why; and justice mapping, use Geographic Information Systems (GIS) to link together criminal justice expenditure and the neighbourhoods where these resources are deployed. We also consider the challenges involved in data collection, data sharing, data integration and data access. The critical challenge which embraces all of this is the capacity and capability of government and local agencies engaged in JR initiatives to make effective use of data, which must therefore be available in a timely fashion so as to inform investment decisions and to enable the management of performance.

Given the impact of the economic downturn, and subsequent reductions in public expenditure on the shaping of criminal justice policy, it is perhaps no coincidence that JR, in particular its close reliance on economics, has found favour with policy-makers. In Chapter 6 we argue that understanding the cost-drivers in criminal justice systems can lead to an understanding of the potential savings that can be made from JR.

To illustrate this point, we consider a range of economic methods that can be used in JR, including: cost analysis, which focusses just on the cost of an intervention; Cost Benefit Analysis, which places a monetary value on the consequences of an intervention; and economic modelling as developed by Aos and colleagues (2006) in Washington State, which offers criminal justice system investment portfolios based on modelling future costs and benefits. We also examine the challenges inherent in this economic-theory-led endeavour.

In Chapter 7 we consider an important conundrum about the extent to which models of JR can and should be "evidence-based". While one might consider this a rhetorical question, it is not altogether the simple proposition it may at first seem. In this chapter we join the debate about what constitutes evidence and how it is used. We consider the role of politicians, policy-makers, practitioners, the media and the public in influencing and shaping the use of evidence to make decisions about what approaches to adopt in addressing issues of criminal justice. In the USA it appears that the use of evidence has enabled radical reforms to state and county criminal justice systems. For both the USA and the UK we try to determine whether evidence-based policy-making is possible or whether in fact, it is policy-based evidence-making that holds sway.

In Chapter 4, having tried to construct a theory of JR based on existing published work, we conclude that JR has been theoretically under-developed. In Chapter 8 we start the process of developing a new theory of JR. Our starting point is to recognise that one of the things that makes JR distinct is its recourse to economic thinking. So, we start Chapter 8 with "standard" economic theory on crime and criminal justice, specifically considering the concepts of Rational Choice theory and how these apply to offenders. We review the challenges to this model by examining the importance of intrinsic rewards, the impossibility of perfect information, and the notion of non-consensual games. Ultimately we move to a more "humanistic" economic model that has some parallels with the Good Lives model of offender rehabilitation examined in Chapter 4.

Our model suggests that an individual offender has the ability to make choices – albeit constrained ones – and has both rights and responsibilities in relation to the society or community within which they live. Traditional offending-focussed approaches concentrate on targeting offender deficits. Recognising that an individual offender has agency (Maguire and Raynor 2006), our model, in line with desistance-focussed approaches, promotes offender strengths or assets: for example, strong social bonds, pro-social involvements and social capital.

Having worked our way through the principles underlying JR approaches to criminal justice – justice analysis; justice mapping; the application of economic methods, tying rehabilitative theories to economic theories; and the interventions that contribute to JR – we aim to apply these ideas to the real world.

In Chapter 9 we aim to address the question, "How should interventions be provided in a JR approach?" – addressing the question to the world as it presents itself in the latter part of 2012. We argue that JR needs a strong community and social focus on a range of outcomes that allow individuals to live a Good Life. This implies both broad coalitions of services to support offenders and a mixed economy of provision to enable relevant services in the public, private and not-for-profit sectors to collaborate together. In this chapter we also consider recent developments in the commissioning of justice provision in England and Wales, such as Payment by Results and other innovative funding approaches that might also be harnessed to help deliver an effective, mixed economy of JR provision.

We conclude the book by considering the future of JR in the UK and the USA. We present a compelling argument for the consideration of a more holistic view of justice. That is to say, we suggest that the most efficient way to a just society is to reduce criminality at source through investment in social justice. Notwithstanding, we conclude that the strength of JR is that it has something to say about all aspects of criminal and social justice. As an encompassing approach, JR provides a frame of reference in which to couch debate.

This book is based primarily on published material from both sides of the Atlantic relating to JR. However, the authors also undertook interviews with some of those in the USA who have been influential in developing JR or other complementary approaches, and in the UK with some of those involved in developing the Manchester Transforming Justice programme – a project that draws on some elements of JR. Those interviewed are listed in the Appendix.

2 Current challenges for criminal justice policy

On both sides of the Atlantic, although crime has fallen, prison numbers have gone up and public confidence has remained low. Further, there is little evidence that prison is effective in promoting law and order. In the current economic crisis, continuing to invest in more prison beds is not an option and more efficient solutions are needed. However, developments in criminal justice and criminal justice reform must take place within the context of an ongoing political debate about crime and punishment. Moreover, any reforms must address the current structure of the criminal justice system, encompassing the range of organisations and interests responsible for developing criminal justice policy and commissioning and delivering services. Nonetheless, the financial and social imperatives are clear. Ultimately, the citizens of the USA and the UK do not want less justice, but better justice.

Introduction

In any democracy, "the legitimate object of government" according to Abraham Lincoln, "is to do for the people what needs to be done, but which they cannot, by individual effort, do at all, or do so well, for themselves" (Shaw 1950: 136). It is clear that, whatever the political background of the government, the provision of law and order falls within its purview. In practice, the demands of citizens for criminal justice services can be addressed in a variety of ways.

In recent times the UK and the USA have chosen to address the demand for criminal justice by devoting high and rising resources to the incarceration of offenders. Indeed, politicians would have us believe that anything less is being "soft on crime". Yet, strange as it may seem, as recently as the 1970s the national mood in the USA was that prisons might become a thing of the past for anything other than the most serious offence. There are alternatives to increasing incarceration; we have chosen not to employ these alternatives. Yet incarceration costs and the state of the economy have forced our reconsideration of the lessons of the past. Perpetually increasing the resourcing of prisons is no longer sustainable.

To understand the significant shift that turning away from incarceration would represent for criminal justice policy in the UK and the USA requires an understanding of various factors: the size of the increase in the use of prison that has taken place over the last 20 years on both sides of the Atlantic; the policies and drivers for this; the cost of these policies; and their effectiveness – both on crime and on public perception and confidence in criminal justice. This chapter will examine each of these in turn.

The politics and delivery of criminal justice

On both sides of the Atlantic, governments have increasingly turned to the use of custody to deliver criminal justice to the population. Yet there is little, if any, statistical evidence which suggests this increase in the use of custody is more efficient than other methods of promoting the public good of law and order. Whether this increase in incarceration is intended or unintended, it is the inevitable result of sentencers imposing more frequent and longer prison sentences. The reasons for this emphasis are partly to be found in political rhetoric, sometimes reinforced or amplified by the media. However, this is not the whole story in either the UK or the USA. There are many vested interests in the existing framework of the criminal justice system. Therefore the existing system itself – the way it is structured and delivered – must also be recognised as an important factor in any attempt to improve the delivery of justice in our societies.

Criminal justice policy in the USA

There is no one criminal justice policy in the USA as a whole, because of the complex interaction between the federal and state governments. The balance of legislative and political power means that a relatively greater level of consensus is required for change before it can be implemented. However, this arrangement also means that a greater variety of approaches to criminal justice may be tried, as states may often have different priorities and outlooks.

Consistency and inconsistency between federal and state policy

The debate over what works and what does not in criminal justice policy has been raging for several decades. In 2003, Frank Bowman, a former federal prosecutor, noted in the *New York Times* that in many states of the USA "people are scratching their heads and saying, 'You know, incarcerating people for that long doesn't work.'" (*New York Times* 2003). The same article noted that "from Connecticut to California, legislatures and governors are, with a few exceptions, eagerly finding new ways to reduce, rethink or eliminate prison sentences for crimes within their jurisdictions" (ibid.).

However, the political debate on justice policy in the USA is complicated by differences between federal and state policy and political agendas. At the same time state governors were rethinking their sentencing policy and taking steps to reduce imprisonment, John Ashcroft, the attorney general, was beginning to keep track of cases where judges imposed more lenient sentences than those in the range set by federal sentencing guidelines (ibid.). This "get tough" strategy was required by an amendment tacked on to the Protect Act of 2003 and reflected the approach of the Republican party, which had a majority in Congress at the time (The American Prospect 2003).

The politics of being "soft on crime"

The reasons for this discrepancy are to be found to some extent in the requirement, by law, for state governments to balance their budgets – which is not required of the federal government. However, the major factor would seem to be, according to Ohio Governor Ted Strickland, "the silliness of politics" (*The Columbus Dispatch* 2008). There are major political costs of being seen to be soft on crime. As Strickland points out, "There isn't a person in public office that's not sensitive to the accusation of being soft on crime". However, "you don't have to be soft on crime to be smart in dealing with criminals" (ibid.).

It is this latter aim, of dealing with offenders more effectively – especially in the context of the crisis in public finances – which has spurred the development of Justice Reinvestment in the USA. As Drake Bennett, writing for American Prospect, commented: "In theory, society could reduce crime by locking up every first-time offender for life. But even the hardest of the hard-liners knows this approach is neither just nor fiscally possible" (The American Prospect 2003: unnumbered).

Economic paradigms

It might be reasonable to ask from where this hard-line approach has arisen, given that as recently as 1979, *A World Without Prisons* was envisaged quite realistically by Dodge (1979), among others (e.g. Scull 1977, Sommer 1976 and Mitford 1973). Scull (1977) was of the opinion that the policy of "decarceration" was a product of the social organisation of "advanced capitalism" and the associated rise of welfare. In their study of (USA) state-level incarceration rates between 1975 and 1995, Beckett and Western (2001) support this, finding that high levels of incarceration are associated with weak welfare systems. However, the "advanced capitalism" of Scull has advanced further (if advanced is the right word). According to Beckett and Western (2001), there is evidence that the rise of the neo-liberal economic paradigm from the late 1970s to the present has seen the state's response to social marginality shift from welfare support to incarceration. This result is further supported by Cavadino and Dignan's (2006) cross-section analysis of the penal policies in 12 nations. Cavadino and Dignan note that the neo-liberal economic paradigm excludes many people, often whole communities, from the benefits of economic growth and effective citizenship. This leads to the denial of full effective rights of citizenship. In nations which adopt the neo-liberal paradigm, incarceration rates are higher, compared with those of more inclusive nations:

> One theory is that punishment is a sort of "negative reward": societies that are prepared to reward success with higher incomes and greater social status are also more willing to punish failure with both poverty and formal

> sanctions. Or one could say, perhaps preferably, that a more egalitarian society is both more inclusive and less willing to consign offenders to an even more unequally low level of existence.
>
> (Cavadino and Dignan 2006: 452)

The winds of change?

Recently the federal government has begun to recognise the effect on state budgets of a criminal justice sector which over-emphasises imprisonment. In 2010, the US Congress and Senate passed the Criminal Justice Reinvestment Act 2010 (US Senate Judiciary Committee 2010), which aimed simultaneously to increase public safety and reduce the corrections budget.

Criminal justice policy in the UK

There are some parallels between the debate in the UK and that in the USA.

Prison: the political arms race

In the UK, as in the USA, criminal justice policy is driven by the interplay between politicians, public opinion, the media, and sentencers. As the Justice Committee puts it, policy is formed in the context of

> a toxic cocktail of sensationalised or inaccurate reporting of difficult cases by the media; relatively punitive overall public opinion (compared to much of the European Union); a self-defeating over-politicisation of criminal justice policy since the late 1980s and the responsiveness to all these factors of the sentencing framework and sentencers.
>
> (Justice Committee 2010: 5)

The Justice Committee based their findings on research and evidence from criminal justice professionals including prison governors, police, workers in the probation service, academics and politicians. The committee cited a lecture by the Lord Chief Justice, Lord Phillips, who acknowledged that rises in the use of custody and increases in the length of sentences "may well be attributable in part to media pressure" and related this to the fact that it is "part of a sentencer's job to reflect, at least to a degree, the public's view as to the proper response to crime" (Phillips 2008: unnumbered).

However, it is not only sentencers who are well aware of media pressure and the view of the voting public. According to Professor Ian Loader of Oxford University, giving evidence to the Justice Committee, the politicisation of criminal justice has led to

> a political arms race in the field of crime and punishment where the two main parties have decided to try and outdo and outthink, to be, among other

> things, the party that protects victims, that is tough on offenders, that sends more people to prison, that passes more laws, that protects the public from criminals and so on and so forth.
>
> (Justice Committee 2010: 92)

Notwithstanding the USA's experience, which suggests that protecting the public from criminals does not necessarily require more people sent to prison, in the UK between 1991 and 1996 the prison population in England and Wales rose by almost a quarter, from 44,800 to 55,300 (Hicks and Allen 1999). It is perhaps no coincidence that this significant increase took place during the tenure of Michael Howard as Home Secretary (from May 1993 to May 1997); Howard famously declared "prison works" in his speech to the 1993 Conservative Party Conference. Mr Howard served as Conservative Home Secretary until 1997, at which time the Labour Party were elected to govern.

In an age of political sound-bites, Howard's "prison works" was matched by Tony Blair's slogan in 1993;[1] at that time, Shadow Home Secretary, Blair promised that Labour would be "tough on crime, tough on the causes of crime" (Labour Party 1997). Nearly two decades later, the Labour Party remained committed to this position (*The Guardian* 2011).

The legacy of 14 years of Labour government, from 1997 to 2010, is a prison population of 85,000, a 54 per cent increase since Howard's tenure. In 2007, responsibility for criminal justice was reorganised, being divided between the Home Office (responsible for policing) and the newly created Ministry of Justice (responsible for prisons, probation and courts). This followed the contention of John Reid, the incumbent Home Secretary, that the Home Office, which had had responsibility for police, probation and prisons up until 2007, was not "fit for purpose" (politics.co.uk 2007). The subsequent division of responsibility championed by Reid has consequences for the development and implementation of Justice Reinvestment in the UK. These will be considered later in this book.

Under the Coalition government, elected in 2010, the prison population continued to grow, despite the sentencing reforms promised by Ken Clarke, the Conservative justice secretary from May 2010 to September 2012 (Clarke 2010, BBC 2010a, *The Guardian* 2010). These proposed reforms met with less than universal acclaim. Michael Howard, for one, was unconvinced and reiterated his stance on prison during his lecture to the Carlton Club in 2011. However, Clarke did not promise wholesale reform, as Daniel Sandford, BBC News Home Affairs Correspondent, points out:

> It has taken a man who has run the prisons before to publicly question the wisdom of the policy [of prison growth]. Even so, Ken Clarke is not promising to cut the prison population, only to look at cost-effective ways of preventing reoffending. He's not saying prison doesn't work. But he is saying it doesn't always work.
>
> (BBC 2010a: unnumbered)

In closing this section, it should be noted that, like the USA, the UK is a neo-liberal nation (Cavadino and Dignan 2006). As we have mentioned, associated with this paradigm is the increasing use of incarceration as a means of controlling the socially excluded.

The delivery of criminal justice

In the UK, a complicating factor in any attempt to understand why prison numbers are high or how they might be reduced is the complexity of the criminal justice system in England and Wales. It is beyond the scope of this book (or perhaps any book) to describe in detail the workings of the system. However, its convoluted nature may be illustrated by discussing some aspects of the commissioning processes within the criminal justice system and by the development of complex local partnerships designed to manage offenders both in custody and in the community.

To get a sense of the arrangements for commissioning and delivering offender management services in England and Wales, consider the number of organisations involved. Overall responsibility lies with the Ministry of Justice, a central government department. The National Offender Management Service, NOMS, is an executive agency of the Ministry of Justice responsible for commissioning and delivering prison and probation services in England and Wales. NOMS is responsible for the National Probation Service and Her Majesty's Prison Service. Through these it delivers offender services by means of (National Offender Management Service 2012):

- 35 Probation Trusts responsible for the delivery of probation services at local level;
- 119 public sector prisons; and
- several private sector organisations, which between them operate 12 prisons under contract, and which provide other services including prisoner escorts and electronic monitoring of offenders in the community.

Currently the only elected politicians involved in this substantial structure, which employs thousands of staff, are the handful of government ministers in the Ministry of Justice. These include the Secretary of State for Justice, who has overall responsibility for the Ministry, and a more junior minister with a specific brief to cover prisons. Despite the local nature of the custodial work of NOMS, it is noticeable that "local communities, however they are defined, have no sense of involvement in prisons and what goes on in them" (Coyle 2007: 35).

The complexity also extends to criminal justice budgets, where funding is delivered in a series of "silos".[2] This is an approach which sometimes limits the possibilities of innovation and creates perverse incentives (Justice Committee 2010). A good example of this comes from the youth justice system. Although local authorities have traditionally met the costs of managing young offenders in the community, central government, through the Youth Justice Board, have met the cost of incarceration. At the local level, these costs of incarceration have been hidden (Justice Committee 2010), and therefore they have provided no incentive for local authorities to reduce the use of incarceration. Indeed, from a purely economic perspective, this approach arguably creates an incentive for the use of incarceration. However, this is set to change, with custody remand budgets for young people being transferred to local authorities in England and Wales under the Legal Aid, Sentencing and Punishment of Offenders Act 2012.

We turn now to the use of partnership working in offender management. Since 2003, local criminal justice agencies, along with local authorities, health agencies and other local agencies, have sought to improve the way in which persistent and prolific offenders were managed through the government-mandated Prolific and other Persistent Offenders (PPO) schemes. Following the implementation of PPO and other multi-agency approaches such as the Multi-Agency Public Protection Arrangements,[3] a bottom-up approach emerged, labelled Integrated Offender Management (IOM). However, the use of local partnership working to deliver IOM is not straightforward (Senior *et al.* 2011). While the commissioning of offender management services is the responsibility of the Ministry of Justice, the Home Office (which has responsibility for policing and local community safety partnerships), through its Reducing Re-offending Unit, has the lead responsibility across government for Integrated Offender Management.

The overall picture, then, is of a complex system where there is plenty of scope for confusion. Thus the Justice Committee has been concerned that

> [T]he criminal justice system is a complex network of agencies with substantial public funding operating under increasing pressure but the different parts of the system do not seem to be pursuing the same goals or making cogent contributions to an agreed overarching purpose.
>
> (Justice Committee 2010: 5)

According to the Commission on English Prisons Today (2009: 46), "Central government, because of the organisation of ministerial responsibility, encourages a uni-dimensional, single-issue approach to complex and multi-faceted problems such as crime and exclusion".

There is some evidence that the "stickiness" of public sector financing of criminal justice in the UK is being challenged (Downey *et al.* 2010). Historically, when public service providers have funding for services, they tend to keep control of the resource. Therefore, new provision could only be funded through new spending rather than by recycling out of savings from existing funding. According to Downey *et al.* this is one of the factors which have led to a poor rate of growth of productivity in public provision. It is suggested that initiatives in local government which envisage a more mixed economy of provision and which use "Payment by Results" may address this. Notwithstanding, Payment by Results schemes are often also very convoluted, and "simplicity is critical to success" (Commission on English Prisons Today 2009: 47). Perhaps the main attraction to government of Payment by Results is the opportunity for politicians to shift both blame and risk on to the private sector (Clarke and Newman 1997, Fox and Albertson 2011). These are issues we return to towards the end of this book.

The growth in demand for incarceration

As a result of the political imperative to look tough on crime, or at least not to look soft on crime, both USA and UK governments have funded extra capacity over recent years.

Extra demand for incarceration in the USA

In the last three decades, the USA prison population has tripled. According to the Bureau of Justice Statistics (1999) the total number of inmates in state or federal prisons in mid-1985 was 744,208. This had increased to 1,802,496 by mid-1998 (ibid.). By the beginning of 2008, a total of 2,319,258 adults were incarcerated – 1,596,127 in state or federal prisons and another 723,131 in local jails (Pew Center on the States 2008). The US Department of Justice broadly confirms this figure, putting the population of state and federal prisons at 1,598,245 by the end of 2007 (US Department of Justice 2010). According to the Department of Justice, the prison population had increased further to 1,605,127 by the end of 2010 (ibid.).

In their 2008 report, the Pew Center also noted that America was the global leader in the rate of incarceration, outpacing South Africa and Iran. In the USA, 750 people were in prison for every 100,000 residents. This was eight times the rate in Germany, five times the rate in the UK (at 148 prisoners per 100,000), and 11 times the rate in Finland (68 prisoners per 100,000).[4] Indeed,

> The United States incarcerates more people than any country in the world, including the far more populous nation of China. At the start of the new year, the American penal system held more than 2.3 million adults. China was second, with 1.5 million people behind bars, and Russia was a distant third with 890,000 inmates.
>
> (Pew Center on the States 2008: 5)

The title of the Pew report *One in 100: Behind Bars in America 2008* comes from the observation that "With the number of adults just shy of 230 million [in the USA], the actual incarceration rate is 1 in every 99.1 adults" (ibid.). This is disproportionately distributed according to age, gender and ethnicity – the most striking figure is for young black men (aged 20–34), where one in nine were imprisoned.

According to Pew (2008), 36 states reported higher prison numbers in 2008 compared with 2007, and ten states experienced an increase of 5 per cent or more. Kentucky led (for want of a better word), with a 12 per cent increase. Pew

(2008) attributed this to changes in the appointees to the parole board, leading to a reduction in the grant rate for parole. Therefore inmates were incarcerated for longer periods of time.

While the example of Kentucky illustrated one of the drivers of prison growth, the Pew Center report offered Florida as a case study to understand the dynamics of the phenomenon. Between 1993 and 2007, the prison population increased from 53,000 to 97,000. This rise was attributed to changes in the state's correctional policies and practices.

> One of the first came in 1995, when the legislature abolished "good time" credits and discretionary release by the parole board and required that all prisoners – regardless of their crime, prior record, or risk to recidivate – serve 85 per cent of their sentence. Next came a "zero tolerance" policy and other measures mandating that probation officers report every offender who violated any condition of supervision and increasing prison time for these "technical violations". As a result the number of violators in Florida prisons has jumped by an estimated 12,000.
>
> (Pew Center on the States 2008: 9)

The report noted that while crime in Florida decreased significantly during this period, it fell much more in states that had not enlarged their prison systems, or even states that had shrunk them, such as New York.

Extra demand for incarceration in the UK

The UK, like the USA, has seen its prison population rise seemingly inexorably over the last 60 years. Analysis of the prison population in England and Wales between 1900 and 2000 indicates an upward trend from 1946 onwards, following the end of World War II, with decreases from 1951 to 1956 and from 1986 to 1991 (Hicks and Allen 1999); the latter reduction was ascribed to policy intervention beginning in 1989 (ibid.). This increase in the population has continued during the first decade of the twenty-first century.

This unprecedented growth in the level of incarceration has surprised even those most familiar with the criminal justice system of England and Wales.

> I am amazed that the prison population has doubled since I was Home Secretary in the early 1990s. It stands at more than 85,000 today. This is quite an astonishing number which I would have dismissed as an impossible and ridiculous prediction if it had been put to me as a forecast in 1992.
>
> (Clarke 2010)

As Kenneth Clarke suggests, in 1991 the prison population was 44,800 (Hicks and Allen 1999); on 22 June 2012, according to the Ministry of Justice (2012a), the prison population in England and Wales was 86,456, while the operational capacity for the English and Welsh prison system on the same date was 90,310.

Under the current government, the trend towards increasing incarceration has at least been considered, if not reconsidered. For example, as late as March 2010, the Labour government committed the nation to a prison-building programme intended to deliver an overall capacity of 96,000 prison places by 2014 based on a projection of future requirements (Ministry of Justice 2010a). This expansion has been partially curtailed by the Coalition government of Conservatives and Liberal Democrats which took office in May 2010. During 2011 the Coalition committed the nation to reducing the prison population to 2008 levels (81,724) by 2015; and providing 3000 fewer prison places in 2015 than in 2010, through some prison closures (National Offender Management Service 2011). However, this still involves completing a capacity-building programme (commenced under the New Labour government) delivering a further 2,685 places including two new prisons, Belmarsh West and Featherstone 2, over a 12 to 18 month period (ibid.).

Rationalising growth

It seems reasonable to question why prison numbers have risen so sharply. There is little, if any evidence, that the level of criminality in society is driving the increase in incarceration – certainly over the last decade, crime rates have been generally declining, while prison numbers are continuing to increase, as shown in Figure 2.1.

Neither is it the case that the clear-up rate has increased. The number of people found guilty by the courts has remained largely constant over recent years. 1,724,225 people were found guilty in 1996; ten years later (in 2006), 1,771,378 were found guilty (Prison Reform Trust 2009). Analysis of the data suggests that almost all of the increase in prison numbers was generated within

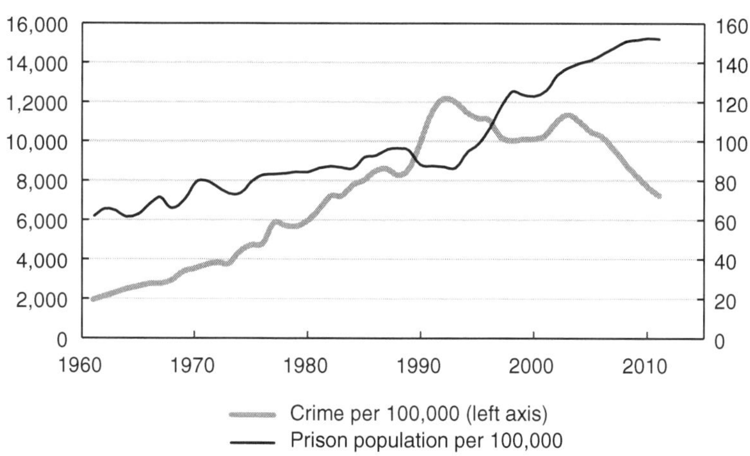

Figure 2.1 Total UK prison population (per 100,000) and total offences (per 100,000) (source: authors' calculations based on Home Office data).

two segments of the prison population: those sentenced to immediate custody (78 per cent of the increase); and those recalled to prison for breaking the conditions of their release (16 per cent of the increase) (Ministry of Justice 2009).

The increase in convictions leading to custody goes along with an increase in the average length of custody. The number of people given custody in magistrates' courts has risen from 25,016 in 1993 to 53,431 in 2006, and the number given custody at the crown court has risen from 33,722 in 1993 to 42,586 in 2006 (Prison Reform Trust 2009). At the same time the length of sentences has increased. For example, the average custodial sentence length handed down for indictable offences across all courts increased by 15 per cent, from 14.3 to 16.4 months, between 2000 and 2004 (Ministry of Justice 2009). Since 2004, average sentence lengths have decreased, but this may be a result of switching from longer determinate sentences to indeterminate sentences. There were 12,228 people serving indeterminate sentences at the end of March 2009, compared to fewer than 4,000 in 1998 and 3,000 in 1992 (Prison Reform Trust 2009). These changes are illustrated by Carter (2003), who notes that a first-time domestic burglar had a 27 per cent chance of receiving a custodial sentence in 1995–1996, but by 2000, this had increased to 48 per cent. At the same time, the average sentence length for burlary had increased from 16 to 18 months (Carter 2003).

Meanwhile, the rate of recall to prison for those who breach the conditions of their release has also increased. Over the period 1995 to 2009, 16 per cent of the overall increase in prison population was due to changes in the law regarding recall to prison. Two factors have contributed to this increase. First, a higher proportion of offenders have been recalled because probation practice has changed in response to changing national standards: the Crime and Disorder Act 1998 and the Criminal Justice Act 2003 (Ministry of Justice 2009). Second, those recalled have spent longer in custody after their recall (Prison Reform Trust 2009).

How much is spent on criminal justice?

We have seen that over the last two to three decades both the UK and the USA have become increasingly reliant on incarceration as a default criminal justice policy. This has resulted partly from political pressure and partly because of vested interests and the complexity of the criminal justice system. When it comes to criminal justice, at least we know what incarceration can deliver. However, it is not clear what is the price tag for this default strategy.

Criminal justice costs in the USA

According to The American Prospect (2003: unnumbered) it is "neither just nor fiscally possible" to lock up every first-time offender for life. Leaving aside, for the moment, the question of whether such an approach is just, it is certainly costly. Expenditure on corrections in the USA has increased rapidly over recent years; total state spending rose from $12 billion in 1987 to $49 billion in 2007

(Pew Center on the States 2008). One of the biggest drivers of cost increases has been medical care for special-needs populations, including HIV-positive prisoners and geriatric inmates serving very long or complete life sentences.

Costs have continued to rise since Pew (2008) was published. The National Association of State Budget Officers (2011) reported that state spending on corrections, which reflects the costs of building and operating prison systems and may include spending on juvenile justice programmes and alternatives to incarceration, totalled $51.1 billion in the 2010 fiscal year. However, this may be an underestimate. A recent study of 40 states in the USA by the VERA Institute of Justice (Henrichson and Delaney 2012) found that not all direct prison costs were included within corrections budgets. A number of direct costs including, for example, underfunded contributions to retiree health care for corrections employees, fell outside corrections budgets. Thus, while the 40 states included in the study had an aggregated corrections budget of $33.5 billion, the total taxpayer cost of prisons was actually higher at $39 billion. Henrichson and Delaney (2012), based on their estimate of the full direct costs of prison, go on to estimate a total per-inmate cost. This average cost is $31,286, although the range was very wide, from $14,603 in Kentucky to $60,076 in New York.

Criminal justice costs in the UK

In 2007, the UK Government spent about 2.5 per cent of GDP on public order and safety (Duffy *et al.* 2007). The Ministry of Justice budget for 2009–2010 was just over £10 billion (Ministry of Justice 2009), of which the NOMS budget, which meets the cost of prisons, is around £4 billion. The Justice Committee (2010) notes that, due to inflation and the rising costs of utilities and food, the costs of custody will keep rising even if the number in custody remains the same. Alongside increases in the marginal cost of a prison place, the fixed cost has also increased substantially. The average capital-build cost per prison place, without adjustment for inflation, has almost tripled to £153,000 between 1998 and 2008 (ibid.). Thus the current criminal justice strategy of planning for increased prison numbers has serious cost implications. The Ministry of Justice has estimated the total cost of the new prison-building programme over 35 years is between £3.2 and £4.2 billion (ibid.).

How effective is prison?

From an economic point of view, interventions may be justified, even if they are costly, by their effectiveness. We therefore consider how much crime rates are likely to have been reduced by current government policy. Michael Howard famously declared "prison works"; however, it is not clear how well it works.

To justify such a large investment in criminal justice, we might expect a large return. This might come from cost savings arising from reductions in crime, whether first offences or re-offending. On the face of it, however, the evidence is not promising. In England and Wales the re-conviction rate for all custodial sentences is 46.8 per cent. For custodial sentences less than one year in duration, the re-conviction rate is even greater at 56.8 per cent (Ministry of Justice 2011). However, prison is not only a deterrent to criminality, it is also a reassurance to the general law-abiding public. Therefore, to consider the effect of prison we must consider both these outcomes.

Incapacitation

The theory behind the incapacitation effect is straightforward. It is clear that once a person is in custody, their potential to commit further crime is dramatically reduced.[5] To measure the strength of the incapacitation effect it must be distinguished from a general deterrent effect. One study which makes this distinction clear is that of Kessler and Levitt (1999). In 1982, a referendum in California known as Proposition 8 led to enhanced sentences being given for various violent and serious crimes. The sentence enhancements were large in magnitude, leading to substantial increases in the lengths of prison sentences. However, even before Proposition 8, the affected offenses were serious crimes for which a conviction almost always resulted in a prison term.

Because a convicted criminal would have been sentenced to prison even without the law change, there was no additional incapacitation effect from the sentence enhancement in the short run. Therefore, any immediate decrease in crime rates would be due to a general deterrent effect. If the passing of Proposition 8 led to an incapacitation effect, the impact of this on crime rates would not be observed until offenders were starting to serve the additional time in prison, that is, over and above that which they would have received prior to the change in legislation. Analysis of the data showed that Proposition 8 appeared to reduce eligible crimes by 4 per cent in the year following its passage and 8 per cent three years after passage. The immediate effects are consistent with deterrence. However, the impact of the law continued to increase five to seven years after its passage, which allows the estimation of the size of the incapacitation effect (Kessler and Levitt 1999).

The evidence from the UK is more equivocal. During the first decade of the twenty-first century, crime rates have generally been falling, and prison numbers have been rising (as shown in Figure 2.1). While a cursory inspection of the data suggests that there might be some degree of correlation between these two trends, there is no evidence to suggest that the rise in prison numbers has caused a *substantial* part of the fall in the crime rate. Based on unpublished research, Carter (2003) claims the 22 per cent increase in the prison population between 1997 and 2003 led to a five per cent decrease in crime; however, as Hedderman (2008) notes, absolutely no evidence is presented to support this claim.

An earlier British study (Tarling 1993) was less optimistic about the scale of incarceration effects. Based on an analysis of incarceration and crimes rates in England and Wales between 1975 and 1986, Tarling concluded that imprisonment reduced recorded crime by between 6 and 9 per cent from its potential value. Taking account of crime and imprisonment rates at that time, Tarling calculated that a 1 per cent reduction in crime would require a 25 per cent increase in the prison population. When considering these estimates, it should be borne in mind that not all crime is successfully cleared up; that only a small proportion of offenders are incarcerated; and that many offenders receive short-term sentences.

It might seem counter-intuitive to postulate that incapacitation has little effect on the crime rate. However, as Shepherd (2006) and Liedka *et al.* (2006) note, more recent studies in the USA have failed to find such a relationship and have even found some evidence that imprisoning people might increase crime.

Shepherd suggests these seemingly contradictory findings can be reconciled, and puts forward the theory that earlier studies examined periods when prison populations tended to grow with the addition of violent and property offenders, whereas later studies examine a period when prison populations were increased by incarcerating drug offenders and increasing sentence lengths for low-level offenders (Shepherd 2006). Shepherd also puts forward a number of arguments as to why longer prison sentences for low-level offenders may not reduce crime, several of which illustrate the difficulties inherent in conceptualising and measuring the concept of incapacitation. For example, she argues that lengthening incarceration periods may have little impact because research on the relationship between age and crime (the age/crime curve) tells us that most offenders will stop committing crime relatively quickly in any case: "Increasing an offender's sentence from 10–12 years will not reduce crime through incapacitation if he would have stopped committing crime after 10 years anyway" (Shepherd 2006: 290). Shepherd also points to empirical evidence which suggests that longer sentences lead to offenders experiencing more alienation from society, greater deterioration of family relations, and further removal from the prospect of regular employment. All of these factors will increase the likelihood of re-offending.

Individual deterrence

It is clear, then, that there is only limited reduction in crime from incapacitation. Further, if Shepherd (2006) is correct, incarceration increases the likelihood of re-offending. This would seem at odds with the generally held view that offenders are unlikely to wish a return to prison. In fact, the evidence of prison being effective at reducing re-offending among released prisoners is very limited. For example, Villetaz *et al.* (2006) look at analyses which test the effects on re-offending rates of custodial versus non-custodial sentences. Their extensive *Systematic Review* covers research, published and unpublished, written in any language between 1961 and 2002. Their preliminary searches identified a "rough inventory of more than three thousand studies", but they eventually identified only 23 relevant and methodologically robust studies, and of these, only five were based on a controlled or natural experimental design. From these 23 studies they were able to extract data to make 27 comparisons between the effect of custodial and non-custodial sentences on re-offending. They found that the rate of re-offending after a non-custodial sanction was lower than after a custodial sanction in 11 significant comparisons. In 14 comparisons there was no significant difference in re-offending rates between custodial and non-custodial sentences, and only two comparisons were significantly in favour of custody. Villetaz and colleagues also undertook a meta-analysis of the five most robust studies (controlled or natural experimental designs) and found no significant difference between re-offending rates after completion of custodial or non-custodial sentences.

Villetaz *et al.*'s study has been updated by Nagin *et al.* (2009). Their study notes that incarceration may have a criminogenic rather than a deterrent effect on some offenders – that is, they emerge from prison more likely to commit crimes than before they were sentenced. Indeed, Nagin *et al.* find that

> the great majority of studies point to a null or criminogenic effect of the prison experience on subsequent offending. This reading of the evidence should, at least, caution against wild claims – at times found in "get tough" rhetoric voiced in recent decades – that prisons have special powers to scare offenders straight.
>
> (Nagin *et al.* 2009: 178))

The UK Ministry of Justice (2010b) undertook a comparison of "proven re-offending rates" (re-convictions in a court) for prisoners serving short custodial sentences (under 12 months) and offenders receiving court-order commencements under probation supervision in 2007. The rationale for comparing these groups was that those receiving a short prison sentence would be the group of prisoners likely to be most similar to those receiving a community sentence. To further improve the comparability of the two groups, individuals serving short prison sentences were matched with individuals receiving community sentences using two different forms of matching (Propensity Score Matching and "mechanical matching"). The results from the analysis showed that court orders were more effective (by seven percentage points) at reducing one-year proven re-offending rates than custodial sentences of less than 12 months for similar offenders (Ministry of Justice 2010b).

General deterrence

Another way in which prison might reduce crime is by deterring others from committing crime (general deterrence). However, there is no strong evidence linking the decline in crime rates with the deterrent effect of increased incarceration. In fact the evidence suggests that prison has, at most, a small impact on overall crime rates (see for instance Liedka *et al.* 2006, Marvell and Moody 1994, Witt and Witte 2000, and Levitt 1996). Summarising three of the strongest econometric studies on deterrence, Liedka *et al.* (2006) note that collectively the studies suggest that a 10 per cent increase in the prison population resulted in a 1.6 per cent to 5 per cent drop in crime rates. Indeed, it has been suggested (Eide 1999) that crime rates vary in a non-linear relationship with severity of punishment and that, beyond a certain point, increases in length of sentences might even increase the crime rate (see also Shepherd 2006, Leidka *et al.* 2006). However, it is also worth noting that researching the deterrent effect is complicated. For example, there is a need to distinguish the concept of "certainty of punishment", where generally empirical studies of punishment show that increasing certainty of punishment leads to increased deterrence, and "severity of punishment", where the empirical evidence is less strong (Von Hirsch *et al.* 1999). Von Hirsch *et al.* argue that "Deterrence concerns desistance from crime through fear of the legal consequences. It is consequently *subjective*, so that changes in criminal justice policies can have no deterrent effect unless they alter potential offenders' beliefs about sanction risks [emphasis in original]" (Von Hirsch *et al.* 1999: 3). They note that there is little research on potential offenders' perceptions of sentence severity. A more general survey of the public (Hough and Roberts 1998) found that the public underestimate the severity of sanctions, which would tend to support the contention that potential offenders underestimate the effect of incarceration.

It cannot be denied that in the UK and the USA there is a crude correlation between increasing prison numbers and reductions in crime. For example, in the UK, over the last 15 years or so crime has dropped substantially as prison rates have risen. Crime rates, as measured by the British Crime Survey (BCS), peaked in 1995 (Hoare 2009). They fell substantially until 2004–2005 and, in 2007–2008, reached the lowest level recorded since the British Crime Survey was first undertaken in 1981 (ibid.). Between 1995 and 2009 the prison population in England and Wales grew by 66 per cent (Ministry of Justice 2009). However, there is little evidence that this reduction in crime is the result of investment in prisons.

Crime has been dropping in many western economies, obviously independently of UK and USA criminal justice policy. To the best of our knowledge, no criminologist or economist predicted the drop in crime, either based on theory or based on a multivariate model. Further, while various criminologists and economists have attempted to provide an ex-post rationalisation of the crime drop, there is no widely accepted explanation:

> The question "Why have crime rates dropped in most developed countries for the best part of a decade?" is one of childlike simplicity but arguably the biggest unsolved puzzle of modern-day criminology. It is embarrassing to criminology that there is no adequate answer, and it implies a fundamental failing of theory and empirical study.
>
> (Farrell *et al.* 2010: 25)

The impact on public confidence

We have seen in the preceding sections that incarceration costs nations dearly, and yet there is little, if any, evidence of any return in reducing criminality. However, we have not yet addressed the question of whether there is a political return. Despite all the statistical evidence to the contrary, it is possible that politicians, in emphasising incarceration, are merely responding to the public's lack of confidence in any other kind of sentence. However, there is little evidence in the UK that higher rates of incarceration have had a positive impact on public confidence. Substantial drops in crime have been accompanied by drops in people's personal level of worry about crime (Hoare 2009). However, as Duffy *et al.* note, "Unfortunately for the government, even though personal levels of worry about crime have decreased, the majority of the public just don't believe that crime rates are actually falling" (Duffy *et al.* 2007: 18). In 2008–2009, 75 per cent of respondents thought the level of crime in the country as a whole had increased over the last two years – the same percentage as in 1996 (Thorpe and Hall 2009). Evidence from the BCS also suggests that people consistently and substantially overestimate their risk of being a victim of crime (Thorpe and Hall 2009). Research by Ipsos MORI (reported in Duffy *et al.* 2007) shows that the proportion of the public that is confident in the government to crack down on crime has fallen from 63 per cent in 1997 to 27 per cent in 2007. This has occurred despite increases in criminal justice expenditure and decreases in crime. Taken as a whole, this evidence suggests that there is no strong case for arguing that the increase in prison numbers has made people feel safer. In sum, there is no evidence that this is a strategy which is reaping political dividends for the government; quite the reverse.

"The economy, stupid"

The phrase, attributed to James Carville, Bill Clinton's 1992 campaign strategist, was one of three key messages which hung on the wall of Clinton's Little Rock campaign headquarters during his successful bid for the presidency. Although intended for the internal audience of campaign workers, it became a slogan for the campaign as whole[6] and has been much copied since (for example, "The problems of a graying population: It's the demography, stupid", *New York Times* 2011).

If anything, the economy was even more an issue in Barack Obama's successful presidential campaign of 2008. Another of Bill Clinton's challenges, "Change vs. more of the same",[7] could equally well apply today.

In the USA, as early as 2003, policy-makers, criminal justice experts and politicians from both mainstream political parties were already engaging in the debate around reducing the incarceration rate through social interventions – in effect attempting to set back the neo-liberal clock (compare Cavadino and Dignan 2006). As The American Prospect (2003) notes, the "state fiscal crisis has put an end to the prison boom", making "strange bedfellows" of Republican and Democrat politicians.

Since the so-called "sub-prime crisis" of 2007,[8] which mutated into a worldwide economic crisis, the ongoing weak state of the economy and consequent fiscal constraints in the UK and the USA appear to have led to an unseating of long-held views about criminal justice policy, particularly regarding increased spending on prison places. At the time of writing, both countries face economic conditions in which every pound and dollar of public expenditure must be properly justified. The "change" called for by Clinton must come, as "more of the same" is no longer fiscally realistic.

In the USA, public debt has been increasing over the last decade and was $16.05 trillion in September 2012.[9] Similarly, the UK public sector has recorded deficits since 2002–2003. In March 2012, UK public sector net debt (excluding the temporary effects of financial interventions) was £1,022.5 billion, equivalent to 66 per cent of gross domestic product (Office for National Statistics 2012b). This compares to £617 billion (44 per cent of GDP) at the end of March 2009 (Office for National Statistics 2010).

The UK Coalition government, on coming to power in May 2010, almost immediately announced a series of spending cuts (BBC 2010a) with a view to reducing the government budget deficit. The criminal justice system is not exempt from the pressure on public finances. Indeed, the need to reduce expenditure was already clear. The cross-party Justice Committee's report on Justice Reinvestment, published prior to the 2010 general election, noted:

> The criminal justice system is facing a crisis of sustainability. Public expenditure generally is under pressure in all areas in the worst economic climate since the Second World War. The Ministry of Justice is no exception, being tasked with finding £1.3 billion worth of cost savings over the next three years. New and existing resources are being pre-empted by planned spending to accommodate a potential prison population of 96,000 by 2014 at enormous capital and running costs.
>
> (Justice Committee 2010: 5)

In November of the same year, the Coalition government announced an ambitious cost reduction of 23 per cent over four years for the two Government departments with joint and sometimes competing responsibility for criminal justice: the Ministry of Justice and the Home Office. Their targets for capital spend were reduced by 50 per cent and 49 per cent respectively.[10]

Conclusion

Since the late 1970s, prison populations and incarceration rates in the UK and the USA have risen steadily. This rise, arguably reinforced by the prevailing economic paradigm, is no longer affordable. In the current straitened national circumstances there are good reasons to reassess the delivery of criminal justice. It is not just that prison costs; there is little evidence that it works. The experiment we have been engaged in – rapidly rising penal populations and escalating prison budgets – has failed to provide sufficient evidence that incarceration is effective. Indeed, there is some evidence that a term of incarceration increases offenders' criminogenic tendencies. Notwithstanding the statistical evidence, the politicised nature of criminal justice reform on both sides of the Atlantic, and – particularly for the UK – the complexity of the criminal justice system, mean that attempts to change the system are unlikely to be straightforward. We have tried getting "tough on crime"; it is time to become "more efficient on crime, more efficient on the causes of crime".

3 What is Justice Reinvestment?

This chapter provides an introduction to the theory of Justice Reinvestment and a brief history of the approach in the USA and, more recently, in the UK. When it was first suggested, the Justice Reinvestment approach sought to widen the debate on what exactly is justice. One view of justice is little more than the apprehension and conviction of criminals and their subsequent punishment. In this paradigm, criminals are "bad" and society must be protected from them. Justice Reinvestment suggests that it is possible to alleviate the social conditions which give rise to criminality. Appropriate analysis and evaluation are required to determine whether interventions which promote social justice actually prove cheaper than traditional criminal justice.

Introduction

In the previous chapter we discussed how the rise of incarceration in the USA and the UK has driven their respective justice systems to a fiscal crisis. This crisis has been heightened by the ongoing global financial situation, but pre-dates it. USA state corrections budgets have been an issue of concern since 2003. Any solution must include consideration of efficiency in delivering justice. In broad terms, we must begin to invest limited resources more wisely so as to create, if possible, greater savings down the line – savings which might be used further to address problems of criminality and reduce overall costs. We should seek to institute a virtuous cycle of criminal justice investment, reinvesting cost savings as they are realised. Such an approach has been used with success in the USA and is now being considered in the UK.

In this chapter we give a short history of the core theory, beginning with an introduction to Justice Reinvestment (JR) in the USA. The term was first used by Tucker and Cadora (2003), and was adopted by the US Council of State Governments for its Justice Reinvestment project (see www.justicereinvestment.org). We go on to discuss early implementation of JR projects in the USA, highlighting three successful case studies.

In the UK, the history of Justice Reinvestment is much more limited – indeed, the application is much more limited. A vision of JR in the UK is described in the Justice Committee's report of 2010. According to the committee, the key concepts of the JR approach are: determination of vulnerable individuals and communities;

provision of options to policy-makers; implementation of options; measurement of impacts, with evaluation and assurance of effective implementation. However, there has been, to date, no full application of this approach. Rather, the government has appropriated the term to motivate innovations in criminal justice delivery.

This leads us to a discussion of the two broad philosophies of Justice Reinvestment. One the one hand, policy-makers might seek to increase social justice. Increases in social justice, it is claimed, will lead to a decrease in demand for criminal justice. As criminal justice is scaled back, the resulting savings are reinvested in vulnerable communities, further lowering future criminality. Alternatively, governments might take the vulnerability (or otherwise) of communities as a given, and seek efficiencies in the delivery of sentences and rehabilitation. To some extent, the approach chosen will represent the view we have of ourselves and our fellow citizens. This will determine the limit of what we call "justice" (Faulkner 2010).

In practice, however, Justice Reinvestment is a broad concept. Many, if not most, interventions will include aspects of addressing social vulnerability and informing efficient sanctions for criminal behaviour. We conclude this chapter with a brief summary of the main issues.

What is justice reinvestment?

Justice Reinvestment seeks to reduce the cost of crime in the most efficient way possible; at its base is the consideration of criminal justice as a problem of the allocation of resources. JR is not a single strategy, project or intervention. It is a multi-stage process, as shown in Figure 3.1, providing a framework for local

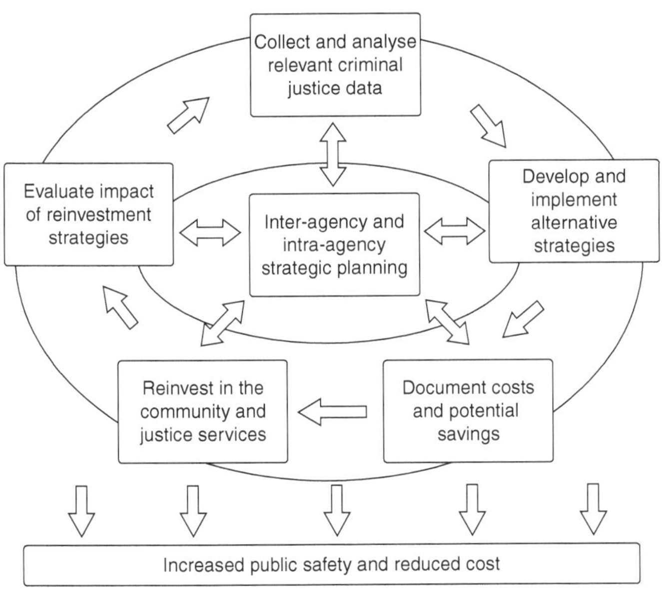

Figure 3.1 A model for Justice Reinvestment (adapted from La Vigne *et al.* 2010).

agencies to work together to identify and reduce the drivers of criminal justice costs (La Vigne *et al.* 2010). A JR approach recognises the potential to create a more law-abiding society in a more effective and less costly way than the traditional detect-convict-punish approach. Many of the cost savings may come from reductions in the crime rate: the crimes which cost society the least are those which are prevented from being committed. Justice Reinvestment proposes moving funds spent on punishment of offenders to programmes designed to tackle the underlying problems which gave rise to the criminal behaviour (Allen 2008a).

The basics

The Justice Center at the Council of State Governments (an organisation which has pioneered the use of JR in the United States) describes Justice Reinvestment as "a data-driven approach to reduce corrections spending and reinvest savings in strategies that can decrease crime and strengthen neighbourhoods" (The Council of State Governments Justice Center 2010: 1). As described by the UK Justice Committee (2010) there are four main stages to a JR approach:

- "Justice mapping": Analysis of the prison population and of relevant public spending in the communities to which people return from prison
- Provision of options to policy-makers for the generation of savings and increases in public safety
- Implementation of options, quantification of savings and reinvestment in targeted high-risk communities
- Measurement of impacts, evaluation and assurance of effective implementation

"Justice mapping" is important, as the likelihood of a person's becoming involved in crime varies with a range of societal, environmental and individual factors. For the purposes of efficiency, it would seem logical that interventions should be put in place where the risk is greatest. Therefore JR starts from a universal criminological truth, that people in prison are not drawn in equal numbers from all neighbourhoods (ibid.). From a criminal justice standpoint, the resource we devote to incarceration might be better spent on investment in reducing the occurrence of crime at a local level. In other words, where budgets are limited, the opportunity cost[1] of incarceration is decreased social support of the community.

Allen suggests JR has two key elements. First, it seeks to develop measures and policies to "improve the prospects not just of individual cases but of particular places" (Allen 2007: 5). Second, JR adopts a strategic approach to the prevention of offending and re-offending by collecting and analysing data to inform commissioning decisions (ibid.).

Key distinguishing features of Justice Reinvestment

There are many community-based interventions and rehabilitation programmes in the criminal justice sector. However, not all of these fall within the framework of the JR approach. For example, the Community Justice concept of Clear and Karp (2000) brings together three major themes in attempting to reduce criminal behaviour: restorative justice; prevention and early intervention; and community strengthening and self-determination. Such an approach may form part of a JR intervention, but by itself it is not JR.

The distinguishing feature of JR is its reliance on economic theory for its validity. The rational approach of economics is employed to address the constraints imposed by the "the silliness of politics" (*The Columbus Dispatch* 2008). By presenting and justifying efficient solutions, the JR approach can attenuate the political costs of being thought "soft on crime" (ibid.) and widen the policy debate.

However, although the analysis which underpins JR often deploys economic principles and methods, not all economics is JR. Consider the approach implemented by the Washington State Institute for Public Policy (WSIPP). Their sophisticated economic modelling project combines analysis of the offending population in Washington State, a wide-ranging Systematic Review of the evidence regarding what is effective in reducing crime and re-offending, and long-term economic modelling (Aos *et al.* 2006). This project has allowed WSIPP to develop a number of long-run economic models for different social and criminal justice strategies characterised according to how "aggressive" their investment is in diversionary measures. Notwithstanding, in an interview with the authors, Steve Aos contended this approach should not be described as JR.

Within an overall economic paradigm, three further factors can be identified which distinguish JR from other approaches to rethinking and reforming criminal justice systems. The first is that JR is generally a data-driven exercise. It is not a coincidence that it came to the fore at the point that modern computing power and sophisticated software for mapping data allowed researchers to develop new insights into the workings of the criminal justice system. This is an issue we return to in Chapter 5.

The second distinguishing factor is related to the first. JR is more avowedly committed to the use of evidence in shaping criminal and/or social justice services than traditional approaches. As such, JR makes a different political pitch for investing in justice services. Most JR projects start with a detailed "justice mapping" exercise and involve close, ongoing analysis of elements of criminal justice practice. JR is, at its heart, a geographically-focussed intervention, involving multiple agencies. This differs from traditional interventions which are geographically diverse, but delivered by a single agency. In essence JR is more interested in "what works" than "what is currently on offer". We return to this issue in Chapter 6.

Finally, the principles that shape JR, whether we take a broad or a narrow view of the project, make clear reference to the concept of efficiency. The current criminal justice response to re-offending is argued to be inefficient because there exist strategies and approaches which will give a better return to society for the same amount of cost. JR addresses the problems which incarceration seems unable to address: the high proportions of re-offenders and the detrimental impact high rates of custody have on the communities from which most offenders are drawn.

A brief history of justice reinvestment

It hardly needs pointing out that the concept of rehabilitating offenders as an alternative to incarceration is not untried. Indeed, as we discussed in Chapter 2, by the 1970s many in the USA thought large-scale imprisonment might become a thing of the past (Dodge 1979, Scull 1977, Sommer 1976, Mitford 1973). Sadly from the point of view of the 1970s, reliance on custody was a thing of the future. Over the last three decades the USA and the UK have seen a return of imprisonment on a large and indeed unsustainable scale. It has apparently seldom occurred to policy-makers to question whether this represents an efficient use of resources. However, the effectiveness of prison can no longer be taken for granted; evidence is required.

Justice Reinvestment in the USA

Social investment and the work of the WSIPP

Justice Reinvestment was pre-dated, and informed by, the work of the Washington State Institute for Public Policy (WSIPP), founded as a non-partisan research group by the Washington State legislature in 1983. Although the approach of the WSIPP is very similar to that of JR, the WSIPP describes its work in terms of portfolio and investment theory.

The current director of the WSIPP is Steve Aos, who joined in the 1990s from a background of energy and utilities modelling. On joining the WSIPP, Steve noticed that the same prudent investment and portfolio models employed in the area of utilities modelling might also be applied in the area of social interventions. The intention is to shift public social investment into areas with the highest return. In an interview with the authors in August 2011, Steve Aos stated that the most significant question on any research project is economic efficiency – "which combination of public policy instruments leads to the desired goal".

This approach need not only be applied to criminal justice, of course, and the WSIPP has been involved in projects in education, child welfare, mental health, and substance abuse. These areas are all, however, interrelated with crime and community well-being.

The WSIPP adopts a three-step approach to costing and evaluating policy issues. Initially, a thorough meta-analytic review of relevant literature is carried out. The focus at this point is on evaluating what works and what does not in the context of the issue under review. In particular, researchers are focussing on identifying causal relationships between interventions and outputs and assessing their size and significance. Part of this process involves determining how well results that relate to other states or nations may translate into the Washington context.

Having identified which interventions have been successful in the past, a Cost Benefit Analysis is carried out on each intervention that is identified as "causing" an improvement in outcomes. Benefits are monetised, and are broken down into two forms: those enjoyed by the taxpayer, for example, reduced prison costs; and those enjoyed by society, for example, reduced victimisation. On the basis of this systematic work, a portfolio of potential interventions is drawn up, ranked from least efficient to most efficient. To determine the sensitivity of potential returns, a risk analysis is also undertaken and interaction effects modelled. Once the likely returns and Cost Benefit ratios are known, interventions and policies are recommended to the state legislature by the WSIPP.

From social investment to Justice Reinvestment

The term Justice Reinvestment was used for the first time by Tucker and Cadora (2003) who, in their opening paragraph, throw down the challenge to incarceration:

> There is no logic to spending a million dollars a year to incarcerate people from one block in Brooklyn – over half for non-violent drug offenses – and return them, on average, in less than three years stigmatized, unskilled, and untrained to the same unchanged block. This unquestioned national dependence on mass incarceration reflects a fundamentalist approach to imprisonment that actually sacrifices public safety.
>
> (Tucker and Cadora 2003: 2)

According to Eric Cadora, by the early years of the twenty-first century, the combination of rising prison numbers and ineffective prisoner resettlement (re-entry into communities and society outside of prison) leading to high recidivism rates "led elected officials to ask what the return on continued investment in prison expansion would be and whether there is a more effective strategy" (Cadora 2007: 9). What was becoming apparent was that the "debilitating pattern of cyclical imprisonment" represents failure:

> From an investment perspective, both our prison and parole/probation systems are business failures. These policies destabilize communities along with the individuals whom they fail to train, treat, or rehabilitate (and whose mental health and substance abuse are often exacerbated by the experience of imprisonment).
>
> (Tucker and Cadora 2003: 3)

For Cadora (2007) two new lines of research opened up the possibility of a new type of response to these challenges. First, increased access to data and associated research was helping to clarify the drivers of increased prison numbers. A major cause of increased use of custody was incarceration triggered by minor infringements of probation and parole requirements. Alongside this, advances in computer mapping enabled the identification of communities from which a disproportionate number of those in prison came: communities in need of additional social support. As Cadora recounts:

> The phrase "million-dollar blocks" was coined to refer to research findings which show that in certain communities states are spending up to a million dollars per block to cycle residents back and forth from prison each year.
>
> (Cadora 2007: 11)

The question Cadora and other pioneers of JR asked was simply whether this million dollars per block might be better spent on other criminal justice and/or social justice interventions: for example, "a retooling of parole and probation for the twenty-first century, transitional supports for people in need of housing and healthcare, and increased sponsorship of civic and neighbourhood renewal initiatives" (Cadora 2007: 10). As Tucker and Cadora suggest: "A basic principle of justice reinvestment is to redefine the notion of public safety. Research proves that public safety is not assured by imprisonment alone" (Tucker and Cadora 2003: 4). Their suggestion and vision is "to invest in public safety by reallocating justice dollars to refinance education, housing, healthcare, and jobs" (ibid.).

Early Justice Reinvestment projects

Early JR projects concentrated on young offenders. Case Study 1 describes a project in Oregon that saw the devolution to local counties of state funds earmarked for incarcerating young offenders.

CASE STUDY 1: TUCKER AND CADORA'S ACCOUNT OF A JUSTICE REINVESTMENT PROJECT IN OREGON

Tucker and Cadora (2003) recount the experience of Dennis Maloney, appointed in the 1990s by the Oregon legislature to their state's prison forecasting committee. The committee estimated the number of prison beds the state would need in the future. Maloney, who was also developing youth programmes as part of Oregon's Commission on Children and Families, found the experience disheartening. "One day I'd be planning children's services, for which there was a pittance of funding, and the next, I'd be projecting prison spending, with politicians eager to throw money in that direction to appear tough on crime" (ibid: 6).

Maloney realised that because the state picked up the prison costs for adults and children, local governments had no political or economic incentive to keep them in the community and out of prison. Working with business leaders (who understood financial incentive models), he developed a community service programme that would make crime prevention a local, not state, responsibility.

With bipartisan support, in 1997, Oregon passed legislation that allowed Deschutes County to supervise, in community programmes, juveniles who would otherwise have ended up in state prisons. At the same time, the state turned over the cost of incarceration to the county. These funds were used by the county to create neighbourhood improvement projects to supervise the juveniles, and to invest in primary prevention programmes. Deschutes County also became financially responsible for each young person subsequently incarcerated.

As Tucker and Cadora (2003: 6) describe it:

> Propelled by a financial incentive, Deschutes County couldn't afford to squander its earned dollars on programs with limited results. Recognising that a majority of Americans prefer that people be held accountable for their actions, Maloney focused on community service as an active alternative to time in custody.

The project was a success:

> Deschutes County emphasised service and got results. Within one year, the community service program reduced youth incarceration in state facilities by 72 per cent, a national high according to the National Center for Juvenile Justice. The youth in the program averaged 204 hours of community service versus the average four hours for incarcerated youth; and their restitution rate was four times higher than that of young people who were imprisoned.
>
> (Tucker and Cadora 2003: 7)

CASE STUDY 2: CADORA'S ACCOUNT OF A JUSTICE REINVESTMENT PROJECT IN CONNECTICUT

Cadora (2007) reports on a project in Connecticut that built on projects with juveniles and used innovative financial incentives to lower the adult incarceration rates in Connecticut. Despite a prison expansion programme costing over $1 billion, by 2000 the state was facing a shortfall of 2,000 beds and the prospect of paying millions of dollars a year to other states to rent additional prison capacity.

Cadora (2007) reports that a "flood" of newspaper editorials published between June 2003 and April 2004 argued that policy-makers should consider alternatives to custody instead of continued prison construction. Public officials sought support from the Council of State Governments, which provided the technical support for a JR project. Their research confirmed that Connecticut mirrored national trends: violations by people on probation and parole were increasing the prison population, with inmates staying in custody longer and various factors delaying their release. They also found that half the prison population came from a few neighbourhoods in three cities in the state, including the city of New Haven, where a single neighbourhood was costing the state $20 million a year, $6 million of which was for probation violators alone (Cadora 2007). Analysis of social services data showed that people returning from prison lived in the same neighbourhoods as those where a disproportionate number of unemployed people and welfare claimants lived (ibid.).

The research helped to create a political consensus for a JR project, and in 2004, the state passed the Act Concerning Prison Overcrowding. It included measures for reducing probation revocations and creating comprehensive community plans for accommodating people returning from prison (ibid.). The state also stopped a plan to pay the state of Virginia to house 2,000 more Connecticut prisoners, reduced the corrections budget by $30 million, and reinvested $13 million in neighbourhood-targeted strategies, including more probation service capacity and additional mental health and substance misuse services (ibid.).

Cadora (2007) reports that the results were encouraging, with Connecticut going from being one of the fastest-growing prison systems in the country to nearly the fastest-shrinking one. Plans to build additional prisons were scrapped and out-of-state contracts cancelled. Drops in probation revocations to prison led the state to follow up with additional funds in 2007 of $6 million for the probation violator programmes and $11 million for community-based and residential treatment programmes. Planning for the future, the state established stronger analytical functions to support further JR initiatives. However, Cadora also notes some obstacles, including inadequate community planning resulting from funding small programmes targeting very small numbers of people returning from prison, instead of a more widespread community initiative.

The role of the Council of State Governments

Many of the early JR projects in the USA were implemented with the support of the Council of State Governments Justice Center. The Justice Center emphasises practical, data-driven and consensus-based strategies in designing and implementing localised criminal justice reform (Council of State Governments Justice Center 2010). As a condition of its involvement in any JR project, the Council requires an invitation from all the three branches of state government (legislative, executive, judicial). This requirement is to ensure that the work will be non-partisan and broadly supported in the state. The Center's approach is comprised of three elements: analysing data and developing policy options; adopting new policies and putting reinvestment strategies into place; and measuring performance.

The first full-time member of staff taken on by the Council of State Governments to work on JR was Marshall Clement. Clement worked with Connecticut – his involvement pre-dates the establishing of the Justice Center – and has since taken part in projects in 14 further states. In an interview with the authors in August 2011, Clement stated that one of the most important aspects of the JR approach is the engagement with stakeholders, involving liaison between different interested parties and criminal justice groups. Unfortunately, there is often a potential conflict of objectives at policy and local level. For example, elected mayors may be held accountable for high-profile cases by the voting public, but effective policy cannot be built on public response to a few cases. Thus the Center emphasises that JR is not itself a policy, but rather an approach to public policy making. Negotiating a JR-based intervention is something of "a dance" rather than a silver-bullet cure which will instantly appeal to all stakeholders. For successful implementation, members of the Justice Center must "speak the language of both the policy makers and the public". Because of this, the Center is careful to maintain its independence and apolitical stance, which is seen as an advantage in keeping "everyone on board".

Case Study 3 is an extract from an overview of JR produced by the Council of State Governments Justice Center (2010). The Center supported many of the early JR projects in the USA, and Texas is widely quoted as an example of what JR can achieve.

CASE STUDY 3: TEXAS

In 2007, the prison population in Texas was projected to grow by more than 14,000 people over the following five years. After reviewing the Justice Center's detailed analyses that revealed the reasons for this trend, along with a set of suggested policy options, state lawmakers enacted a comprehensive policy package to avert the anticipated growth and save $443 million. As part of their efforts – and to improve the success rates of people under supervision – the legislature reinvested $241 million to expand the capacity of programmes dealing with substance abuse and mental health treatment, and to ensure that the release of low-risk individuals was not delayed due to lack of in-prison and community-based treatment programmes.

> Since the enactment of the new policies, the number of people on probation and parole who have been returned to prison decreased significantly. The prison population has stabilized and has not been projected to grow, allowing the state to cancel plans to build any additional prisons for the foreseeable future. While these developments occurred, crime rates in nearly every major urban area in Texas have declined.
>
> (Source: Council of State Governments Justice Center 2010: 3)

Recently the federal government has begun to recognise the effect on state budgets of a criminal justice sector which over-emphasises imprisonment. In 2010, the USA Congress and Senate passed the Criminal Justice Reinvestment Act 2010 (US Senate Judiciary Committee 2010) which aimed simultaneously to increase public safety and reduce the corrections budget. According to Senator Whitehouse, one of those who introduced the legislation in November 2009,

> The Criminal Justice Reinvestment Act would create a two-part grant program for governments to analyze criminal justice trends, develop policy options to address growth in the corrections system, and implement and measure the impact of the policy changes.
>
> (Whitehouse 2010: unnumbered)

The grant fund in total is on the order of $30 million. It should be noted that it is designed to promote interventions to support those already convicted for criminal activity; thus it is promoting rehabilitative interventions.

Justice Reinvestment in the UK

Although the UK has not experienced the high incarceration rates seen in the USA, it is nonetheless clear that the level of incarceration in English and Welsh prisons is unsustainable. A possible solution is that the US experience of JR may be translated to the UK context and thus inform more rational policy than that currently employed.

The Commission on English Prisons

As part of their comprehensive review of the prison service in England (and, to some extent, Wales), *Do Better, Do Less*, the Commission on English Prisons Today (2009) note the unsustainable increase in demand (and supply) for prison places – and this despite the falling rate of criminality in the nation. Looking abroad (and to Scotland), the Commission concludes it is possible to reduce both prison numbers and criminality. To achieve this, the Commission recommends a three-fold approach: public fears on law and order must be challenged; moderation rather than excess should be a philosophy of punishment; and a new framework must be realised through practical and appropriate interventions.

The Commission notes (somewhat optimistically) the English characteristics of being "reserved, moderate, prudent, considered, pragmatic, tolerant, temperate and forgiving" (p. 32) and suggests these, together with the lack of confidence the public has in the current criminal justice system, allow the foundation of a desire for change in the prison system. In practical terms, the policies which might be employed are also three-fold: localisation; Justice Reinvestment; and restorative justice.

The policy of localism allows the addressing of two issues simultaneously. According to the commission, while the people of England feel their communities are increasingly disempowered (Watts 2008), there is good evidence to show that justice functions are more efficiently delivered at the local level (Mulgan and Bury 2006, Local Government Information Unit 2008, Stern and Allen 2007). It is argued that localising services and service providers also leads to an increase in trust (Lappi-Seppälä 2009, cited in Commission on English Prisons Today 2009), which is associated with a reduction in the proportion of the population who are incarcerated and, we might expect, a more effective series of interventions. The commission also argues that cooperation between stakeholders is more likely to be achieved at a local, rather than national, level (p. 51). Localisation is, therefore, an approach which will lead to more correctly aligned incentives as well as making it more likely that interventions will be supported and be successful.

To the Commission, the policy of restorative justice is about reintegrating offenders into communities. For restoration to occur, offenders must acknowledge the damage they have done and make some kind of reparation. Although, in the UK, restorative justice has primarily been used for "conflicts in schools, community and neighbourhoods" (p. 57), the Commission note that in New

Zealand, "some 25% of the most serious cases (excluding murder and manslaughter) and all repeat young offenders have been offered the opportunity of restorative justice" (p. 58). However, it is the case that "embracing restorative justice has not prevented New Zealand experiencing dramatic rises in both rates of imprisonment and the use of community sentencing" (ibid.).

It is also worth noting that the supposed benefits do not follow automatically from the application of restorative justice. As with all interventions, it is no magic bullet, but needs to be used only where appropriate. For example, Davis *et al.* (1988) are concerned that the accommodation between restorative justice and criminal justice

> is dishonest because many proponents of "reparation" are principally interested in diversion, or in the imposition of less severe punishments, but they have difficulty convincing police and magistrates of their case. So they invite the offender to jump through certain hoops which are believed to be consistent with the values of those key decision-makers.
>
> (Davis *et al.* 1988: 133)

For this reason, it seems reasonable to suggest that restorative justice might be useful as a component of evidence-based policy, but that its application requires very careful monitoring.

In their consideration of the strengths of the Justice Reinvestment approach, the Commission on English Prisons Today (2009) argues (p. 49) "Justice Reinvestment is not about alternatives within the criminal justice process, it is about alternatives outside of it". To the Commission, the JR approach allows the holistic consideration of the problem of criminality. It is in the interlinking of localised costs and benefits – including social costs and benefits – where real opportunities arise for innovation.

The Justice Committee report

JR was thoroughly reviewed by the House of Commons Justice Committee and was given a broad endorsement by that cross-party body (Justice Committee 2010). The committee began by noting a "crisis of sustainability" (p. 5) in criminal justice. They considered three main drivers of the need to evaluate JR as a more economically efficient alternative to the current approach. In sum, these are: the complexity of the current system and the difficulty in setting overarching efficient objectives; the government's ongoing commitment to building more prison places; and the relative efficiency of local authorities and other non-criminal-justice agencies in delivering reductions in offending and re-offending.

The committee welcomed the government's abandonment of the programme of building "Titan" prisons, which would have been capable of housing up to 2,500 offenders each; however, it noted that the government remained committed to increasing the stock of prison places. Indeed, the suggested alternative to three prisons capable of holding 7,500 inmates in total was a building programme of five slightly smaller prisons with the same total capacity. Once these were available, the committee felt it would be almost inevitable that they would be used, and thus the demand for prison places would rise passively with the supply. Once criminal justice expenditure is "invested" in further prison places, it will become increasingly difficult to divert funds into community alternatives because of the sunk costs of prisons (and, we might speculate, the political costs of such a change of focus).

Rather than focussing on an incapacitative approach to criminal justice, the committee recommends an emphasis on rehabilitation and – doing some degree of injustice to the English language (though in a good cause) – "prehabilitation" (para. 129), which they describe as interventions designed to head off the drift into crime before it happens. This is to say that vulnerable individuals and the communities in which they find themselves require support to reduce the likelihood of criminality. In this they go beyond the current emphasis in the USA, which is broadly rehabilitative.

As has been shown to be the case in the USA, the process of reducing offending and re-offending through community interventions, apparently so rational and efficient, can be sidelined by politics and ill-informed public opinion (para. 192). Notwithstanding, there is some evidence the British public are not so reactionary as they might be thought. Lord Dubs (para. 208) is of the opinion that public perception is a "political problem", and the committee suggests that the government has acquiesced to the media portrayal and must to do more to foster rational debate. HM Council of Circuit Judges (quoted in para. 214) are concerned that "senior political figures appear to publicly accept as correct reports that are clearly wrong". The committee suggests that the government must do more to take charge of the debate on rehabilitation and non-custodial sentences with a view to creating a more efficient and rational justice system.

In sum, the committee recommended to the government a holistic approach summarised in four steps: justice mapping, to determine where reinvestment is required; devising options; quantifying savings and reinvestment; and measuring the impact of interventions. In addition to this, the committee suggests, there needs to be a national debate on criminal justice spending.

As we have seen, the Commission on English Prisons Today (2009) consider localism an important aspect of a renewed approach to criminal justice. However, the Justice Committee note the squeeze that government policy puts on smaller local organisations in favour of larger commercial enterprises. They suggest:

> Government contracting policy has sometimes put an unacceptable level of pressure on such organisations which are squeezed by a departmental wish to cut overheads while contracting with larger bodies or with commercial organisations rather than with a larger number of smaller organisations which are closer to the coalface.
>
> (Justice Committee 2010: para. 95)

They suggest that local models are more responsive to local needs and recommend that the government "reject any move away from contracting with small organisations with proven track records" (para. 237). Sadly, as Fox and Albertson (2011) discuss, Payment by Results, which forms a mainstay of the government's approach to JR, is likely to squeeze out smaller providers and true innovation.

There is a further issue relating to localism, which is whether the UK public as a whole will be altogether happy with much local variation in law enforcement or sentencing (Faulkner 2010). There is also a concern that local, but unrepresentative, pressure groups may come to exert undue influence on localised criminal justice services (ibid.). For this reason, it is very important that national standards also be maintained. No offender or victim of crime should be forced into participation in a local scheme which will disadvantage them relative to traditional criminal justice services.

The "rehabilitation revolution"

One of the first of the new generation of Conservative politicians to recognise the link between (the lack of) social justice and the demand for criminal justice services is Iain Duncan Smith, leader of the Conservative Party (in opposition) from 2001 to 2003. In 2004, Smith established the Centre for Social Justice with a view to seeking effective solutions to the high levels of poverty in parts of Britain. The Centre's research has established five pathways to poverty: family breakdown; economic dependency and worklessness; educational failure; addiction; and personal indebtedness (Centre for Social Justice 2006). Although primarily concerned with poverty, the Centre has also published work in the area of criminal justice, as, according to Smith:

> the criminal justice system, particularly our overflowing prison system, picks up the pieces of this breakdown [in British society] on a daily basis. Each of the five pathways to poverty has fuelled an unprecedented prison population increase in the last decade.
>
> (Iain Duncan Smith in Centre for Social Justice 2009: 7)

The Centre's analysis indicated that the "spectacular failure" (ibid.) to rehabilitate prisoners while in prison cost the country £12 billion each year. In response, the Centre suggested that National Offender Management System (NOMS) be abolished and the management of custody and rehabilitation devolved to the local level. They further called for a collaboration between criminal justice professionals, the private sector, and voluntary and community sector organisations to rehabilitate prisoners, in the process helping them find employment and accommodation after release. These interventions, though targeted at rehabilitation rather than "prehabilitation" (Justice Committee 2010), are clearly cast in the same mould as the original vision of JR: that is to say, a community approach which supports neighbourhoods from which offenders come, with a view to reducing both offending and re-offending (Tucker and Cadora 2003). Although they do not mention the JR projects in the USA, the Centre for Social Justice refer to the work of the WSIPP with respect to Dedicated Drug Courts; general and vocational prison education, motivated by the "carrot" of earned release from prison; and prison work in the community. Citing evidence from the WSIPP, the Centre for Social Justice (2009) demonstrated the significant cost savings that can be made from these interventions.

Although they did not mention social justice or JR directly, the Conservative Party, in the run-up to the 2010 general election, cited the role of rehabilitation as a way of reducing criminal justice costs (Conservative Party 2009). Noting that "[c]rime will not be reduced by cutting the prison population. The prison population will be cut by reducing crime" and that "[h]alf of all crime is committed by previous offenders" (p. 45), the Conservatives' vision was of cutting the demand for prison by reducing re-offending.

Under a Conservative government, prisons would become "places of education, hard work, rehabilitation and restoration" (Conservative Party 2009: 46). The four principles of reform were to be: the decentralisation of the prison service and the NOMS; accountability of local probation chiefs and prison governors to locally elected politicians; an increased role for the private and voluntary sector; and Payment by Results (pp. 48–49). Thus the means of rehabilitation was to be fragmentation of the public service and an increased emphasis on private sector support.

In 2010, the Conservative Party and the Liberal Democrats agreed to form the UK's first formal Coalition government for 55 years. By this time, the vision for criminal justice reform had shifted yet further from state and private sector partnership. The first bullet point under the "Justice" heading in the Coalition Agreement reads: "We will introduce a 'rehabilitation revolution' that will pay independent providers to reduce reoffending, paid for by the savings this new approach will generate within the criminal justice system" (Her Majesty's Government 2010: 23). As indicated by the Conservative Party (2009), one of the priority areas for reform was the introduction of Payment by Results for the rehabilitation of offenders. That is, provisions would be put in place to hold providers of rehabilitation services to account for the outcomes achieved. Referring to Payment by Results, the Ministry of Justice stated:

> This is a radical and decentralising reform which will deliver a fundamental shift in the way rehabilitation is delivered. It will make the concept of justice reinvestment real by allowing providers to invest money in the activity that will prevent offending rather than spending money on dealing with the consequences
>
> (Ministry of Justice 2010c: 38)

However, it should be noted that Payment by Results, while it might form a part of a JR project, is not, in isolation, capable of making the concept of JR real. We discuss this issue further in Chapter 9.

Partial implementations of Justice Reinvestment

A number of projects in the UK have implemented discrete elements that could be associated with JR. However, to date, none represents a full implementation in the terms of the US Council of State Governments' four-stage approach to JR, as described earlier in this chapter.

The Diamond Initiative, for example, was a two-year scheme (ending in March 2011) piloted by London Probation and the Metropolitan Police Service, working as part of the London Criminal Justice Board and using elements of the JR approach, specifically justice mapping. The Initiative brought together multi-agency teams of police, probation, and local authority officers to resettle offenders back into the community following prison sentences of less than 12 months. The project was focussed primarily on offenders in custody and after release from custody (Allen 2008b) rather than taking the broader view, characteristic of some projects in the USA, of offending careers rooted in deprived communities. Thus the Commission on English Prisons Today (2009) argue that rather than re-directing resources into communities, Diamond Initiative resources were used for the management of individual offenders, and that in this sense the Diamond Initiative was simply a reinvention of after-care schemes for short-term prisoners and an extension of the existing Multi-Agency Public Protection Arrangements. According to Rob Allen (interviewed by the authors in May 2011), because of the multicultural make-up and population churn of London, it was unclear how many of the offenders on the programme were UK citizens from the neighbourhoods where the project teams worked. The geographical focus of the project therefore was not as significant as intended.

CASE STUDY 4: THE GATESHEAD PROJECT

In 2005, the International Centre for Prison Studies at Kings College London, with the backing of the Gateshead council, began a pilot of a JR-style approach in financing and delivering services to offenders and ex-offenders. Gateshead is a town in northern England, close to Newcastle, with a population of 191,000 according to the 2001 census. The unemployment rate for Gateshead is higher than the national average, and those employed receive lower wages than the national average; the borough is ranked the twenty-sixth most disadvantaged out of the 354 in England (Allen *et al.* 2007).

The aim of the project was to divert money from the criminal justice budget into community support, and then to collect data and thus determine whether the approach was practicable in the sense of delivering economic efficiencies. However, the project met with only limited success. Allen *et al.* describe the difficulties which the project struggled to overcome.

The first step in much JR work is justice mapping; however, as Allen *et al.* note, the prison service was unable to provide information on where the offenders lived prior to imprisonment or where they lived on release. This lack of data was exacerbated by the practice of giving prisoners an additional discharge grant if they reported that they had no fixed abode on release. A data set of sorts was accessed through the probation service but, as the service generally does not support those on short-term sentences, it is likely that the data is incomplete. Therefore, although justice mapping was carried out, it is likely that the coverage was limited.

Second, the possibility of a neighbourhood-based approach to resettling prisoners was discussed with the probation service, with the local authority and with the project's advisory board. However, it proved difficult to obtain a consensus about the appropriate form of intervention. It became clear that local residents would not be happy with facilities for released prisoners being located in their midst; neither did released prisoners wish to visit local services, possibly for fear of stigma. Also, it was suggested that resources were not necessarily available to relocate probation staff from a headquarters (ibid.).

Although Allen *et al.* (2007) do not express this explicitly, the Gateshead project seems to have struggled with the limited financial incentives available to encourage local agencies, particularly local authorities, to invest in preventative programmes or community-based alternatives to prison. This was despite an explicit aim of the project being the shifting of "the distribution of decision-making power from national to local in promoting local solutions to local problems" (Gateshead Housing Company 2005). A close reading of Allen *et al.* (2007) suggests that the project team could not develop the kinds of sophisticated economic modelling of different options which is characteristic of some JR projects in the USA. Such analysis might have been useful in pressing the JR case. Another point of contrast with JR work in the USA is the notion of bipartisan support: where the Justice Center of the Council of State Governments undertake JR, they require bipartisan support from the beginning.

A further and related problem is to do with the scale of the project. Arguably, it was unrealistic to expect that such an approach would or could work effectively at the level of a single local authority given that funding decisions about the criminal justice system are made primarily at a national and regional level. Moreover, in an interview with the authors in May 2011, Allen suggested that a geographic focus is perhaps more problematic in the UK than in the USA. Allen argued that while there was some correlation between people who go to prisons and concentrations in neighbourhoods, in the UK "we don't have million dollar blocks".

Devolution of budgets

One of the key issues of JR is an increased emphasis on localism; a particular case has been made for the devolution of youth budgets to local level. This has underpinned several ongoing initiatives, including The Youth Justice Reinvestment Pathfinder Initiative and Transforming Justice.

The Youth Justice Reinvestment Pathfinder Initiative in part foreshadows the partial devolving of youth custodial budgets in England and Wales. This has been legislated for in the Legal Aid, Sentencing and Punishment of Offenders

Act 2012. Part 3, Chapter 3, Sections 91–107 of the act provide for the transfer of financial responsibility for remands for young people (aged up to 18) to local authorities from April 2013. Ministry of Justice (2010c) states:

> Specifically, we are proposing that local authorities should share both the financial risk of young people entering custody, and the financial rewards if fewer young people require a custodial sentence. We therefore propose to run a small number of pilots, each working in partnership with a consortia of volunteer local authorities. We will agree a target reduction in the use of custody with the consortia and provide a reinvestment grant, on top of the standard grant to Youth Offending Teams, to help them achieve this.
>
> (Ministry of Justice 2010c: para. 256, 257)

The pilot areas are Birmingham, West London, North and East London and West Yorkshire.

At the heart of the Transforming Justice pilot, run in Greater Manchester and London, is a local approach using financial incentives which will reward a successful reduction in re-offending (House of Commons 2011). Specifically, the Financial Incentive Model (FIM) provides financial returns to local areas for reducing demand on the criminal justice system. The intervention has its roots in the Justice Reform Agenda, set out in the Justice Green Paper published in Ministry of Justice (2010c). In essence, the Ministry of Justice has undertaken to pay back half of their calculated cashable savings if a 5 per cent reduction in adult demand is achieved (with an upper threshold of 20 per cent reduction in demand). For the youth FIM the threshold is 10 per cent. At the time of writing, the scheme is ongoing; however, the authors understand from stakeholders (interviewed in May–June 2011) that Transforming Justice is unlikely to get the money required to "reinvest" because cashable savings do not include the savings made by crimes averted. Interventions may often take time to achieve savings; even then, it is not clear that all, or even the major part, of savings will be "cashable". This is partly because the pilots are on too small a scale. The economies of scale required to close the wing of a prison, for example, may be beyond the scope of a single project.

Different approaches to justice reinvestment

It is clear that the implementation (or partial implementation) of JR by the UK government is less comprehensive that that envisaged by the Justice Center at the Council of State Governments. In an interview with the authors in 2011, Rob Allen, an early UK proponent of JR and Special Advisor to the House of Commons Justice Committee when it produced its influential report (Justice Committee 2010), expressed dismay and frustration about the lack of development of JR in the UK. While he welcomed the interest in JR from national and local policy-makers, including civil servants and politicians from across the political spectrum, he observed that JR was like "motherhood and apple pie".

No-one is going to disagree with it; however, if you ask individuals what they mean by JR, this is a different matter. In an interview with the authors Allen posited that conceptualisations of JR varied considerably – "Three or four people will give you five or six definitions of what it is".

In general, we suggest it is possible to distinguish between two broad approaches to JR; crudely: "being more efficient on crime"; and "being more efficient on the causes of crime". The seminal paper by Tucker and Cadora (2003) addresses the latter approach and locates the delivery of criminal justice within a wider set of social issues and policies focussed on the communities which generate a high proportion of prisoners. That is to say, Tucker and Cadora see criminal justice arising, at least in part, from a failure to deliver social justice. As Marlowe (*The Long Goodbye*, Chandler 1953, Chapter 47) puts it, "Crime isn't a disease, it's a symptom. Cops are like a doctor that gives you aspirin for a brain tumour".

The social justice model

In social justice models, JR aims to prevent criminality arising in the first place. By investing in vulnerable communities – those at risk of damaging themselves as well as society – we may reduce the demand for criminal justice by increasing social justice. Clearly, social innovations based on rehabilitation cannot reach those individuals who are at risk of becoming first-time offenders. Therefore, interventions based on "prehabilitation" (Justice Committee 2010) must take a holistic view of the society from which offenders come. Interventions of this kind will favour support, compassion, and help for individuals to achieve legitimate aspirations, to the benefit of society as a whole. As Churchill put it:

> There is an injury to the individual, there is a loss to the State whenever a person is committed to prison for the first time, and every care, consistent with the maintenance of law and order, must be taken constantly to minimise the number of persons who are committed to gaol.
>
> (Hansard 1910)

There is good evidence that those nations with the weakest social security systems, and those nations more reliant on the neo-liberal economic paradigm, resort more easily to incarceration (Beckett and Western 2001; Cavadino and Dignan 2006). Where social institutions are weak, there is more social fragmentation, and hence there are more temptations to crime and fewer inhibitors. In this model, JR would seek to strengthen the legitimacy of social mores and the rewards of engaging positively with society.

Justice Reinvestment as criminal justice system redesign

Latterly, a more narrowly focussed model of JR has concentrated on "being more efficient on crime" (or, to extend Marlowe's simile, searching for a cheaper or more effective aspirin). This limited model seeks to reduce the use of incarceration by analysing demand for prison places and identifying opportunities at different points in the system to divert offenders from custody and reduce the likelihood of re-offending. This model of JR – which we may describe as a criminal justice system redesign approach – places little attention on what is happening beyond the criminal justice system. This limited vision is at the other end of the continuum from social justice models.

In the UK, at the time of writing, no JR has been implemented fully. However, generally, JR has been discussed in the narrower sense of redesign of criminal justice systems with a view to reducing costs, primarily through demand for custodial sentences.

Justice Reinvestment as a continuum

While we have aimed to typologise JR by describing two types or approaches – a broader social justice approach and a narrower approach focussed on the criminal justice system – our experience of collecting data for this book suggests that these are not mutually exclusive models. In fact, what they represent is JR as a continuum, where the approach that is adopted by local, regional or national agencies is shaped by dynamic factors – factors which can and do change over time. For example:

- Political acceptability – in these straitened times, it may be easier to justify and describe JR as offering a cost-effective criminal justice system than it is to champion social justice.
- Ability to re-direct budgets for public services – in the UK, budgets which might be brought together to offer a more holistic social justice approach to JR are retained within individual Government departments. This constrains their reallocation at a regional and local level.
- Short-termism versus long-termism – redesigning the criminal justice system offers a quicker fix than a redesign of social welfare interventions.

Real-life experience suggests that JR is a journey – an observation made by Jennet Peters during an interview for this book. Peters was until recently the lead on reducing re-offending at Government Office North West, and the Strategic Advisor to the Greater Manchester Transforming Justice pilot. When the authors spoke to her in 2011, her view of the Greater Manchester Transforming Justice Programme was that they were on a journey taking a step towards JR, as a broader public service management approach focussed on social justice. At the time, it was narrowly focussed on efficiency measures to divert individuals from more expensive interventions within the criminal justice system. This was a rational response to funding that was available at the time. Twelve months on, the Transforming Justice Programme is part of a Greater Manchester pilot study, which is aiming to break down the spending and funding constraints among government budgets. This would allow local agencies the flexibility to allocate funds for more upstream "prehabilitation" work, and would integrate criminal justice services more closely with other services such as accommodation and employment, through the development of new service delivery models. This latter development moves Transforming Justice along the continuum towards the broader, social justice end of the JR spectrum.

Conversely, the scope of JR in the USA has started to narrow. According to Tony Fabelo, who was involved with the Council of State Governments' 2007 Texas initiative, and was interviewed by the authors in August 2011, JR was initially seen as a way of "reweaving the fabric of society". Fabelo acknowledged that JR is a changing concept and that use of the term varies from state to state in the USA; it is also changing in line with the current political fabric of the USA. In the early JR interventions, a unifying theme was to intervene in neighbourhoods to reduce incarceration and "free up" resources for further investment (reinvestment) at neighbourhood level. It will be noted, however, that before funds are "freed up", interventions must take place. There is, therefore, an inherent lag in the system. More recently, money saved from successful interventions is more likely to go on closing the fiscal gap.

Notwithstanding the changing nature of the debate, in neither the USA nor the UK is it correct to characterise government at national, state and local level as having one and only one policy goal. Even if we might, it is certainly not true the electorate will hold so uniform a point of view. As Faulkner puts it:

> Public attitudes may reflect a generally optimistic view of human nature, a belief that there is some good in everyone and that people can change for the better and the country's condition can always be improved; or a view which is conscious of human imperfections, a belief that there is potential for danger in everyone and risk in every situation, and sees a broken society and a country in decline. Both views will always be present among people, communities and institutions, and governments will have to respond to them.
>
> (Faulkner 2010: 26)

Conclusion

JR represents a shift in criminal justice policy on both sides of the Atlantic. First, there is much greater emphasis on holistic responses to reducing crime and re-offending. JR has developed from the concept of the "million dollar block" and attempts to reduce re-offending are seen in terms not just of resettlement and post-release rehabilitation (known as "prisoner re-entry" in the US) but in addressing the underlying causes of offending and re-offending that are located in communities and even particular families. JR therefore requires improved links between criminal justice interventions and work with complex family situations. Second, JR is based on localism and the idea that criminal justice policy needs to be tailored to local areas and communities. Third, JR suggests a greater role for communities in tackling crime.

In order to be politically acceptable, JR requires a data-driven and evaluative approach. As Tony Fabelo puts it, often a successful intervention may not result in reducing spending – it might mean spending less than would otherwise have been spent without the intervention. This is a concept which is difficult to sell and requires framing the debate in very clear terms.

The cumulative effect of such an approach might be to establish close links between criminal justice policy and broader policy on social justice. This has certainly been an aim of much JR work in the USA. To date, the JR narrative favoured by UK policy-makers has tended to have a narrow focus on reducing re-offending. However, the real-life experience of JR on both sides of the Atlantic suggests that JR is a continuum with the social justice and criminal justice redesign approaches operating at different ends. Shifts in policy and practice between these two are determined by public expectations; political expediency; the ability to re-direct resources for public services; the capacity to adopt short-term or longer-term interventions; and – perhaps having the loudest voice of all of these – the state of public finances.

4 Theorising Justice Reinvestment

In this chapter we consider the theoretical underpinnings for Justice Reinvestment. The movement began from the pragmatic observation that social justice might prove a cheaper alternative to criminal justice (Tucker and Cadora 2003). To see how this fits into the overall framework of social policy, we frame Justice Reinvestment in the context of a slightly modified version of Ward and Maruna's (2007) framework for rehabilitation theory. We go on to develop this by considering the implicit assumptions made in the literature on Justice Reinvestment and attempt to make more explicit the assumed theoretical underpinnings. Having established a reasonable basis of current theory, we suggest some further theoretical developments of the approach. We return to these later in the book when we attempt to develop a new theory of Justice Reinvestment.

Introduction

In this chapter we examine the extent to which Justice Reinvestment (JR) has a theoretical underpinning. In the seminal paper by Tucker and Cadora (2003), the concept of JR is presented fully fledged and justified by practical examples. However, an exploration of the theoretical basis for JR is necessary to establish the coherence and logical consistency of the approach. Through the unearthing of the theoretical foundations of the movement, we may establish an approach to build on this model further and thus provide a stronger justification and intervention base for implementation. By way of a parallel, consider the example of offender rehabilitation.

When Ward and Maruna (2007) came to consider established practice in rehabilitation they found a lack of theory underpinning much of the work which goes on. They articulate two problems with this lack of theory:

> First, it has meant that the rehabilitation work that goes on inside and outside prisons today is too haphazard and ill-planned ... Second, even those interventions that are explicitly modelled on evidence-based correctional models (i.e. what works) frequently fail because of the program's inability to implement the intervention as designed.
>
> (Ward and Maruna 2007: 28)

While JR is (potentially) a much broader approach than offender rehabilitation, there are obvious similarities also. Our attempt to elaborate the theoretical basis of JR presents us with three initial challenges:

- First, as we described in the previous chapter, there are different versions of JR in operation and so it is likely that they draw on different theoretical underpinnings. It is unlikely therefore that we will arrive at a single, unified theoretical understanding of JR.
- The second challenge is that, to date, there has been relatively little discussion in either the academic literature or among policy-makers about the theory that underpins JR. JR is a strategy, in some cases a very broad-brush one, developed by criminal justice policy-makers and practitioners with relatively little input from academics. Perhaps not surprisingly, there has therefore been relatively little attention paid to what theory or theories might underpin JR and whether these theoretical underpinnings are coherent.
- The third challenge is deciding which theoretical framework to adopt in analysing JR.

We address the third of these challenges first, in the following ways. We argue the case that using Ward and Maruna's (2007) framework for theorising rehabilitation may be extended to encompass JR. We then consider the clues available in current literature on JR regarding its possible theoretical underpinnings. Finally, we start to outline some possibilities for further theoretical development of JR; we expand these further in Chapters 8 and 9.

Justice reinvestment, rehabilitation and "prehabilitation"

What theoretical framework should we use to analyse JR as theory? As we have discussed in Chapter 3, an intervention described as Justice Reinvestment may be drawn from a continuum of approaches. At its most limited extreme, JR might appear to be little more than a criminal justice system redesign formulation. In such cases, JR may be seen as an innovative commissioning strategy designed to improve the efficiency of the criminal justice system, with superficially limited impact on reducing re-offending or delivering better rehabilitative services. However, as we discuss later in this chapter, the interventions that are typically associated with system redesign, while intended to deliver greater efficiencies, do offer some rehabilitative impact. So, even in its most narrow implementation, at its heart JR is about reducing offending and re-offending.

However, at the other end of the spectrum we can conceive of JR as a strategy for delivering social justice, where effective rehabilitation is clearly an important, albeit not the only, aim. This is made clear by Tucker and Cadora, who argue that:

> with justice reinvestment the role of the formerly incarcerated will change. As utopian as it may sound, the cycle of incarceration can be broken.

> Residents of low-income communities of color, now relegated to permanent consumers of correctional services, can – through public reinvestment in individual capacity and community institutions – become builders and restorers of healthy, safe communities.
>
> (Tucker and Cadora 2003: 5)

La Vigne *et al.* (2010), in their guide to planning and implementing JR programmes in the USA, also put rehabilitation at centre stage. As well as being concerned with strategies to reduce the number of people entering the criminal justice system and to expedite the criminal justice process, La Vigne *et al.* place considerable emphasis on reducing re-offending through the greater use of prisoner re-entry programmes before and after release. They also advocate the use of recidivism as a measure of programme success in a local jurisdiction (in particular see La Vigne *et al.* 2010: 71), again emphasising that the reduction of re-offending arising from more effective rehabilitation is an important component of JR.

In the UK, Lanning *et al.* (2011) set out a vision for JR in which offenders are diverted from the criminal justice system where possible, and, within the criminal justice system, more offenders are diverted away from custody to community alternatives. However, there is, at the heart of their model, a redesigned offender management system which will be more effective at cutting re-offending rates: "The goal, if it can be reached, is a great one: a criminal justice system that both punishes offenders and rehabilitates them, that costs less and is more effective at tackling crime and protecting the public" (Lanning *et al.* 2011: 3). Community sentences are recommended precisely because Lanning *et al.* feel they are more likely to be effective in rehabilitation than custodial sentences – particularly short-term custodial sentences. (ibid.: 10)

While JR is a more universal approach than rehabilitation, it is broadly based on "prehabilitation" and rehabilitation – that is, the reduction of offending and re-offending. Therefore it is reasonable to begin to outline our theoretical justification by considering Ward and Maruna's (2007) rehabilitation framework.

In their analysis, Ward and Maruna found that there are theories to explain how specific types of therapy should work – for example, cognitive behaviourism involves psychological principles and strategies applied in clinical settings to change the behaviour of individuals (ibid.). However, these are really "local theories of change" (Ward and Maruna 2007: 33) and do not amount to a broader theoretical framework within which more strategic approaches to rehabilitation can be placed. The framework they develop is designed to perform this function.

The structure Ward and Maruna develop is a generic one. In brief, they argue that a rehabilitation theory needs to set out general principles; etiological assumptions (that is, assumptions about causation); and practical implications. This structure would, with only minor adaptations, be applicable to analysing a wide range of social policy interventions. This latter point will hopefully become clearer as we look in more detail at the theoretical components Ward and Maruna describe.

In sum, while JR is not simply an approach to offender rehabilitation, offender rehabilitation is sufficiently central to it (across the continuum of JR approaches) to justify using Ward and Maruna's theoretical structure to analyse the component parts of JR.

Components of a useful rehabilitation theory

Rehabilitation, from its beginnings, grew in an organic way; not exactly atheoretically, but with an over-arching paradigm of operation – informed by an intuition of what might work and by informal case history. As Ward and Maruna note: "for much of its history the practice of rehabilitation has taken place within a theoretical vacuum, with no clear explanation for how the process is supposed to work" (Ward and Maruna 2007: 27–28). They go on to argue that:

> a good theory of offender rehabilitation should specify the aims of therapy, provide a justification of these aims in terms of its core assumptions about etiology and the values underpinning the approach, identify clinical targets, and outline how treatment should proceed in the light of these assumptions and goals.
>
> (ibid.: 32)

The clinical language used by Ward and Maruna reflects their interest in the Good Lives model of offender rehabilitation, which has its roots in positive psychology (Ward and Maruna 2007). They also apply their theoretical framework to the Risk-Need-Responsivity model (see, for instance, Andrews *et al.* 1990, Andrews and Bonta 2006, Andrews and Bonta 2007); this approach also has its roots in psychology, albeit a different psychological paradigm. However, as we shall see, Ward and Maruna's framework can be applied to a broad range of rehabilitation approaches. As they elaborate on the components of their theoretical framework, the language they use is not discipline-specific. They argue that a theory of rehabilitation has a structure comprising three levels:

- A set of general principles and assumptions that specify the values and views that underlie rehabilitation practice and the overall aims for which clinicians should be striving. These form the foundation of the theoretical structure.
- Etiological assumptions (assumptions about causation) that serve to explain offending and identify its functions. Such assumptions give support to intervention-specific theory.
- The practical implications of the general principles, and etiological assumptions on the nature and working of the interventions.

These three levels are hierarchically structured, the first two each supporting the level above, as set out in Figure 4.1.

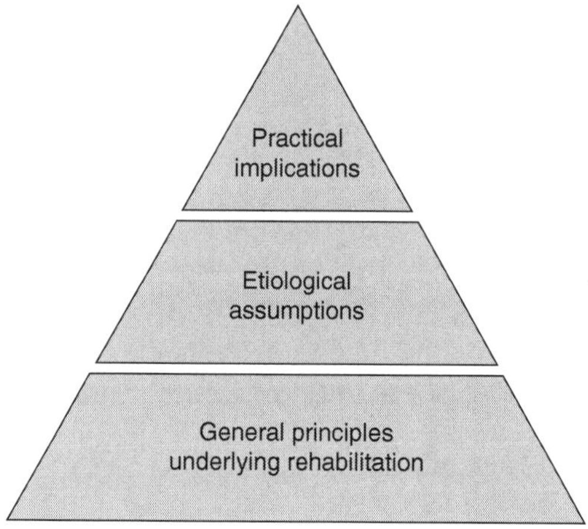

Figure 4.1 The components of a theory of rehabilitation (based on Ward and Maruna 2007: Figure 2.1).

General principles

The underlying principles and assumptions of Ward and Maruna (2007) cover a range of concerns and are not limited to a criminal justice framework: "As rehabilitation is an inescapably human enterprise – with humans helping other humans – the core metaphysical concern is with human nature in general" (Ward and Maruna 2007: 35). Rehabilitative theory will lead to different implications if based on humans being naturally selfish (the Hobbesian model) or naturally social beings (Rousseau's model). Thus the theory interacts with the nature-versus-nurture debate and with the question of whether risk resides in the person or the situation. It must also be considered *who* does the rehabilitating and for what purpose. That is, it should be considered whether a medical model is presumed, whereby practitioners rehabilitate passive clients, or whether a process of self-help is presumed (Ward and Maruna 2007).

It is also useful to consider how we go about the process of building the core theory – that is, setting out the epistemology of the approach. Epistemological assumptions "spell out what constitutes knowledge and how research that informs practice should be undergone" (Ward and Maruna 2007: 36). An example of the importance of epistemology is to be found in the debate about the merits of qualitative versus quantitatively derived data. Constructivist approaches to knowledge give weight to personal or lived experience; conversely, positivist or empirical theories favour more objective data yielded by psychometrically robust[1] measures (ibid.).

The motivating principle of any attempt at rehabilitation must be a coherent set of normative principles: the ethical justifications for one person to intervene in the life of another. For Ward and Maruna, core issues here include the question of coercion and the interplay between rehabilitation and punishment, needs and deserts. Justifications will range from the purely socially driven (where an individual's actions are damaging society, they must be induced to change) to the co-production of an individual's self-awareness and their ability to engage with society in a positive way. Motivation for those who require intervention will thus range from fear of punishment to desire for increased life opportunities – vulgarly, we may term the range of inducements "stick and/or carrot".

Therefore, interventions which are focussed on individuals must reflect social mores: ethical values which represent "foundational or core standards used to construct ways of living" (Ward and Maruna 2007: 36). In this context, moral values can be defined as humanly caused benefits provided to others and which can be described (by social approval or approbation) as right or wrong, good or bad (ibid.). Similarly, prudential values can be described as humanly caused benefits that people secure for themselves, or naturally occurring benefits resulting in enhanced well-being (ibid.). That is to say, moral values influence individuals to behave in such a way as to benefit society, while prudence influences individuals to behave in a way beneficial to themselves. It will be clear that there will be some circumstances where morality and prudence do not necessarily indicate the same course of action.

Etiological assumptions

Etiology[2] is the study of causation. In our current context, etiological assumptions serve to explain offending and identify its functions, thus acting as a "bridge" between general principles and practical applications (Ward and Maruna 2007). Clearly these assumptions must be based on – and be consistent with – the established general principles. However they need not amount to a fully developed theory of the causes of crime. As a component of a rehabilitation theory, an etiological theory

> only serves to sketch out the causal factors that might increase the likelihood of criminal actions and to depict their relationships with each other. In a sense it provides an *overview* of the kinds of factor that are likely to cause crimes and on its own does not constitute a complete explanation.
>
> (Ward and Maruna 2007: 38)

Practical implications

The intervention implications of the general principles and etiological assumptions are the "'how to' guide for effective interventions" (Ward and Maruna 2007: 39). Whereas the first two levels are often implicit or implied, this level is the most overt:

> Every rehabilitation theory needs to specify the most suitable style of treatment (e.g. skills-based, structured, etc.), inform therapists about the

> appropriate attitudes to take toward offenders, address the issue of motivation, and clarify the role and nature of the therapeutic relationship. Intervention implications include the recommended screening mechanisms for the matching of the individual participant with intervention type, the criteria on which to base decisions about "dosage" … and "intensity" of the intervention.
>
> (Ward and Maruna 2007: 39)

The theoretical underpinnings of justice reinvestment

In this section we use the theoretical framework set out above to analyse JR. This is not a straightforward business. Clearly, work around JR to date has paid relatively little attention to theory and, as we saw in the preceding chapter, there are different conceptions of JR – "being efficient on crime"; "being efficient on the causes of crime". Notwithstanding, in what follows we will develop an encompassing theory which allows us to treat JR as a single approach. From this basis, we will draw out instances where application of the theoretical framework suggests contradictions between different versions of the model.

Underlying principles

Following Ward and Maruna (2007) we begin by considering the underlying principles and assumptions of JR. The first of these is the set of metaphysical assumptions about the nature of the entities involved in the rehabilitation and reinvestment process.

The individual and society

Advocates of JR stress the need to rebalance the use of custody and community-based alternatives away from custody. In part this is driven by a desire to reduce the cost of criminal justice; it may also be justified on the grounds of the relative economic efficiency of the two models. These are positivist, value-free arguments. We may also consider the normative perspective. In this context JR seeks to reduce social exclusion and marginalisation because these are "societal bads". JR interventions may also reflect a desire to give local communities a greater role in and ownership of the delivery of social and criminal justice. Hence, Tucker and Cadora argue that "Justice Reinvestment seeks community level solutions to community level problems" (Tucker and Cadora 2003: 2). At the level of the individual, we must also consider the normative principles setting out the justifications for intervening. As mentioned above, for Ward and Maruna, core issues here include the question of coercion and the interplay between rehabilitation and punishment, needs and deserts. In broad terms, JR seeks to change the balance between rehabilitation and punishment in favour of rehabilitation or "prehabilitation".

Ward and Maruna also draw our attention to the importance of ethical, moral and prudential values. It is probably pushing the literature on JR too far to try and extract clear statements in these areas, but the emphasis in some of the literature on community and building social capacity might (at least implicitly) suggest a model of human well-being rooted in the relationship between individuals and their families and communities.

Objective data and subjective data

Regardless of where a particular intervention sits on the continuum, JR is an evidence-based approach. Therefore, we must start with an analysis of criminal justice data. This might suggest an epistemology broadly in line with the positivist (i.e. scientific or objective) paradigm. This would in turn suggest a view of human nature as passive or determined by social structures and processes. The tendency of some proponents of JR to work primarily at the level of the criminal justice system, to base analysis on criminal justice statistics, and to concentrate on identifying the cost implications of different cohorts of offenders and applying interventions accordingly, might provide further support to this position.[3] In other words, the positivist approach is broadly in line with the narrow view of JR.

At the other end of the scale are those proponents of JR who engage with that part of "localisation" leading to greater involvement of communities in the criminal justice process. Interventions in this context are mechanisms which can help to build social capacity within communities and hence increase the individual capacity of (potential) offenders to desist. Most models of social capacity assume that individuals have a degree of agency. Therefore the relationship with social networks and structures is reflexive – individuals can act against or in accordance with the influences of socialisation; they exercise a degree of autonomy. This potential to exercise agency is illustrated by Tucker and Cadora in their suggestion that previously incarcerated individuals "can – through public reinvestment in individual capacity and community organisations – become builders and restorers of healthy, safe communities" (Tucker and Cadora 2003: 5). In broad terms, as we have noted, proponents of JR tend to prioritise quantitative data, generated by criminal justice agencies (objective data), over data which might provide individual insight, such as qualitative data gathered from offenders, communities, or indeed those working in the criminal justice system (subjective data). Thus La Vigne *et al.* (2010), in their guide to planning and implementing JR, devote considerable space to outlining how data generated by the criminal justice system, at different points in the criminal justice process, can be used to identify the drivers and costs of the system and as the starting point for thinking about possible solutions that will reduce the use of criminal justice resources.

We look at the process of "justice mapping" in detail in Chapter 5, but it suffices to say here that data that is central to the process includes arrest information, offender demographics, risk and needs assessments, case processing information and sentencing data. The data analysis envisaged is largely quantitative or economic. As discussed above, La Vigne *et al.* (2010) also advocate the use of recidivism as a measure of programme success. Typically these measures take the form of measuring re-offending over a one-year period, perhaps measured using re-arrest or re-conviction.[4] Evaluating effectiveness using this form of outcome measure might suggest an approach which is closer to the positivist paradigm compared to, for instance, an approach to research located within a constructivist or realist paradigm.[5] In the latter case, we might conceive of outcomes in more individualised or subjective terms giving greater weight to the goals of the (potential) offender and their account of the impact of an intervention.

Summary

The principles of JR may be justified from both the positivist and normative paradigms. The former will be more likely to emphasise solely objective, quantitative data. The latter will consider a broader range of data, and these different philosophical positions might, in turn, suggest different approaches to reducing offending and re-offending – an issue we return to in Chapter 8.

Etiology

As discussed above, etiological assumptions serve to explain offending and identify its functions. Ward and Maruna see etiology as an important component of a theoretical framework to explain rehabilitation, but do not require a fully developed theory of crime. Any proposed etiology will therefore provide a "sketch" of the causal factors that increase the likelihood of crime (Ward and Maruna 2007).

Models of JR that concentrate on the criminal justice system have relatively little to say about the etiology of crime. Perhaps in emphasising the value of measures to divert people from different stages of the criminal justice process, there might be an implicit reference to the dangers of "labelling" (Bernburg and Krohn 2003). In general, however, the criminality of the offender is taken as a given, and the narrow view of JR merely considers how the state might respond to this in an efficient manner. In what follows, we are assuming that society can intervene to shape the (potential) offender's life chances in such a way as to reduce their propensity to commit crime.

Individual criminality

An approach to JR that includes investing in measures to prevent or reduce offending (as opposed to re-offending) may draw implicitly on developmental criminology and/or the importance of the life course. Developmental crime prevention focusses on the causes of individual criminality from pre-conception through childhood and into early adulthood. This perspective moves us away from the criminal justice system response to crime, and from the situations where crimes occur, to mobilise resources that shape the individual's development.

Homel suggests that "Developmental prevention involves the organised provision of resources in some fashion to individuals, families, schools or communities to forestall the later development of crime or other problems" (Homel 2005: 71). There is a substantial evidence base that underpins much of the thinking around developmental crime prevention. In particular, the approach draws heavily on longitudinal research into risk factors that predict future criminality. In a longitudinal study, cohorts of children are tracked over time through adolescence and, in some cases, through much of their adulthood. Data is gathered on a range of factors that might contribute to criminality, and statistical analysis is used to identify which factors are best able to predict future offending. These "risk factors" are the focus of developmental crime prevention. Chambers *et al.* explain that "The predictions of delinquency based on these risk factors are about as accurate as predictions of epidemiologists forecasting who will get lung cancer based on weight, income, or smoking habits" (Chambers *et al.* 2009: 33). The theory and evidence that underpin developmental crime prevention can be interpreted in different ways. Of particular importance is the debate between researchers who characterise the development of a propensity to commit crime as a "pathway" and those who characterise it as a "life-course". This important distinction is made clear by Laub and Sampson:

> Developmental accounts, especially from developmental psychology, focus on regular or lawlike development over the lifespan ... The resulting emphasis is on systematic pathways of development (change) over time, with the imagery being one of the execution of a program written at an earlier point in time ... In contrast, life-course approaches, while incorporating individual differences and notions of lawlike development such as aging, emphasize variability and exogenous influences on the course of development over time that cannot be predicted by focusing solely on enduring individual traits ... or even past experiences ... A life-course focus recognizes emergent properties and rejects the metaphor of "unfolding" that is inextricably part of the developmental paradigm.
>
> (Laub and Sampson 2003: 33–34, quoted in Homel 2005)

This debate is important because, as Homel (2005) explains, if a propensity to commit crime is established in early childhood in such a way that a "trajectory" is irrevocably set during these early years, then the main focus of prevention should be on these early years. If, however, childhood risk factors have very modest predictive power into adulthood, and if human agency, situational factors and other life events are of greater importance, then prevention resources should be deployed across the individual's life course (ibid.).

Social injustice

Approaches to JR which advocate reinvestment in the local communities from which the majority of offenders come include further suggestions of a possible etiology of crime. These approaches highlight a range of programmes and social institutions which are needed to address offending, including education, health care, housing and employment. The implication is that poor social provision of these is a factor in offending. For instance, the early JR movement in the USA stressed the importance of integrating work on employment into rehabilitation. Thus, offending results not only from poor education, poor health, poor housing and lack of employment, but also because of social structures which have failed to alleviate these social and economic conditions. In short, a lack of social justice may be a precursor to much criminal activity.

An institution which has contributed further to this state of affairs is the criminal justice system itself. From the JR perspective, there is a reciprocal relationship between communities from which many offenders are drawn and the criminal justice system. Thus, Tucker and Cadora argue that:

> [B]oth our prison and parole/probation systems are business failures. These policies destabilize communities along with the individuals whom they fail to train, treat, or rehabilitate (and whose mental health and substance misuse are often exacerbated by the experience of imprisonment) … The "coercive mobility" of cyclical imprisonment disrupts the fragile economic, social, and political bonds that are the basis for informal social control in a community.
>
> (Tucker and Cadora 2003: 3)

In the early theory of JR, much consideration is given to the communities from which offenders are drawn in disproportionate numbers. This version of JR seems to have its roots in "environmental criminology" and theories of crime such as Social Disorganisation Theory. This theory is at least 80 years old; the Chicago School working in the 1930s and 40s established links between environmental factors and crime. One element of this work is to characterise a zone of transition within cities, where residents suffer poor quality housing, high levels of residential mobility, high levels of poverty, and poor levels of health. This zone was typically the first home for newly arrived immigrants who, once economically established, would move out to more prosperous neighbourhoods, making way for the next immigrant group. The zone of transition was an area of social disorganisation, and Shaw and Mackay's (1942, 1969) empirical work found that it was the area of a Chicago associated with the highest delinquency rates. Generalising, Hale (2009) suggests that it is logical to posit that, in times and neighbourhoods where unemployment is high or economic prospects are poor, then "it will be difficult to muster the necessary resources to combat social disorganisation and maintain informal social control" (Hale 2009: 368).

Social capital

One of the most influential recent concepts to emerge from sociological theory and research is that of social capital (Putnam 2000). In holistic models of JR, such as that of Tucker and Cadora (2003), there are references, sometimes explicit, sometimes implicit, to the literature on social capital.

Social capital derives from the informal and formal array of social relationships between individuals, groups and/or organisations. It depends for its growth on trust, cooperative behaviour, inclusiveness and openness, and is driven by a sense of equity and justice (Office for National Statistics 2001, Smith and Kulynych 2002). Civic engagement is critical to its growth, and social capital is generally understood as the property of the group rather than the property of the individual. As such the concept of "reciprocity" between individuals is particularly important in explaining social capital (Office for National Statistics 2001). Under these conditions, social capital fosters an ability to coordinate for mutual benefit and a larger common purpose (Smith and Kulynych 2002).

High social capital, in the form of social trust and associational networks, is linked with many desirable outcomes. The Office for National Statistics (2001) reviews the literature and finds positive outcomes that include:

- lower crime rates;
- better health;
- improved longevity;
- better educational achievement;
- greater levels of income equality;
- improved child welfare;
- lower rates of child abuse;
- less corrupt and more effective government;
- enhanced economic achievement through increased trust and lower transaction costs.

Focussing in particular on the link between (lack of) social capital and crime in Chicago, Sampson *et al.* (1997) found rates of violence to be lower in urban neighbourhoods that were able to activate informal social control, a concept they characterise as "collective efficacy": "Extending the concept of community cohesion, collective efficacy refers to mutual trust among neighbours, combined with willingness to intervene on behalf of the common good, specifically to supervise children and maintain public order (Sampson *et al.* 1997: 1). Their findings are important because they provide evidence that rates of neighbourhood crime are not just a product of factors such as poverty. Sampson *et al.* (1998) found that some Chicago neighbourhoods that were poor also had low crime rates. In these neighbourhoods, the researchers found collective efficacy was the most powerful influence keeping violent crime low.

Putnam (2000) describes the decline of social capital in the USA. In 2001, the Office for National Statistics, reviewing the literature, declared that:

> The decline in social capital in America recorded by Putnam is not mirrored in the United Kingdom. ... Some civic organisations have declined (e.g.

> membership of the Women's Institute) but other forms of engagement are rising, particularly single issue groups.
>
> (Office for National Statistics 2001: 3)

However, some more recent studies suggest a UK decline. For example, in 2008, the Joseph Rowntree Foundation (Watts 2008) published a survey which considered the attitude of the British people on what they regarded as the greatest challenges faced by their communities. One of these was the feeling that neighbourhoods were losing capital or capacity, as a sense of individualism grew and individuals became increasingly isolated from each other. This growing isolation has eroded the well-being of members of society: "[s]ociety has changed, it is a lot more selfish and 'me, myself and I'" (Watts 2008: 3). Watts also noted that participants felt social mores had been eroded and there was increasingly "a lack of tolerance, compassion and respect" towards others (Watts 2008: 1). A similar study has been carried out by Whiteley (2012), who considers the increase in dishonesty and anti-social activities in UK society. Whiteley finds that in general, survey respondents scored lower on integrity than their peers in a similar survey conducted ten years previously.[6] Whiteley notes that, in general, older participants exhibited more moral integrity than the young, and speculates that this could be one or the other (or both) of an aging effect – older people in general having more integrity than the young – or a cohort effect – the younger generation having a more relaxed attitude to low-level anti-social behaviour, which will remain relaxed as they age.

Summary

There is a range of theoretical underpinnings which may inform the etiology of crime and thus support a JR model. We may choose to consider the individual offender, whose lack of capacity to resist anti-social influences may draw them into a criminal lifestyle or prevent their escaping from such. A holistic approach would suggest the consideration of the social capital of a neighbourhood, with a view both to understanding how cohorts of inhabitants might be drawn into crime and also to considering the impact of crime. The former approach we might classify as informing a typically criminal justice approach; the latter, an approach focussed on the increased provision of social justice.

Interventions

It will be clear from the preceding discussion that the intervention or interventions chosen as the core of a JR model will depend on how broad a view is taken of criminality and capacity – whether we are concerned more with individuals or with communities and whether we are more concerned with efficient criminal justice or the provision of social justice. In the following, we discuss interventions which might be implemented at the various stages of the criminal career. It should be noted that we do not intend this to be an exhaustive list, but rather a framework through which future interventions may be considered. Within the framework, we sketch examples of interventions which have already been, or are in the process of being, evaluated.

We begin by considering interventions which may divert an individual from a criminal lifestyle altogether. Further interventions encompass diversionary measures within the criminal justice system and rehabilitative interventions designed to reduce re-offending. La Vigne *et al.* (2010) propose that agencies adopt a framework to implement interventions (to improve outcomes for offenders) at six key points in the criminal justice system: arrest; pre-trial; case processing; sentencing; re-entry (in the UK release back into the community); and community supervision. In describing interventions associated with dealing with offenders, we use this schema as a basis for discussing typical interventions often associated with JR on both sides of the Atlantic.

We begin, then, with a section considering "prehabilitative" interventions and move on to considering diversion within the criminal justice system and rehabilitative intervention.

'Prehabilitation'

We begin our discussion of interventions that might be associated with JR by recognising that some approaches to JR would imply a wider range of interventions than others. When we looked at what JR suggests about the etiology of crime (see above), we noted that those models of JR that make a stronger link between offenders and communities are likely to make reference, at least implicitly, to the potential to reduce offending through early intervention in offenders' lives. This may be done by the building and strengthening of a range of community institutions and resources as part of the reduction of both offending and re-offending. For example, Tucker and Cadora (2003: 4) argue that "A basic principle of justice reinvestment is to define the notion of public safety". Specifically, they advocate taking a geographic approach in which the low-income communities from where most offenders are drawn are targeted with programmes to address education, health, job creation and job training.

Implied in this approach is a strong strand of "localism", whereby solutions to public safety issues are "locally tailored and locally determined" (Tucker and Cadora 2003: 4); in the USA, this approach has also involved the devolution of spending from the state level to the local level. This broader view of JR implies a much broader range of, often, non-criminal-justice interventions. In particular, there will be more emphasis on social investment and reinvestment in preventative measures. Clearly, those interventions which reduce the likelihood of future offending are also those likely to reduce re-offending; however, we cover them here under the topic of "prehabilitation" as they will impact on all inhabitants of a community, including those who have not yet fallen into a criminal lifestyle.

There is an extensive evidence base on the risk factors that are associated with future offending. Chambers *et al.* (2009), in a report published by Policy

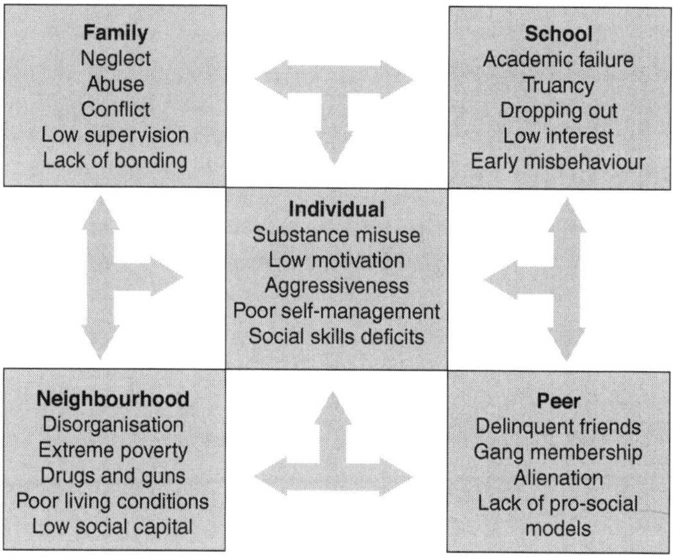

Figure 4.2 Risk factors for future offending (source: Chambers *et al.* 2009: Figure 12).

Exchange, a right-of-centre think tank, provide a useful overview of the most widely accepted risk factors, grouped according to domains such as "individual", "family" and "school" (see Figure 4.2). There is significant evidence to suggest that the greater number of risk factors in a young person's life, the greater the chances that they will go on to commit crime.

The correlation between risk factors and criminality is shown by the Home Office's *Youth Lifestyles Survey* (Campbell and Harrington 2000), a large cross-sectional self-report survey of young people aged 12 to 30. The study found only 6 per cent of boys under 18 had at least four adverse risk factors. Of this 6 per cent, over three-quarters had committed at least one offence at some point in their lives, and more than half were currently serious or persistent offenders[7] (ibid.). Among 18- to 30-year-old men, only 1 per cent had at least four risk factors; all of that 1 per cent had committed an offence at some point in their lives, and more than half were serious or persistent offenders (ibid.). In sum, those youth who were most at risk committed a disproportionately high number of crimes. Therefore it is possible to identify those young people who are most likely to adopt a criminal lifestyle and provide additional social support to change their likely life-course.

There is particularly compelling evidence for the efficacy of social support of the very young – so-called "early intervention", defined by Allen as referring to

> the general approaches, and the specific policies and programmes, which help to give children aged 0–3 the social and emotional bedrock they need

to reach their full potential; and to those which help older children become the good parents of tomorrow.

(Allen 2011: xiii)

In his influential review of "early intervention", Allen notes:

> Science illustrates that well-meant attempts to understand and tackle social problems have often failed because they have taken little account of the fact that children's early experiences lay the foundation for their future development. This is a fundamental issue: the way people respond to situations is rooted in their early years, a time when they rarely have contact with social service agencies unless there are very significant problems in their lives, which often result from parental mistreatment.
>
> (Allen 2011: 13)

The Allen review identifies early interventions that are robustly evaluated, have demonstrable impact, are underpinned by a clear "theory of change", and are "system ready" in the sense that they can be integrated into existing public service infrastructure and have the potential to realise economic benefits. The review identifies 72 programmes which meet these criteria, with 19 in the top category (Allen 2011); see Figure 4.3.

In summary, holistic models of JR tend to emphasise preventing offending and reducing re-offending, and place less emphasis on diverting from a custodial sentence those individuals who do offend.

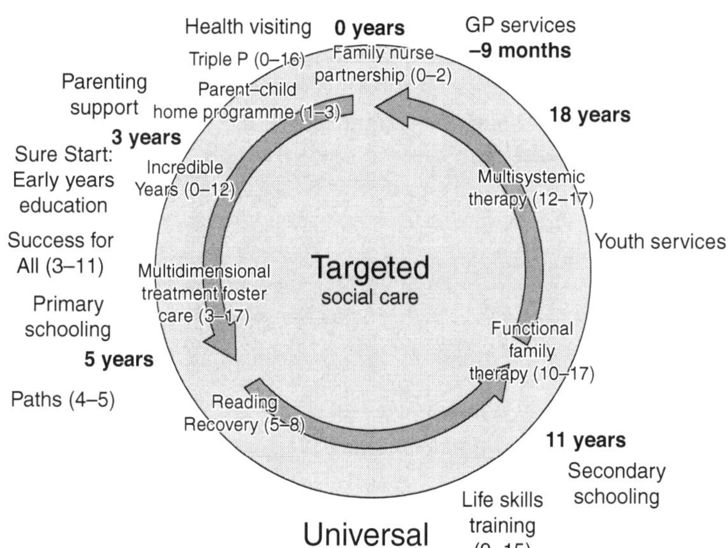

Figure 4.3 Examples of effective early interventions identified in the Allen Review, organised by age (source: Allen 2011: Figure 6.1).

Arrest

Where an offence has taken place, the emphasis of JR necessarily turns to mitigation of the costs of criminal justice, including remand, trial, punishment and re-offending. In the first instance, it is worth considering whether the offence committed requires and warrants the expense of the traditional criminal justice process.

The legal process is a costly one; at the point of arrest, measures might be implemented which would divert individuals from custody and a court hearing. In the USA, one approach used is "citation release" procedures for low-risk individuals. For example, in Bernalillo County, New Mexico, the sheriff's office has been issuing citations for non-violent offenders since the 1980s (La Vigne *et al.* 2010); this policy has expanded to include the police department in Alberquerque (ibid.). The point of these early interventions is to reduce the numbers of arrests and bookings in county jails. La Vigne *et al.* describe a number of further examples, including Jefferson County, Kentucky, where citations have been used as an alternative to custody for individuals arrested for shoplifting, public intoxication, criminal trespass, disorderly conduct, operating a vehicle on a suspended or revoked licence, and unlawful possession of less than eight ounces of marijuana.

There are also possibilities for diversion away from the criminal justice system altogether. A wide range of possibilities are used on both sides of the Atlantic. In the USA this range includes:

- Diversion to mental health services – Crisis Intervention Teams in Memphis, Tennessee, deploy liaison officers who work with the police with a view to referring individuals with mental health problems to mental health professionals and hospitals. In other jurisdictions, such as Miami-Dade County, Florida, mandatory crisis intervention training for all police and corrections officers has facilitated the diversion of mentally ill individuals to community-based treatment facilities (La Vigne *et al.* 2010). In the UK, while the reduced use of institutional settings in the health and social care sector has sometimes resulted in gains in well-being for service users (see for instance, Fox 2012), the running-down of hospital provision for the mentally ill has sometimes resulted in the inappropriate and expensive incarceration of some of the most vulnerable members of UK society (Dalrymple 2005).
- Diversion to homeless and alcohol services – the provision of a 75-unit dedicated emergency centre in Seattle, Washington, allows inebriated homeless individuals semi-permanent accommodation and access to services which assist them in reducing their alcohol consumption. Provision of this centre has paid off in significantly reduced costs. The city spent $86,000 on each individual while they were homeless, compared with $13,440 for each person enrolled at the centre (Larimer *et al.* 2009).

In the UK, approaches to divert people away from the criminal justice system at the point of arrest include:

- Restorative justice – the UK Government Green Paper (Ministry of Justice 2010c) signalled their commitment to extending restorative justice as an alternative to formal prosecution for low-level offenders. An example of this is the South Yorkshire Restorative Justice Programme implemented by South Yorkshire Police in conjunction with the local Criminal Justice Board. The model targeted low-level offending such as criminal damage, assaults, theft, public order, and anti-social behaviour, where the offender had no previous convictions (other than fixed-penalty notices). The process requires the (supposed) offender to admit guilt and to consent, with the victim, to the restorative justice process. Trained police officers facilitate "street" restorative justice interventions with offenders and victims, which involves victims communicating the impact of the offence to the offender and the offenders making an apology to the victim and some form of reparation either to the victim or the community. Meadows *et al.* (2012) found that the programme could lead to cost savings and efficiency improvements within the police and the wider criminal justice systems. They also found some indication that those who admitted responsibility and received a restorative justice disposal (as opposed to a conviction) were less likely to re-offend than those in a comparator cohort who were convicted and received a traditional sentence.[8]
- Conditional cautioning by police officers – the Greater Manchester Transforming Justice Programme (mentioned in Chapter 3) is piloting the use of conditional police cautions (instead of prosecution) as one means of establishing whether police might change their way of dealing with some kinds of lower-level offences. The conditional caution is implemented as an incentive to those adult offenders admitting minor alcohol and drug offences to undertake education and support rather than be prosecuted. A second pilot will focus similarly on offering education and support to adult females involved in low-level offences. Such support will be implemented in collaboration with voluntary sector agencies which specialise in working with women offenders.
- Custody triage for young people – an example of this scheme is run by Hackney Council in London, one of the local authorities involved in the Youth Justice Reinvestment Pathfinder scheme referred to in Chapter 3. If a young person is arrested for a minor offence, and there is a low likelihood of their re-offending, they are diverted into a custody triage programme. Such participation means they can avoid getting a criminal record for the presenting offence. The programme involves restorative justice and, in addition, a youth worker will work with the young person and their family to ensure that the young person is in placed in school, training or a job. If they are homeless, have drug and alcohol problems and/or have mental health problems, the youth worker will ensure that they receive appropriate support.

Pre-trial

Where it is determined that a criminal trial is the appropriate response to the offence, the state may consider how the interval between arrest and the trial may most efficiently be used to reduce costs and/or the likelihood of future repeat offences. La Vigne *et al.* 2010 identified three types of schemes in the USA at the pre-trial stage which aim to minimise criminal justice resources in the pre-trial stage.

The first, and indeed most obvious, is to increase the efficiency of bail; where judges refuse bail or set unreasonably high bail, the cost of remand increases significantly. Pre-trial agencies can facilitate the use of bail by collecting all the information which might impact on a defendant's likelihood of appearing for court, such as: their employment status; living arrangements; family environment; physical and mental health problems; and previous criminal history. Such factors will allow the assessment of the defendant's likelihood of failing to appear in court; minimise the need the need for judges to re-evaluate bond recommendations; increase the use of bail for people who qualify for pre-trial release; and reduce the time it takes to post bail (La Vigne *et al.*). Other ways to increase the use of bail include a 24-hour bail magistrate to facilitate bail setting and payment, thereby reducing the time spent in pre-trial custody. The use of technology to facilitate bail payments, for example self-pay, credit-card-pay online or payment over the phone, are also likely to reduce the length of time spent in pre-trial custody.

A second set of interventions is those designed to reduce "failure to appear" rates. Pre-trial officers can provide defendant referrals and facilitate linkages to community-based services for detainees who may have conditions attached to their bail. Such officers may also maintain contact with defendants who are on bail, to reduce their likelihood of failing to appear at trial. Further, more effective monitoring of data in automated systems will allow improved tracking of individuals who fail to appear in court (ibid.).

A third set of interventions is that of comprehensive diversion programmes. For example, in the 1990s, Birmingham, Alabama, implemented a case processing system for individuals charged with drug offences. This facilitated early intervention, case management treatment, and release. The approach was based on referring detainees to service providers on the basis of their required level of supervision and treatment. It was overseen through judicial review to ensure compliance with programme, treatment and testing requirements (ibid.).

Similarly, in the UK, arrest referral schemes for substance misuse operate in the period between arrest and trial. Drug arrest referral schemes have been in operation in police forces areas in England and Wales since the early 2000s. Similar schemes have followed in Scotland. They provide an opportunity for drug users who have been arrested to engage with drug treatment and/or other appropriate services with the aim of reducing their offending behaviour. Engagement can take place in the police cell or at court. The policy intention in Scotland is that arrest referral is regarded as a "pathway into services" rather than a diversion scheme or community disposal.[9] However, evidence from England and Wales suggests one of the outcomes of the scheme has been to reduce re-arrest rates for the majority (two-thirds) of those who had contact with an arrest referral worker (Sondhi *et al.* 2002). Preliminary economic analysis by Sondhi *et al.* suggested that the economic and social benefits of arrest referral schemes amounted to £4.4 billion over an eight-year period, with a ratio of social and economic benefit to cost of 7:1. Thus, while these schemes have not been explicitly established to reduce demand on the criminal justice system, evaluations indicate that they can contribute to minimising criminal justice resource costs.

Alcohol arrest referral schemes piloted and evaluated in England and Wales demonstrated less positive results. Eight schemes operated between November 2008 and September 2010. These typically involved a single brief intervention by an arrest referral worker with follow-up sessions in some cases. The first interventions were delivered on a voluntary basis in custody. Overall, McCracken *et al.* (2012) found these schemes did not appear to be effective at reducing re-arrest rates. Only one of the eight schemes was found to deliver a statistically significant reduction in re-arrests post-intervention (ibid.)

Case processing

Once a defendant is brought to trial, it is rational to consider how to ensure that the case progresses in the most efficient and effective manner. In the USA, examples of minimising case processing costs identified by La Vigne *et al.* (2010) have focussed on ways that county jurisdictions can exert control over case processes, particularly where case processing also involves state and federal jurisdictions.

One way such control might be exerted is to set prison population caps. When the population limit is reached, the jail administrator has the authority (or is required) to release certain types of prisoner and/or to expand eligibility for bond releases or diversion programmes. La Vigne *et al.* acknowledge that this needs to be implemented carefully and strategically to ensure only those appropriate are considered for such early release.

Another way is by reducing the number of continuances, that is to say, requests to the court for the trial to be delayed. There are costs to the state of allowing excessive continuances when the defendant is held in custody. La Vigne *et al.* (2010) report that when Seminole County, Florida, published court data on the detainees with the longest length of stay in jail (including the judge assigned to the case), the length of stay of detainees was halved due to reductions in the number of continuances in each case.

Setting time limits on case processing for detainees can speed up processes and reduce costs, as can assigning a case to the same attorney and judge throughout the process (referred to as "vertical processing"); and fast track "rocket and docket" systems to deal with pleas and simple cases (such as technical probation violation hearings) when continuous judicial oversight is not statutorily required (ibid.).

While many actors are involved in case processing, La Vigne *et al.* (2010) argue that court administrators and judges have the greatest influence over the speed of case processing. They suggest that judges can ensure that cases are dealt with as quickly as possible by working with prosecutors and defence attorneys and by evaluating individuals immediately on booking, directing them towards the earliest possible release route and actively monitoring their progress towards the release date.

In the UK, the Government have similarly driven through systems change to speed up case processing with a view to managing cases more efficiently. In the following we briefly describe the impact of this on youth justice.

In *Misspent Youth*, a landmark report by the Audit Commission[10] (Audit Commission 1996), an analysis was made (among other issues) of the inefficiencies in the way in which young people were processed through the youth justice system. The youth court process could take from 70 days in some areas to 170 in others. On average a young person appeared in court four times in the course of one case, and four out of five youth court cases were adjourned. Of those cases which were adjourned, the most frequent reasons were: youths/parents were not present; a defence lawyer was not present or briefed; advance disclosure was inadequate; or a pre-sentence report was required. It was clear that young people were spending far longer in pre-trial custody than was efficient either for them or the criminal justice system.

The Labour government (which took office in 1997) introduced measures to address these shortcomings in the youth justice system through the Crime and Disorder Act 1998. The Act established Youth Offending Teams (local-authority-based multi-agency partnerships) to deliver youth justice; the Youth Justice Board to set and monitor national standards; and the setting of national targets, for example reducing the time taken from arrest to sentence. A further review of youth justice (Audit Commission 2004) found that, by August 2001, the average time from arrest to sentence had halved to 71 days from 142 days in January 1997.

While the later report was generally positive, the Audit Commission identified other potential improvements that could also be made. These included fewer and more specialised magistrates; making sentencing more cost-effective; and more effectively addressing the wider needs of young offenders. A later review by Solomon and Garside (2010) was even more critical. They concluded that, while the time between arrest and sentencing had been reduced, at the time of their writing, performance in relation to case processes was mixed. In the youth court, the time taken for guilty pleas had increased and the performance for committals had worsened compared with what had been achieved four years earlier. Further, any cost savings to the public purse from greater efficiencies in case processing may have been offset by a reported 45 per cent increase in youth justice spending following the establishment of youth offending teams and the Youth Justice Board in 2000–2001(Solomon and Garside 2010).

The current UK Government's white paper on criminal justice system reforms (Ministry of Justice 2012b) proposes a number of measures to improve case processing and reduce costs. These focus principally on "simple, straightforward and uncontested matters that represent the majority of cases prosecuted through the criminal courts" (ibid.: 6). The proposed system changes include: fast tracking cases where a guilty plea is anticipated; simplifying and extending police-led prosecutions, for example for low-level traffic offences when there is no plea or where the defendant fails to appear; avoiding adjournments; and the handing of cases over to the Crown Prosecution Service. In addition, more flexible court sittings are proposed including early morning, evening and weekend sittings for certain types of hearings. This latter proposal is based on the way that courts responded to the processing of cases arising from the disturbances in London, Manchester and other English cities in 2011.

Sentencing

In the UK and the USA (as discussed in Chapter 2) there has been a growing recognition among policy-makers and politicians that imprisonment represents the most significant cost to the criminal justice system. Reducing the use of custody and the length of custody would deliver considerable savings to the public purse.

La Vigne *et al.* (2010) identify three ways in which costs can be reduced at the sentencing stage in the USA to reduce the length of imprisonment.

- Judges may prescribe alternatives to custodial sentences, such as probation supervision; a suspended sentence; a fine; community service; work release; education release; or electronic monitoring/home confinement.
- The courts linking defendants' sentences to services in the community upon release can reduce rates of recidivism and thereby reduce demand for future criminal justice resources.
- Community courts, such as those which commenced in New York City in 1993, help individuals charged with low-level offences out of jail by providing them with links to social services. Typically, "resource coordinators" were deployed to ensure that defendants accessed appropriate services and followed the conditions of their sentences.

The development of community courts has continued in the USA, with the implementation of problem-solving courts dealing with specific types of offenders or offences (La Vigne *et al.* 2010). For example, drug courts can allow a detainee to be released on bail (with conditions based on compliance with court recommendations) or receive an alternative sentence that reduces the likelihood of recidivism (ibid.). Similarly, family violence courts can use alternative sentencing to address the factors which lead offenders to commit violent behaviour and reduce recidivism. Newark *et al.* (2001) report that the Brooklyn Felony Domestic Violence Court, founded in 1996, was successful in reducing the violation rate of court participants by approximately 50 per cent. There was also an improvement in the level of services offered to victims. It has also been shown that mental health courts, which focus on addressing the mental health needs of seriously mentally ill defendants, can produce cost savings over time (Ridgely *et al.* 2007). However, this requires the effective coordination of services through case management, treatment plans and continuity of care (Thompson *et al.* 2007).

On the basis of their apparent success in the USA, specialist drugs courts and domestic violence courts have been trialled in the UK. The drugs court pilot met with limited success. Although there was evidence that costs were reduced through gains in efficiency, their role in reducing re-offending was limited. This is because of the significant role played by the quality of drug treatment and other issues in the lives of the offenders (Kerr *et al.* 2011). The evaluation of domestic violence courts found that they delivered value in terms of reducing repeat victimisation; delivering efficiencies in the way that cases were processed; and delivering benefits to victims (Cook *et al.* 2004).

These interventions were implemented as a means of providing more effective management of the offender (for both drug and domestic violence courts) and delivering better responses to victims (domestic violence courts). They offered more effective management of sentencing and other processes (which provided potential cost reductions), rather than being a point of sentence response which could deliver significant cost reductions to the criminal justice system. These may, where appropriate, be supplemented with the development of explicit, robust (and less expensive) community sentences as an alternative to the costlier option of imprisonment.

As reported by Wong *et al.* (2012a), there has been an increasing recognition among policy-makers (most recently dating back to a Ministry of Justice Penal Policy paper, Ministry of Justice 2007) of a "growing prison population and increased use of short-term custody (characterised by limited rehabilitation work and high levels of re-offending)" (Wong *et al.* 2012a: 1) for adult offenders. Policy-makers acknowledged the relative ineffectiveness of short-term custody, particularly in relation to cost.

In response to Ministry of Justice (2007), the Labour government established a pilot programme to provide courts with a robust and realistic alternative to short-term custody (i.e. sentences of less than 12 months) for adult offenders. These Intensive Alternative to Custody (IAC) pilots operated in seven probation areas in England and Wales and were funded by the Ministry of Justice from 2008 to 2011. IAC orders combined intensive supervision in the community with punishment, such as unpaid work orders and electronic tagging, along with rehabilitative elements such as employment, training and education, support to address drug or alcohol misuse, and behavioural programmes. The orders were imposed (at the point of sentencing) on individuals with a high number of previous convictions (on average at least 29) where they would otherwise have received a short-term custodial sentence (Wong *et al.* 2012a).

The evaluation of five IAC sites found that only one in four IAC orders were revoked because requirements were breached. This suggests that previously persistent and prolific offenders had engaged with the orders (Wong *et al.* 2012b). Importantly, sentencers regarded IAC as a robust alternative to custody (ibid.). Hansbury (2011) reported that the compliance rate of IAC orders was 56 per cent; that the estimated average weighted cost of an order per offender was £5,000; and that a break-even analysis demonstrated that IAC orders were likely to be more cost-effective (in terms of reducing the costs of each sentence and the likely costs of future offending) provided they do at least as well in rehabilitating offenders as short-term custodial sentences.

Similar high-intensity community orders, Intensive Supervision and Surveillance (ISS), have been available in the youth justice system in England and Wales since 2009, promoted by the Youth Justice Board as a robust alternative to custody (Youth Justice Board 2009). An ISS includes core elements of education, training and employment provision; restorative justice; addressing offending behaviour; family support; and work on interpersonal skills. The supervision is enhanced through an electronically monitored curfew. The typical duration of an ISS is six months, although 12 months is an option. A similar approach to ISS, the Intensive Support and Monitoring Service (ISMS), was piloted and evaluated in Scotland. Evidence of the efficacy of the ISSP (a similar scheme to ISS) in England and Wales and the ISMS high-intensity community orders is mixed. A review of the evaluations of both schemes by the Institution for Research and Innovation in Social Services (IRISS 2010) concluded both programmes may be more suitable to some young people as an alternative to secure care or custody. While a sentence requiring ISS may have led to some reduction in the frequency and severity of offending of those on the programme, it is unclear if the intervention is more or less successful than other less intensive (and less costly) community disposals. The evidence suggests that the intensive support may be the most effective component of the programmes (ibid.).

Discharge

In the UK and the USA, policy-makers have recognised the importance of intervening with offenders at the point of discharge from prison in order to reduce the likelihood of re-offending. In the USA,

> The costs of failed reentry can proliferate throughout all the agencies that comprise the criminal justice system. These costs are particularly significant within community supervision agencies, which can consume a great deal of time and resources on probation and parole violators (many of whom are unsuccessful because of a lack of reentry planning) … In addition, emergency services agencies in the community could be over-used if effective discharge planning is not implemented (for example, through the overuse of detoxification facilities and emergency rooms if individuals are released without sufficient medical plans).
>
> (La Vigne *et al.* 2010: 46)

Discharge interventions in the USA identified by La Vigne *et al.* (2010) include:

- re-entry courts to improve the accountability of court clientele, increase access to community-based support services and family involvement, and provide links to specialist services such as mental health and substance misuse;
- employment, training and education programmes in prison;
- programmes targeted at reducing the incidence of specific offences, for example, the six-week programme for individuals charged with domestic violence operating in Davidson County Jail, Tennessee;
- work release programmes allowing offenders to continue working and maintain their jobs while in prison;
- study release programmes which allow temporary release of offenders to undertake coursework or training outside the prison; and
- systematic re-entry planning, for example the scheme implemented in Montgomery County, Maryland, which enabled re-entry planners to release the vast majority of programme participants into the community with housing and employment.

In the UK, Prison Service Order (PSO) 2300 (Her Majesty's Prison Service 2001) sets out mandatory requirements to prisons on the provision of resettlement provision for prisoners. This is taken to operate throughout their time in custody, including the pre-release period. PSO 2300 prescribes a similar range of provision to the examples of USA discharge interventions detailed above.

Subject to PSO 2300, the focus of UK policy-makers has increasingly been the effective resettlement of short-term prisoners (serving custodial sentences of less than 12 months). As reported by Lewis *et al.* (2003):

> Short-sentence prisoners – those sentenced to less than 12 months and normally released at the mid-point of their sentence – constitute the majority of adult prisoners. This group has the highest re-conviction rate among released adult prisoners, but as a consequence of their short sentences, few are able to take advantage of offending behaviour programmes and pre-release services designed to improve their prospects of resettling successfully and leading law-abiding lives in the future. Unlike longer-term prisoners, moreover, they are not subject to statutory post-release supervision and are thus dependent upon voluntary after-care services for help with the multiple problems which research demonstrates are a consistent feature of the profile of short-sentence prisoners.
>
> (Lewis *et al.* 2003: iii)

Community supervision

It must be recognised that offenders, upon release, often present with complex and varied needs, ranging from educational needs to housing, drug and anger management, and employment. One way to provide a more coordinated, and ideally a more effective, response to managing offenders in the community and on release from prison was put forward in the UK government's 2010 Green Paper (Ministry of Justice 2010c). This offered a robust approach to rehabilitating offenders under the Integrated Offender Management (IOM) programme. Currently in the UK, IOM represents the most developed attempt to operationalise the concept of end-to-end offender management with extensive coordination between agencies (Senior *et al.* 2011).

The principles of Integrated Offender Management are:

- All partners tackling offenders' needs together – local partners and agencies both within the criminal justice sector and outside the sector develop a multi-agency problem-solving approach by focussing on offenders, not offences.
- Delivering a local response to local problems – all relevant local partners are involved in strategic planning, decision-making and funding choices.
- Offenders facing their responsibility or facing the consequences – offenders are provided with a clear understanding of what is expected of them.
- Making better use of existing programmes and governance – this involves gaining further benefits from programmes such as the PPO programme, DIP and Community Justice to increase the benefits for communities. This will also enable partners to provide greater clarity around roles and responsibilities.
- Keeping all offenders at high risk of causing serious harm and/or re-offending "in scope" – intensity of management relates directly to severity of risk, irrespective of position within the criminal justice system or whether statutory or non-statutory.

(Home Office 2010: 2)

Senior and his colleagues found that the proportion of non-statutory offenders (those sentenced to less than 12 months custody, and generally discharged after six months) who were being managed under IOM was between about two-thirds in one pilot area to a quarter in another pilot area. The inclusion of "through the gate" provision to non-statutory offenders has been adopted by other schemes across England and Wales, for example in Sussex, where "through the gate" non-statutory offenders have been explicitly identified as one of the target groups for IOM (Wong *et al.* 2011). At the time of writing, it is too early to say whether the programme has achieved cost reductions or improvements in the recidivism rate.

The principles underpinning IOM in the UK are broadly reflected in the USA interventions identified by La Vigne *et al.* (2010), which they suggest can deliver more effective community supervision of offenders. These include:

- Re-entry partnerships between the police and community supervision agencies, which focus on high-risk individuals with histories of recidivism, balancing harsher sanctions with efforts to link individuals to required support services.

- Better liaison between community supervision agencies and correctional facilities to improve re-entry processes and reduce the likelihood of individuals violating their community supervision requirements and returning to prison.
- Community supervision officers establishing behavioural contracts with offenders and offering a compliance credit system for rewarding good behaviour. In the UK, comparable contracts referred to as "offender compacts" have been established between criminal justice agencies and non-statutory offenders managed under IOM.
- Graduated sanctions for violations of behavioural contracts, allowing officers to deploy sanctions based on the violator's risk level and type of violation.
- Offering alternatives to mandatory in-person probation reporting for low risk individuals, such as probation kiosks.

In closing this section, it should be borne in mind that many of the interventions which were described above as "prehabilitative" also serve effectively as rehabilitative. That is to say, the establishing of strong communities with high levels of social capacity will serve both to divert potential offenders from crime, and to assist successful re-entry of those who do fall into criminality.

Summary

We have outlined and briefly discussed the points in the (potential) offender's career where diversion from crime and custody may be effected by appropriate interventions. This is by no means intended as an exhaustive list. As JR progresses, further interventions will be developed, subjected to pilot studies, evaluated and, potentially, rolled out. However, the listings above give something of an outline of the current state of play.

Conclusion

If we review our attempt to place JR in the theoretical framework provided by Ward and Maruna (2007), a number of issues are apparent.

- At a theoretical level, JR is under-developed. We have had to take a fairly broad approach to identifying possible underlying principles and an etiology of crime and criminality.
- As discussed previously, there are different models of JR. The underlying theory is more or less well developed, depending on the model considered.
- Those theoretical elements that we have identified or intuited are not all logically consistent with each other. For example, while much of the literature on JR suggests an approach which sits, broadly, within a positivist paradigm,

there are hints of a model of human agency that does not fit comfortably within this.

- The theoretical framework provided by Ward and Maruna (2007) may be too detached from the political context of the implementation of criminal justice policy, as outlined in Chapter 2, to inform the development of a theoretical approach to JR. For example, their framework does not include commissioning as a dimension of a complete theory, and yet we have seen some evidence that the approach to commissioning services has an influence on the kinds of services that are commissioned.

We suggest there is potential for the further theoretical development of JR, and this is a topic that we return to in Chapters 8 and 9. However, before we turn once again to considering interventions, we look in more detail at three other distinct elements of the JR approach: its use of data analysis (Chapter 5); its use of economic methods (Chapter 6); and its application of the evidence base and interface with politics (Chapter 7).

5 Data analysis and justice mapping

Justice Reinvestment stands out among approaches to criminal justice reform in the extent to which it is driven by data. We distinguish data analysis from justice mapping and discuss both in detail. Justice Reinvestment approaches require the analysis of data from a wide range of agencies including arresting agencies, prisons, pre-trial services, the court system, and community supervision agencies. We outline some of the key challenges in collecting and analysing criminal justice data. Also important is the analysis of criminal justice costs. Key issues here include disentangling fixed and marginal costs and accounting for the costs of decisions made within the criminal justice system that are borne by non-criminal-justice agencies. Justice mapping is one of the building blocks of Justice Reinvestment and uses computer mapping to "visualise traditional criminal justice data in new geographic dimensions" (Cadora 2007: 11). We briefly discuss the wider use of Geographic Information Systems, particularly in relation to crime mapping, before describing the justice mapping process. Key challenges to justice mapping are discussed, and we finish the chapter by describing some case studies of the use of data analysis and justice mapping in the USA and the UK.

Introduction

One way to distinguish Justice Reinvestment (JR) from other approaches to criminal justice reform is the extent to which it is a data-driven approach, requiring a capacity and capability to collate data, analyse it, and make decisions based on interpretation of the results. Justice Reinvestment is not about speculation on what might work in corrections, or at least it is not only that; it requires proof of efficacy and a positive benefit-cost result. In this sense it is more positivist than traditional criminal justice, which relies on appeals to normative arguments such as the imposition of a "fitting" punishment.

As we described in Chapter 3, different versions of Justice Reinvestment have been implemented which operate along a continuum. At one end, criminal justice system redesign uses data analysis primarily to gain a better understanding of the flows and costs of offenders moving through the criminal justice system. At the social justice end of the continuum, data analysis tends to have a strong spatial element to it, with the use of Geographic Information Systems to organise and display data, and the term "justice mapping" often preferred.

Clearly, then, there are different data collection and analysis processes to discuss. There is also the gathering together and analysis of justice data produced by a range of agencies to evaluate the costs associated with offenders moving through the criminal justice system. We start this chapter by discussing the process of justice analysis in detail, identifying some of the key challenges that may be encountered and how they might be overcome.

Sometimes a key element of the data gathering and analysis process is the use of spatial analysis to understand better the relationship between the criminal justice system and specific localities and communities. As part of this work, Geographic Information Systems (GIS) provide a powerful tool for the visual presentation of spatial analysis. We discuss the increasing use of spatial analysis and GIS and show how they have opened up new possibilities in analysing criminal justice data and have been instrumental to the development of justice mapping and the wider Justice Reinvestment movement.

We then go on to look at some specific examples of justice analysis and justice mapping in the USA and the UK, before concluding with a short discussion of why data analysis and justice mapping have been critical to the success of Justice Reinvestment and suggesting some future directions in justice mapping.

Justice analysis

Justice Reinvestment is built, in large part, on an understanding of "the drivers of the local corrections costs and learning where cost savings can be achieved so that resources can be reinvested locally" (La Vigne *et al.* 2010: 4). This requires a data-driven approach that draws on data from a wide range of agencies including arresting agencies, prisons, pre-trial services, the court system, and community supervision agencies (ibid.). For La Vigne *et al.*:

> Two distinct types of criminal justice data inform justice reinvestment: cost data and population data. Cost data enables jurisdictions to determine the scope and size of criminal justice spending at various points in the system at any point in time … Population data describe who enters the system, how they move through it, and the time between stages.
>
> (La Vigne *et al.* 2010: 16)

Criminal justice drivers

For La Vigne *et al.* (2010), the starting point in justice analysis is determining what the drivers of criminal justice spending are. Very often this will entail consideration of the drivers of prison populations, because the use of prison will account for a substantial proportion of criminal justice costs (La Vigne *et al.* 2010). A range of factors is likely to be important in analysing prison populations. To a large extent, these are driven by the decisions of sentencers about how often to use custody and how long custodial sentences will be. However, pre-trial decisions about whether to remand in custody, and post-sentence decisions about when to recall prisoners released on license into the community and when to incarcerate offenders who breach community sentences, can also have an effect on the prison population.

For example, in the UK, the Ministry of Justice (2009) have demonstrated that the recent rise in prison numbers is due to longer, harsher sentences and an increase in breaches of community sentences. In the USA, the Council of State Governments (undated) describe how their Justice Center supported a Justice Reinvestment project in Kansas. In 2007 the state prison population was expected to increase by 22 per cent by 2016. Analysis by the Justice Center found that parole and probation revocations accounted for 65 per cent of prison admissions (ibid.). This led to a Justice Reinvestment strategy in which state policy-makers implemented policies to reduce the risk of individuals under supervision and to strengthen probation and parole (ibid.). The Council of State Governments (undated) credits these strategies with reducing the the state prison population by 4 per cent between 2007 and 2009.

Once the drivers of the prison population are understood, La Vigne *et al.* (2010) suggest that attention should then be focussed on a number of key intervention points in the criminal justice system: system entry, pre-trial processing, case processing, sentencing, and re-entry (or release back into the community in the UK).

Understanding offenders

As data is gathered, the following questions should be answered about offenders in the system:

- Who is involved in what parts of the criminal justice system (courts, jails, diversions, alternatives, etc.)?
- For what reasons or charges?
- For how long are they in the system?
- How do they exit the criminal justice system?
- Who returns and why?

(La Vigne *et al.* 2010: 23)

Data to answer these questions will come from a wide range of criminal justice and some non-criminal-justice agencies. For the USA, La Vigne *et al.* (2010) suggest the agencies and data set out in Table 5.1. In the UK, we might add to this list agencies such as Youth Offending Teams, who would assist with understanding the transition from the youth justice system to the adult system; Drug Action Teams, who would provide data on treatment episodes; and Registered Social Landlords, who might provide additional data on accommodation needs and services.

Table 5.1 Potential data and data sources for a local Justice Reinvestment initiative

Data source	*Potential data*
Courts and court services	• Case processing • Case histories • Sentencing data • Charge, conviction and plea records • Bail records
Law enforcement agencies	• Criminal histories • Arrest records • Arrest diversions
Jail or detention facilities	• Bookings, admissions and commitments • Unique bookings • Length of stay • Programme enrollment, participation and completion • Housing and classification status • Screening and assessment data • Discharge information • Charges and sentences • Population over or under design and rated capacity
Alternative and diversion programmes	• Programme enrolment and capacity • Recruitment methods • Outcomes
Community organisations	• Programme enrolment and capacity • Needs addressed • Outcomes
Pre-trial agencies	• Risk and needs assessments • Background information • Bail recommendations • Failure-to-appear rates
Probation and parole agencies	• Revocation sanctions • Capacity and enrollment • Outcomes • Violations • Successful completions

Source: La Vigne *et al.* 2010: 24.

In addition to collecting and analysing criminal justice data, a Justice Reinvestment initiative must also analyse criminal justice costs. Key issues here include disentangling fixed and marginal costs and accounting for the costs of decisions made within the criminal justice system that are borne by non-criminal-justice agencies.

As data is amassed and analysed it will be possible to answer La Vigne *et al.*'s key questions, thus building up a detailed understanding of the populations, flows and cost-drivers within the system. The challenge, however, will be making sense of the sheer volume of data, not all of which will be of the same quality, and many elements of which will be difficult to reconcile. Reflecting on the experience of putting together profiles of different groups of offenders in the UK, Fox (2010) suggests taking account of the existing research literature on offenders and using this, and local professional knowledge, to develop key questions and hypotheses that may then be tested through a process of data collection and analysis. This can make the analytical task a more manageable one. La Vigne *et al.* (2010) suggest some of the key questions and hypotheses that are likely to apply in a USA context. For example, in relation to the question "Who is involved in the criminal justice system?" they suggest that, although there are many individuals in the criminal justice system who pose significant risk to the public,

> The bulk of the population in county custody, however, may pose minimal risk and only touch the system for a brief period of time, often lasting just a few hours or days. Understanding the criminal justice population, especially that portion within the jail, can help stakeholders decide whether resources are being allocated effectively to ensure an appropriate balance between public safety and criminal justice spending.
>
> (La Vigne *et al.* 2010: 25)

Similarly, in a UK context, much discussion of Justice Reinvestment has tended to concentrate on offenders serving prison sentences of less than one year. Nationally, over 60,000 adults per year receive custodial sentences of less than 12 months, and on any given day these make up around 9 per cent of all prisoners but account for some 65 per cent of all sentenced admissions (Ministry of Justice 2010d). Prisoners released after serving short-term sentences are more likely to re-offend than any other group. Data from the Ministry of Justice suggests that 36.2 per cent of adults who are discharged from custody or start a court order under probation supervision are re-convicted within one year (Ministry of Justice 2011). The re-conviction rate for all custodial sentences is 46.8 per cent (Ministry of Justice 2011), which rises to 56.8 per cent for custodial sentences less than one year in duration (Ministry of Justice 2011). Re-offending by short-term prisoners, according to the National Audit Office, costs the country up to £10 billion per year. Despite such offenders being the most likely to re-offend, the short duration of their period of incarceration means they are less likely than other prisoners to receive the help they need to change their patterns of behaviour.

Criminal justice costs

Understanding the flow of people through the criminal justice system is an adjunct to understanding the costs of the criminal justice system. As we discuss in Chapter 6, a key issue here is to disentangle fixed and marginal costs (La Vigne *et al.* 2010), but this is rarely straightforward (Cohen 2000). In the context of a criminal justice intervention, the fixed costs are those that do not vary with the number of participants on a programme or intervention, whereas costs that do vary are incremental or marginal costs (Cohen 2000). An added complication is that the costs of decisions made within the criminal justice system are not just borne by the criminal justice system. Costs also fall on other agencies which might support the delivery of particular sentences: for example drug treatment. The risk of recidivism also introduces another set of costs, those incurred by victims and potential victims.

Those who are the victims of recidivism might experience both direct costs, such as loss of or damage to property, and less tangible costs incurred as a result of physical and psychological injury (Dolan *et al.* 2005). Moreover, those who are not themselves victimised but are apprehensive about crime also incur costs as a result of the risk of recidivism. Studies (for example, Dolan and Peasgood 2007) have sought to establish the cost of fear of crime. But the impact of potential recidivism goes further than this, because crime will also impact on people's general sense of "well-being". Thus, Cohen argues that when attempting to place a value on the benefits of crime control, a key element in estimating the cost of crime, "a holistic approach should consider the impact of crime on the 'quality of life' in a neighborhood or city" (Cohen 2007: 1). A further challenge is then to distinguish where savings might come from. La Vigne *et al.* (2010) distinguish between actual savings and averted savings. Actual savings are tangible savings that represent budget decreases from previous years, whereas averted savings reflect anticipated expenditures that a jurisdiction will no longer have to incur because of Justice Reinvestment activity. Calculating the marginal costs associated with individuals in the criminal justice system is crucial to calculating both types of saving (La Vigne *et al.* 2010).

Key challenges

Data collection

Data collection systems are often imperfect, and an important element of the data analysis process is to understand whether problems with data coverage and/or quality might be skewing results. La Vigne *et al.* (2010) highlight the importance of establishing clear definitions for data when requesting it, and also of establishing the best processes for analysing data for justice analysis and justice mapping.

Data sharing

An early challenge to data collection is often that of data sharing between agencies. Justice Reinvestment will always involve collaboration among different agencies. While some criminal justice agencies may have a track record of sharing data, with processes and protocols in place to facilitate such sharing, this is often not the case. Where there isn't a history of sharing data, agencies may have concerns about data security and use (La Vigne *et al.* 2010). The consent of offenders to their information being shared might also limit data sharing. La Vigne *et al.* (2010) suggest the implementation of a "universal release form" to obtain the consent of criminal justice clients for agencies to share client-level information.

In the UK, Section 115 of the Crime and Disorder Act 1998 provides a legal basis for sharing information between Community Safety Partnership agencies including the police, probation services and local authorities (Chainey 2010). This includes sharing personal information without the permission of the person to whom it refers. Further, Section 17A of the Act places some of the partner agencies within a Community Safety Partnership under a duty to share depersonalised information with all other relevant authorities, including crime data recorded by the police, and health service data on hospital admissions relating to various types of violent and drug-related crime[1] (Chainey 2010). However, even with such structures in place, many local Community Safety Partnerships "continue to struggle and come up against barriers that constrain them in making better use of the rich sources of information that can be shared between partner agencies" (Chainey 2010: 5). Given the structures and processes that have been put in place in the UK for data sharing between agencies, one might interpret continued difficulties in information sharing as sometimes being the result of unwillingness to make information available, and one might thus conclude that the barriers are more perceived than actual. However, there is some evidence that some of these barriers may be real. For example, in relation to delivering Integrated Offender Management, where information sharing between agencies is critical:

> interviewees from both [Voluntary and Statutory] sectors held the view that there were cultural and practical barriers to information sharing. These perceptions included a feeling reported by both VCS [voluntary and community sector] and statutory interviewees that some statutory staff held a view that VCS agencies could not be "trusted" with sensitive data on offenders. This was either because they were not used to dealing with it or because of the limitations of their IT equipment, which lacked appropriate security and storage systems (for example secure email addresses).
>
> (Wong *et al.* 2012b: 22)

Data integration

As La Vigne *et al.* (2010: 4) note in relation to the US: "In most jurisdictions, data management systems are not integrated, precluding agencies from accessing each other's data". In our experience, the same statement applies in the UK. However, integration of data is not just an issue of systems integration. Different agencies may use different definitions that are unfamiliar to other agencies. For example, in the UK, police data on "offenders" might cover data on those "suspected" of an offence, those "arrested", those "charged" and, in some cases, those "convicted". A common problem in this field is how to define recidivism. As La Vigne *et al.* (2010) note, in the USA there are multiple definitions used, including re-arrest, re-booking, re-incarceration or re-conviction. In the UK, the measure of re-offending rates has changed over time. This has moved from re-arrest rates, as used by the Audit Commission (1996), to the use of Police National Computer (PNC) data on re-convictions. In 2011, the Ministry of Justice defined 'proven re-offending' as "any offence committed in a one year follow-up period and receiving a court conviction, caution, reprimand or warning in the one year follow up or a further six months waiting period" (Ministry of Justice 2011: 3).

Data access

In the UK, the focus on reducing re-offending as a policy aim (for both New Labour and Coalition governments), and the use of PNC data on re-convictions as the gold standard for measuring re-offending, have had some unintended outcomes. Chief among these has been the unprecedented demand from public, private and voluntary sector agencies in England and Wales for PNC data. This reflects the desire by these agencies to show quantitative evidence of the impact of their services, as means of protecting those services – given existing and planned cuts in public sector finances. The measure of choice is re-convictions based on PNC data, following the approach set by government. This increase in demand for PNC data has also been augmented by agencies involved in the Ministry of Justice Payment by Results pilots (see Chapters 2 and 9).

Accessing PNC data is not straightforward; normally this can only be done via the Ministry of Justice. At the time of writing, the demand for PNC data, along with staff reductions within the section of Justice Statistics Analytical Services responsible for providing the data, has led to considerable delays (on the order of 3 to 4 months) in data provision. If there is to be a wholesale shift (Ministry of Justice 2010c) to commissioning all services by Payment by Results, and if reducing re-offending (the key policy goal) as measured by PNC data is the primary outcome that services need to work to, the demand for such data can only increase. This has significant resource implications for government and also for service providers.

Justice mapping

Justice mapping, one of the building blocks of JR, uses computer mapping to "visualise traditional criminal justice data in new geographic dimensions" (Cadora 2007: 11). As La Vigne and Cowan argue: "Given the local context of prisoner reentry, it is particularly important for communities to have a clear spatial understanding of the characteristics of reentry within their jurisdictions" (La Vigne and Cowan 2005: 6). In the USA these are more than simply maps showing the residential addresses of offenders. They are " 'Geographic audits' [that] make connections between criminal justice expenditures and the well-being of neighbourhoods on behalf of whose inhabitants those resources are deployed" (Cadora 2007: 11).

Crime mapping

To some extent, Justice Reinvestment has been made possible by the increased availability and power of computing. It has built on the development of "crime mapping", a distinct subdiscipline within criminology and an important tool used by a range of practitioners within the criminal justice system, particularly the police. According to Wilson (2007), "crime mapping" involves three distinct techniques. GIS allow geographic data to be visualised and manipulated such that data can be prepared for statistical analysis and the results of that analysis displayed graphically. Spatial analysis is "the analysis of geographic objects in relation to other geographic objects across space" (Wilson 2007: 137). Spatial *data* analysis is "the combination of spatial analysis with associated attribute data of the objects" (ibid.). Boba describes "crime analysis mapping" thus: "The process of using a geographic information system in combination with crime analysis techniques to focus on the spatial context of criminal and other law enforcement activity" (Boba 2001: 20).

History of crime mapping

Crime mapping is not a new concept. Boba (2001) notes that it can be traced back to the early 1800s and that one of the first police departments to use mapping was New York City in the 1900s. In the 1940s crime mapping was used by Shaw and McKay (1942) in the development of their theory of social disorganisation (Wilson 2007). They overlaid residences of juvenile offenders with the concentric zone model of urban land usage developed by Park *et al.* (1925) and discovered a correlation between impoverished areas and juvenile offender residences (Wilson 2007). The growth of environmental criminology in the 1980s (see for example, Brantingham and Brantingham 1990) "allowed geography to make inroads into criminological theory" (Wilson 2007: 138), and criminological theories with a geographic component are now part of the criminological canon. Consider, for instance, concepts such as defensible space, situational crime prevention and routine activities theory (Wilson 2007).

Crime mapping using computers first occurred in the 1960s (Boba 2001, Wilson 2007). Although by the 1980s more advanced technology and desktop computers became more widely used, the quality of computerised mapping was limited because of slow processing speeds and poor printing quality (Boba 2001). By the 1990s, desktop GIS had become widely available and was more generally used by law enforcement agencies and criminologists in the USA and the UK (Boba 2001). Today crime mapping is an important tool for practitioners such as the police, and for social scientists exploring the relationship between crime and place.

Geocoding

The crime mapping process usually starts with "geocoding". This is the process of bringing tabular data, such as police calls for service or the locations of crime, together with geographic data based on a common geographic unit of analysis (Boba 2001). This unit of analysis might be a postcode (zip code in the US), an administratively defined area such as a police beat, or an enumeration district or grid.

The validity of data will be a key concern in the early stages of a crime mapping exercise. Many issues can affect data validity, including the accuracy of data entry, whether records are up-to-date, and how "missing" data has been treated. Boba (2001) gives the example of a citizen phoning 911 (the USA police emergency response number) to report that they have been "robbed"; the dispatcher enters the code for a robbery, but does not update the crime category when the actual crime is determined (perhaps the citizen was actually the victim of a burglary). Fox (2010) reports on an exercise conducted by the Greater Manchester Against Crime team in the UK to map prisoner releases in Greater Manchester using Prisoner Intelligence Notification System (PINS) data. One limitation in this work was that a substantial number of prisoners did not have a recorded postcode (zip code) that could be used to map their release address. There were various reasons for this, including that some prisoners who did have an address to return to declined to provide it, because of the incorrect belief that the grant they would receive on release would be higher if they were classified as being of "no fixed abode".

As another example, one of the authors recalls working with a Crime and Disorder Partnership in the UK to undertake geographical analysis of crime data as part of a crime audit. One unexpected finding to emerge from the initial analysis was a "hotspot" of violence, including domestic violence, located on a road going through some disused gravel pits on one of the borders of the local authority area. Initial speculation within the partnership about whether local residents were driving out to the gravel pits to conduct acts of violence were cut short when it became clear that the hotspot was an artefact of administrative practice. Incidents of crime occurring on a long road that ran through the local authority and where a postal address had not been recorded were automatically geocoded to one end of the road, and this happened to be the point at which it ran close to the gravel pits.

Subject to issues of data validity, the process of geocoding allows tabular data to be assigned to a location on the earth's surface (Boba 2001). A key issue will be how closely data can be linked to real-world coordinates. For example, a crime incident may be placed at an address point on a street within the range of the street number, or at the centre of a polygon that represents the police beat within which the crime was recorded (Boba 2001).

Analysis

Once data has been geocoded, the results can be viewed on a map. Another potential challenge at this point will be the accuracy of the digital map being used, and in particular how up-to-date it is.

Analysis can take many forms. At its simplest it may consist of single-symbol mapping, where data such as crime incidents or the addresses of offender accommodation are mapped as single points on to a map, the result being akin to sticking pins into a paper map on a wall. This approach is only really useful with small amounts of data. For larger amounts of data, single-symbol mapping will not identify geographical points with multiple data attached to them, and the density of data might make interpretation difficult. Therefore, graduated mapping is more commonly used, where the size, style or colour of symbols indicates the distribution of data.

Visualisation

Crime mapping has the potential to make complex data analysis accessible to a wide audience. However, whether this potential is realised will depend upon the way in which data is visualised, presented and contextualised.

Mapping offender rehabilitation after release (prisoner re-entry)

Crime mapping has been an increasingly important tool for agencies involved in policing and community safety over recent years. Crime maps identifying crime hotspots and their temporal dimensions have become a key tool for operational policing managers deploying front-line police officers (the best-known example being "Compstat" in the US). The same is true for those concerned with crime reduction strategies. In the UK, for example, Community Safety Partnership Strategic Assessments often use crime mapping to help identify areas and neighbourhoods that will be the focus of strategic crime reduction activities. However, the application of crime mapping techniques and know-how to the wider criminal justice sector, and in particular to understanding the post-release rehabilitation of offenders (generally referred to as "prisoner re-entry" in the US), is a more recent development.

In this section we describe the process of mapping offender rehabilitation and some of the key challenges encountered, before going on in the next section to set out some examples from the USA and the UK.

A range of uses for GIS in the criminal justice system

Karuppannan (2005) describes various uses of GIS in the criminal justice system, including applications within custodial institutions to track incidents such as bullying or violence, and applications to map custodial institutions themselves for planning purposes. Within the community justice field he also identifies a number of potential applications for GIS, including mapping offenders to allow for more efficient planning of home visits by probation officers, as well as more efficient allocation of caseloads so that a probation officer's caseload is geographically focussed. Analysis of this type is described by Cadora *et al.* (2002). As part of a justice mapping exercise in Brooklyn, New York, they mapped data from a police precinct where there were 218 offenders on probation who were classed as "high risk". They found that these offenders were assigned to 43 different probation officers. Given that a typical probation officer managed 76 offenders, these could have been assigned to three specialist probation officers, who could then have built closer links with the local neighbourhood. La Vigne *et al.* (2008) also find examples of mapping being used to manage re-entry for individual offenders. Thus "[u]sing maps, caseworkers can identify resources that align with an individual's needs and his or her location" (La Vigne *et al.* 2008: 4).

Using GIS in the development of Justice Reinvestment

Our primary interest here is in the more strategic use of GIS, where it has been used in the development of Justice Reinvestment to map prisoner re-entry into a community setting. La Vigne and Cowan (2005) identify three benefits of mapping prisoner re-entry. The first is that analyses of prisoner re-entry which are limited to the county or city level may "obscure important patterns and trends occurring within the community" (La Vigne and Cowan 2005: 10). GIS analysis can help local policy-makers and community organisers target interventions more effectively (ibid.). Second, mapping released prisoners in conjunction with services available to them can illustrate which areas contain adequate services and where there is a mismatch between need and service delivery (ibid.). Third, analysis of the demographic and socio-economic characteristics of neighbourhoods with high numbers of re-entering prisoners can "help determine the extent to which communities are equipped to address reentry challenges" (ibid. 12). La Vigne and Cowan illustrate this last point with an example from Baltimore in the USA, where the six communities that were home to the greatest number of returning prisoners also had rates that were much higher than the city average of unemployment, households headed by females, poverty, and crime, suggesting that these neighbourhoods were relatively ill-equipped to cope with relatively high numbers of returning prisoners (ibid.). Fourth, mapping can contribute to assessing the effectiveness of interventions. For example, La Vigne and Cowan discuss mapping changes in employment rates over time as part of assessing the effect of an intervention to attract new businesses into a community with a high concentration of returning prisoners.

An early example of justice mapping is work undertaken by the Community Justice Project in the USA (part of the Center for Alternative Sentencing and Employment Services). It brought together information about the locations and characteristics of crime and offenders with measures of neighbourhood well-being (e.g. employment rates, community assets and local services). Community mapping was used to assess the correctional resources devoted to managing offenders on a block-by-block basis for any given neighbourhood (Karuppannan 2005). The intention was designed to help correctional administrators rethink their investment policies, and work with community constituents to plan more strategic, neighbourhood-based correctional programmes (Karuppannan 2005, citing Cadora *et al.* 2000). Other investments in these neighbourhoods were also mapped, enabling policy-makers to examine the effectiveness of expenditure.

The ultimate aim of these early projects was to encourage policy-makers to consider the proper balance of investments in preventative and punitive responses to crime (La Vigne *et al.* 2008).

Thus, mapping offender re-entry is more than an analytical tool. It provides new opportunities for understanding the relationship between criminal justice policy and social policy in relation to place:

> Mapping not only serves as a powerful tool for analyzing and displaying data, it also encourages new place-based approaches to problem solving. Rather than focusing on a topic or question in isolation, a place-based approach uses location as the key unit of analysis to explore the ways in which various social and political forces interact and affect neighborhoods and communities. In the justice arena, mapping helps us understand the impact of crime and justice policies on the communities in which we live and enables us to visualize the overlapping nature of challenges such as crime, reentry, poverty, poor health, low levels of education, and homelessness.
>
> (La Vigne *et al.* 2008: 1)

Further, mapping can help to highlight the public, private and not-for-profit resources available to meet these challenges (ibid.). Thus, mapping is not the end goal (La Vigne 2007) of a re-entry programme. Maps should be used to engage a range of stakeholders, including agencies which deliver services and local communities.

Key challenges

To some extent the challenges for justice mapping reflect those for justice analysis (see above) and for the wider use of GIS in the criminal justice sector.

Working in partnership

Justice mapping will involve bringing together partners with mapping expertise and access to data on offenders (particularly prisoner re-entry), and data on the range of social issues relevant to prisoner re-entry and offender rehabilitation (La Vigne and Cowan 2005). La Vigne and Cowan envisage a broad partnership involving the following constituencies:

- community stakeholders;
- corrections agencies;
- law enforcement;
- policy-makers;
- service providers;
- victims' advocates;
- other nonprofit organisations;
- universities.

This will pose challenges of project management, partnership working and data sharing that have already been alluded to above. For La Vigne and Cowan, the solution is to create a sustainable re-entry mapping partnership:

> Reentry mapping partnerships that rely on a broad base of stakeholder participation are well positioned to leverage the data they collect and the relationships they establish to continue their work on addressing re-entry challenges in their communities.
>
> (La Vigne and Cowan 2005: iv)

Data on offenders

The sources of data on prisoners, ex-prisoners and offenders serving community sentences or on license in the community will vary from country to country and will not be discussed in detail here. Depending upon the nature of the data that is available, different types of analysis will be possible. Challenges for those undertaking a justice mapping project will be to understand what data is available and to frame requests for data precisely. Based on experience from projects they have worked with, La Vigne and Cowan (2005) outline different data sets on prisoner releases that are commonly analysed, each of which has different advantages and limitations.

- Release data over a specific time period. La Vigne and Cowan (2005) suggest that the main advantage of requesting data on all those released during a given period of time (typically the most recent fiscal or calendar year) is that it represents a discrete set of data for population of interest, and thus provides "tremendous value for analyzing and understanding current spatial patterns of re-entry" (La Vigne and Cowan 2005: 30). The main limitation is that the data represents only those released from prison most recently, and it becomes outdated relatively quickly, requiring subsequent data requests in the future (ibid.).
- Cross-sectional data on current correctional populations. This approach is similar to the first, but less specific because it includes all individuals on supervision at a given point in time, regardless of when they were released (La Vigne and Cowan 2005). The result is that maps derived from the data will depict different spatial concentrations than those produced by analysing locations of recently released prisoners, and this may in turn have implications for how the maps inform service provision (La Vigne and Cowan 2005).
- Longitudinal data on correctional populations. La Vigne and Cowan (2005) discuss a justice mapping project which obtained biannual data snapshots of all sentenced persons who were incarcerated or on post-release supervision over a number of years. This provided a "a powerful data set for tracking the reentry population over time" (La Vigne and Cowan 2005: 30–31) but requires significant additional effort to analyse and use (ibid.).

Once data has been received, appropriate analysis can also present challenges. As La Vigne and Cowan (2005: 32) note "Each data variable provided … is likely to have important background and context needed for accurate interpretation". Those undertaking data analysis may therefore need close cooperation from their partners (see above) in understanding data and interpreting the results of analysis. Common questions about data, identified by La Vigne and Cowan (2005), include:

- If a person is released from prison twice during the period of time covered by the data, are two records included in the data, or just one?
- If data on past offenses are provided, how are cases with multiple offenses coded?
- How are probation, parole and other supervision statuses designated?
- How are race and ethnicity coded?
- How often are records updated? Are multiple databases used to generate the complete data set? If so, when are data fields and databases updated?

Other data

While much of the contextual data required for a justice mapping exercise will be available on publicly accessible websites,[2] gathering and analysing data on current service provision might prove more problematic. One challenge here will be finding a unit of measurement or analysis that conveys in sufficient detail the nature, reach and intensity of available services. For example, pinpointing the location of a service may not be sufficient without also providing some indication of how accessible it is from different neighbourhoods, where transport links will vary. Similarly, we must take account of outreach services and the intensity of a service. A second challenge, one particularly familiar to local policy-makers in the UK, will be making sense of – and conveying the sheer number and complexity of – services that operate in many local areas. In addition to statutory, publicly funded and delivered services, such as policing, probation, health, and education, a wide range of often public funded, not-for-profit services covering areas such as housing, social care and advice will sit alongside myriad small, community-based organisations offering a vast range of idiosyncratic services of widely varying quality.

In the UK and in some cases in the USA, one challenge to the mapping of provision by neighbourhoods and other jurisdictional boundaries as defined by public agencies is that the use of services by offenders and their families may not align to the boundaries within which agencies work. For example, an offender may live in one local authority area, access health care in another local authority area, and receive education, training and employment provision in another area. This poses challenges for the allocation of resources among localities and is a factor that needs to be considered when determining the size of geographical area over which justice mapping and Justice Reinvestment can and should take place. In practical terms, there may be a mismatch between the boundaries and size of a geographical area and the boundaries and size of the most efficient service-user usage areas. Inevitably it will be difficult to align the two, but the closer the match, the more likely it is that the most appropriate services can be aligned to the right offenders.

Accurate geocoding

The process of geocoding (described above) is obviously of critical importance in a justice mapping exercise. La Vigne and Cowan (2005) caution against taking at "face value" geocoding exercises where the proportion of data geocoded successfully is relatively low,[3] because this might indicate systemic problems with the data being used. For example, all cases might be excluded from one area. From our own experience, we would also add a caution about the reliability of postcode (zip code) data assigned to prisoners' return addresses. In our experience in the UK, this data is often incomplete and sometimes inaccurate. Interviews by the authors with some of those involved in the Transforming Justice Programme in Greater Manchester highlighted that is that there is no single source where such data can be accessed; instead, it requires data from all the prisons which return prisoners back to Greater Manchester. Some of these are within the geographical and jurisdictional boundaries of Greater Manchester, while others are not. As an example, the "local" Women's prison for Greater Manchester, HMP and YOI Styal, is in Cheshire, just outside the boundaries of Greater Manchester. Within the adult male secure estate, there are specialist national prisons which house specific types of offenders from across England and Wales, such as prisons which specialise in housing and working with sex offenders. Partnership arrangements and data-sharing protocols between agencies in England and Wales tend to be based on geographical areas, within local authority boundaries for community safety partnerships or "county" boundaries for criminal justice boards. This makes for a tension in governance arrangements, as observed by Senior *et al.* (2011) when it comes to integrated arrangements for managing offenders and also the sharing of data. Prison data tends to fall outside of these arrangements unless specific and individual arrangements are made with prisons – there is no standard approach to this.

From the USA, La Vigne and Cowan (2005) cite the example of a project in Chicago, undertaken by Urban Institute researchers, where a map of the addresses of all prisoners released to the city produced a density map that depicted an unusual concentration in one part of the city, so that one specific address was associated with over 1,000 released prisoners: "A quick check of the address revealed that it was the location of the county jail, where 'released' prisoners were transferred to await other pending charges" (La Vigne and Cowan 2005: 40).

Communicating key messages

As La Vigne and Cowan (2005) note, in order for prisoner re-entry maps to be useful to stakeholders, they must meet a set of criteria designed to ensure that they communicate effectively and are easy to interpret. Key questions to ask during the design of maps will include "what is the intended audience?" and "what is the intended purpose of the map?" Answers to these questions will guide decisions about the type and level of detail to use for each map. Another key decision that will follow from answering these questions is about the type of map to produce (ibid.). Different maps will be suitable for different purposes (ibid.). Point maps display accurate data that might help in understanding resettlement in a particular neighbourhood, but will raise difficult issues regarding the anonymity of individual offenders (ibid.). Thematic maps may be useful for displaying information across an entire jurisdiction and may also allow the layering of different types of data (ibid.). Thematic maps display aggregate data and may therefore be well suited for depicting rates versus volumes (ibid.). Density maps enable the depiction of multiple offenders living at the same address (ibid.) with less risk to the anonymity of individuals. They also allow for the layering of different data sets (ibid.).

Examples of justice analysis and mapping

In this section we provide some examples of justice analysis and justice mapping. Both are from the USA and have been selected because they provide good illustrations of what can be achieved during a justice data analysis and mapping exercise.

Criminal justice and health and human services – overlapping needs, resources and interests in Brooklyn neighbourhoods

Cadora *et al.* (2002) describe in detail a justice mapping exercise undertaken in Brooklyn, New York. It was one of the first, if not *the* first, studies to identify and map the so-called "million dollar blocks". The study's starting point was that:

> Traditionally, criminal justice and other public policy analysis takes place on either a case-by-case basis or on the broad jurisdictional level. However, both these analytical ends of the spectrum miss the cumulative impact that individual decisions have on neighborhoods. To register that important dimension, data must be mapped at the census tract or block level.
>
> (Cadora *et al.* 2002: 150)

They therefore mapped a range of socio-economic factors including single-parent households, concentrations of young people under 18, and concentrations of people from different ethnic groups. Using measures such as Temporary Assistance for Needy Families (TANF) and children receiving Public Assistance, Cadora *et al.* identified that the recipients of needs-based programmes and services are concentrated in particular neighbourhoods and that these are the same places that have high concentrations of youth and single-parent families.

When they mapped the neighbourhoods of serving and returning prisoners, Cadora *et al.* (2002) found that residents who were admitted to jail and prison were highly concentrated in a few neighbourhoods. In Brooklyn between 1998 and 2000,[4] the neighbourhoods with the highest incarceration rates experienced nine times as many admissions to jail and prison each year as those with the lowest (ibid.). This was in contrast to crime patterns, where police crime data for the same period, when mapped, showed that overall crime rates were more evenly distributed across neighbourhoods. Thus, the police precinct with the highest crime rate had a rate that was only about three times higher than the lowest (ibid.).

Also of interest is Cadora and colleagues' finding that offender incarceration and return takes place over a relatively short period of time. Thus, 66 per cent of incarcerated residents return home in less than three years, "producing a potentially destabilizing migration pattern in these neighborhoods" (Cadora *et al.* 2002: 155).

Thinking in terms of criminal justice resources, Cadora *et al.* report that

> In some neighborhoods, we find "million dollar blocks," in which more than a million dollars are spent to incarcerate and return residents from that block in a single year. Cumulatively, upwards of $50 million dollars are spent each year to remove and return residents from the highest incarceration rate neighborhoods.
>
> (Cadora *et al.* 2002: 157)

Perhaps unsurprisingly there is a strong correlation between these neighbourhoods and those with high concentrations of residents receiving TANF and Public Assistance. For Cadora *et al.* this suggests the "opportunity for economy of scale collaborations between criminal justice and health and human services" (Cadora *et al.* 2002: 161).

A portrait of prisoner re-entry in New Jersey

Travis *et al.* (2003) describe in detail the process of prisoner re-entry in the state of New Jersey. Their extensive report describes the policy context surrounding prisoner re-entry in the state, the characteristics of returning inmates, the geographic distribution of returning prisoners, and the social and economic climates of the communities that were home to the highest concentrations of returning prisoners. Travis and colleagues report that they drew on data from several sources including the Bureau of Justice Statistics, the New Jersey Department of Corrections, the New Jersey State Parole Board, the New Jersey State Police, the Division of Probation in the Administrative Office of the Courts, the Juvenile Justice Commission, the Department of Human Services, and the US Census Bureau. They found that between 1977 and 2002, the New Jersey prison population more than quadrupled; the growth was attributed to rising prison admissions and longer lengths of stay in prison (Travis *et al.* 2003). Rising prison admissions were the result of rising numbers of arrests for drug offences, the increased use of mandatory minimum sentences, and the rising number of individuals returned to prison as a result of parole revocations (ibid.). Most of these revocations were thought to be the result of technical violations rather than new offences committed while on parole (ibid.).

Focussing on the 2002 release cohort, Travis *et al.* (2003) found that over three-quarters of the population were between 20 and 40 years old at the time of release, with an average age of 34. Over one-third had been in prison for drug offenses, and about a third had been diagnosed with at least one chronic and/or communicable physical or mental health condition, not including substance misuse (ibid.). A key finding of the study was that almost one-third of prisoners released in 2002 came from two counties within the state of New Jersey – Essex and Camden (ibid.). These were counties that faced greater economic and social disadvantage than other parts of New Jersey (ibid.). Travis *et al.* found that the median household income in the central cities of these two counties was less than 50 per cent of the state-wide median household income, that unemployment in the central cities in these counties was significantly higher than in the rest of the state, and that large shares of the population lived in poverty and in single-parent households. Based on this analysis, Travis *et al.* highlight the policy challenge:

> [M]ore and more returning prisoners are faced with the many challenges of reentry, including finding jobs, housing, and substance abuse treatment; reuniting with family; and reintegrating into the community. Given the increasing numbers of returning prisoners and the fact that they are returning to a small number of communities in the state, the impact of reentry on communities is a particularly pressing problem. Clearly, prisoner reentry is an important policy issue and one that has significant implications for public safety and quality of life across the state.
>
> (Travis *et al.* 2003: 65)

UK examples

There are relatively few examples of comprehensive justice analysis and mapping exercises to draw on in the UK. Some national pieces of analysis have been undertaken that give insight into the geographical patterns of prisoner resettlement. For example, Houchin (2005) undertook research for the Scottish Prison Service that showed that, on the night of 30 June 2003, 25 per cent of those in Scottish prisons came from homes situated in just 53 of the 1,222 local government wards in Scotland. Houchin calculated that the mean number of people in prison from that group of wards was 29.7 per ward. In comparison he calculated that the 25 per cent of the prison population from the wards with the lowest density of prisoners came from 870 wards, and that these wards had, on average, 1.7 people in prison. Further, there were no people in prison at all on that night from 269 of the wards (ibid.).

There has also been some local analysis. For example, recent work in Greater Manchester, being undertaken as part of the Transforming Justice project there, has involved extensive analysis of offender needs and services that offenders might access. This has attempted to bring together mapping and other forms of analysis, including economic analysis. Thus, agencies have a developed service delivery framework which maps interventions across the three transition points of arrest, sentence and release. The analysis has then brought together the geographical footprint of the interventions, commissioning arrangements and evidence of effectiveness. The performance of the project is based on reducing demand for criminal justice services at different points in the overall system, and agencies have undertaken "waterfall" analysis to map throughputs in the criminal justice system and to assess the likely impact of the interventions on demand. As reported in an interview between the authors and Julian Cox,[5] an economist supporting the Transforming Justice project, re-configuring resources through joint investment agreements between local agencies has presented particular challenges around data integration and analysis. For example, tracking (anonymised) individuals and groups of individuals, and obtaining data sets around their employment and their use of drug and alcohol services, has been difficult. Cox observed that the biggest difficulty in data sharing was around obtaining (anonymised) individualised data.

In the UK, the most developed example of justice analysis and mapping is probably the work undertaken in Gateshead as part of a Justice Reinvestment project. This is described in detail by Allen *et al.* (2007). While some justice mapping work was ultimately undertaken, Allen and colleagues' account is partly of interest because of the challenges it identifies to justice mapping in a UK context. For instance, they report that:

> [T]he prison service at national and regional level was unable to provide information which would enable us to know the post code either where prisoners had lived prior to imprisonment or where they would live on release.
>
> (Allen *et al.* 2007: 20)

Some data was collected from the probation service, and the home addresses of offenders known to probation were mapped and showed that offenders tend to live in neighbourhoods with high levels of deprivation. Data from the Youth Offending Team produced a similar picture for offenders under 18 years of age. However, the overall sense is of a justice mapping exercise that was more valuable as a demonstration of the challenges in undertaking justice mapping in the UK than in terms of the new insights it delivered.

Conclusion

Seeing the big picture

Justice mapping is more than a new analytical process. It can help to re-shape the criminal justice policy debate:

> Researchers have not previously put together the big picture that shows the absurdity of the current system. Bits of research are done, but no one sees the big picture. When they see the big picture then politicians start to change their views and buy in to JR.
>
> (Authors' interview with Tony Fabelo)

> Mapping can inject empirical, data-driven analysis into justice debates that are often heavily influenced by political and ideological drivers.
>
> (La Vigne *et al.* 2008: 4)

In researching this book, one of the issues we were interested in was why Justice Reinvestment has been so successful in the USA. One factor that comes across clearly is the power of the analysis, done as part of the Justice Reinvestment process, to carry an argument. The power of the analysis does not primarily come from uncovering new truths about crime and criminal justice. Many of the key findings from Justice Reinvestment analysis would probably be known, at least intuitively, to many of those who do research on and work in crime reduction and criminal justice. Rather its power comes from establishing the "big picture" and presenting it in ways that politicians and key decision-makers can understand easily.

> Maps can communicate large amounts of information quickly and simply. They can demonstrate truths about our communities – such as the fact that crime and incarceration disproportionately affect certain neighborhoods – in a powerful way that narratives and statistics often fail to accomplish.
>
> (La Vigne *et al.* 2008: 1)

Future directions

La Vigne *et al.* (2008) see various possibilities for justice mapping to help change and shape the debate on criminal justice policy reform:

> Mapping can inject empirical, data-driven analysis into justice debates that are often heavily influenced by political and ideological drivers.
>
> (La Vigne *et al.* 2008)

In practical terms they suggest that one way to integrate mapping into the process is to require the inclusion of geographic impact statements with proposed new criminal justice policies. For example, before a new sentencing law is passed or a new prison is constructed, legislators could consult geographic impact statements to obtain a place-based understanding of the expected impact of the policy change (La Vigne *et al.* 2008). In this way legislators would be aware of where resources will be spent, which populations will be affected, how the new policy will interact with existing community factors, and what obstacles may prevent its success (ibid.).

La Vigne *et al.* (2008) also suggest that justice mapping can have a powerful impact on the attitudes and perceptions of communities.

> Mapping can help open a dialogue between neighboring communities, increase awareness of the causal factors underlying pressing community problems, and begin to address the negative stereotyping and labeling that occurs both within and between neighborhoods.
>
> (La Vigne *et al.* 2008: 5)

La Vigne *et al.*'s suggestion is that as people begin to understand the interconnectedness of problems such as prisoner re-entry, substance misuse, homelessness, joblessness, and poor health,

> [T]hey will expect more place-based information from the organizations that work in their communities, the lawmakers that ask for their votes, and the advocates that enlist their support in community development processes.
>
> (La Vigne *et al.* 2008: 5)

This is a view that is very much in accord with ideas put forward by Cadora and Tucker (2003: 4), who argue that an offender's "[r]eentry must be a geographically targeted partnership of public and private interests – penal, social services, health providers, and educational institutions. No [one] size fits all". In policy terms this fits well with an increasing emphasis within policy-making, on both sides of the Atlantic, on recognising the importance of "place" in the development and delivery of services. In the UK this is very much a developing area, the full potential of which has yet to be seen. For example, in England and Wales local information on crime and anti-social behaviour based on neighbourhood-level policing team boundaries has been available to the public since 2011. However, the extent to which this has influenced public views about crime or opened up "dialogue between neighboring communities", as posited by La Vigne, is unclear. A randomised control study by Quinton (2011), undertaken before the above initiative, compared the provision of local crime maps and policing information to residents against the alternative of providing no information to an equivalent group of people. He found that it had a modest positive effect on the perceptions of neighbourhood policing and a small positive impact on perceptions of the crime rate, although it did lead to a slight increase in the proportion of people who thought they would be a victim in the next 12 months. So, while justice mapping and data visualisation promise much, this is still a developing area.

6 Economic methods

The use of economic methods in criminal justice research, evaluation and policy-making is a developing area. However, it is clearly key to Justice Reinvestment. In this chapter we discuss the key methods surrounding the use of economic methods – their strengths and limitations. We start by looking at how the costs of different elements of the criminal justice system can be estimated. This will be key to all Justice Reinvestment programmes because, through an understanding of the cost-drivers of a system, can come an understanding of the potential for savings. We highlight the complexities of costing interventions in the criminal justice system and the implications of this for Justice Reinvestment. We go on to look at Cost Benefit Analysis. Not all Justice Reinvestment programmes involve a formal Cost Benefit Analysis, but where it is used it is a potentially powerful tool to put at the disposal of policy-makers – who must however, have a good understanding of its limitations in order to make appropriate use of the results. We then look at the use of econometric studies, often used in situations where long-term follow-up studies and evaluations involving control groups are not possible. We highlight potential advantages and disadvantages of such approaches. Finally we look at the use of meta-analysis to support modelling studies and in particular explore the work of the Washington State Institute for Public Policy.

Introduction

One of the dimensions to Justice Reinvestment that makes it distinct from other criminal justice reform programmes and philosophies is its close association with economics. All Justice Reinvestment programmes will involve work to estimate the costs of different elements of the criminal justice system. Only through an understanding of the cost-drivers of a system can come an understanding of the potential for savings. Economists generally refer to this activity as "cost analysis" – a partial form of economic evaluation that deals only with the costs of an intervention (Drummond *et al.* 2005).

Often Justice Reinvestment projects will also involve either a Cost Effectiveness Analysis or a Cost Benefit Analysis. The former is a form of economic evaluation where the consequences of an intervention are measured in the most appropriate natural effects or physical units (Drummond *et al.* 2005), such as burglaries avoided or drug-free years resulting. The consequences are not valued, and the results are expressed as a cost-effectiveness ratio such as £1,000 per burglary avoided. The latter is a form of evaluation where the consequences are valued in monetary terms (Drummond *et al.* 2005). Potentially this makes it the broadest form of economic evaluation method; however, as we will discuss later, difficulties in capturing and measuring wider consequences of an intervention mean that, in reality, its scope can be limited (Roman 2004). In this chapter we concentrate on Cost Benefit Analysis. This is because the stages in completing a Cost Benefit Analysis include – and then go further than – those involved in completing a Cost Effectiveness Analysis.

In some more economically-driven models of Justice Reinvestment, particularly those designed by economists, detailed economic models to predict future costs and benefits may be constructed. The best example of this approach is probably that developed by Aos and colleagues in Washington State (Aos *et al.* 2006).

Cost analysis

> When a jurisdiction commits to making changes within the stages of the criminal justice system … it should do so in a manner that enables the quantification of costs and potential savings. In the absence of the identification of net savings, justice reinvestment cannot take place.
>
> (La Vigne *et al.* 2010: 6)

In this section we explore the process of costing criminal justice interventions and highlight some of the challenges likely to be faced.

Viewpoint

The starting point for a cost analysis is to establish the viewpoint for analysis (Drummond *et al.* 2005): in other words, "who pays?" The viewpoint taken could have a radical effect on the analysis undertaken. For example, consider a drug arrest referral project operating in police stations with a primary aim to identify offenders who may have substance misuse problems and refer them to appropriate drug treatment services operated by the UK National Health Service (NHS). There are several ways of considering the costs of this intervention. If we consider only the costs to the criminal justice system, the intervention costs will be the project costs, together with costs incurred by the police in facilitating the delivery of the service. However, if the point of view of the public sector is considered, we must in addition consider the costs incurred by the NHS in providing services to those offenders referred by the intervention. As the criminal justice budget is distinct from the NHS budget, considering only the former implies that NHS services are (so far as the intervention is concerned) a "free good", and thus a greater than optimal number of offenders is likely to be referred.

Different viewpoints that are commonly used in economic evaluation relating to crime include a criminal justice perspective, a public-sector (government) perspective, and a societal perspective. In the latter, costs incurred by individual victims and/or offenders will be included, whereas in the first two perspectives only costs incurred by the criminal justice system or the wider public sector will be included.

Different types of cost

As Roman (2004) notes, criminal justice programme costs are generally divided into four areas. The first is direct project expenditure. Often, in crime reduction and criminal justice interventions, a substantial proportion of the direct project expenditure goes on staff (salaries and employer contributions such as – in the UK – National Insurance and pensions). The second area consists of estimates of the value of public resources used by the intervention (ibid.). These might include costs resulting from a referral to another agency made as part of the intervention. For example, a project working with young people at risk of offending might make a referral to a social service provider. The third area consists of estimates of the costs of services or facilities used by the intervention which are "free"[1] or discounted (ibid.). An example of this would be the use of (unpaid) volunteers' time or where an intervention makes use of (formerly surplus) office space provided *gratis*.

The fourth cost category is more subtle. Evaluators must also identify where resources have been diverted as a result of the intervention. Resources which would have been mobilised anyway, in the absence of the intervention, are generally excluded from cost analyses (Dhiri and Brand 1999). This fourth category of costs is comprised of those relating to "changes in the use of program resources by program participants as compared with the counterfactual (comparison) condition" (Roman 2004: 258). This relates to the concept of "additionality of costs" (Dhiri and Brand 1999). To illustrate the concept of additionality, Dhiri and Brand (1999) take the example of a change of approach to policing that could involve: (a) hiring additional police officers; (b) reallocating officers from one activity to another; or (c) a more effective approach to existing tasks. They suggest that while (a) involves a clear additional resource need and therefore should be included as a cost of the intervention, (b) and (c) may well not constitute additionality; that is, there are no additional costs incurred. In other words, replacing one intervention with another or working more efficiently (through the upgrading of existing technology, for example) requires no additional resource. Roman (2004) considers that such costs should be included in the analysis; however, he notes when discussing Cost Benefit Analysis (CBA) that "few CBAs explicitly study this fourth cost category" (Roman 2004: 259).

In the short run, economists generally break the costs of any good or service into two, so-called "fixed" costs and "marginal" costs. Consider the decision whether or not to commit an offender to a period of incarceration. In this context, the fixed cost would be the purchase, staffing and maintenance of the prison.

This cost is fixed in the short run, which is to say, it will not change if another single offender is imprisoned. However, marginal costs are those associated directly with another prisoner, for example, processing, extra meals, and so on. These costs will vary with the additional prisoner. A further concept is that of average cost. In this context, the average cost of incarceration would be the total cost of the prison (fixed and marginal cost) divided by the number of prisoners. Because the fixed costs are unchanging, the fixed cost per prisoner decreases as the population of the prison increases.

In the context of a criminal justice intervention, the fixed costs are those that do not vary with the number of participants on a programme or intervention, whereas costs that do vary are incremental or marginal costs (Cohen 2000). Thus the concept of additionality makes a distinction between incremental or marginal costs on the one hand and fixed costs on the other. As Cohen notes:

> Conceptually, all costs of a crime prevention program should be included in a cost analysis if those costs would not otherwise be incurred.... There is a fundamental economic principle at work here: only the costs (and benefits) that vary with the decision should be considered.
>
> (Cohen 2000: 278)

A complicating factor is that a cost which is incremental for one decision might be fixed for another (Cohen 2000). Cohen illustrates this using a decision about whether or not to increase the average sentence for violent offenders. If there is spare prison capacity, then the incremental costs associated with this decision will primarily be the cost of food, medical care, and so on. However, if the policy decision will require additional prison capacity to be built, then the annualised cost of prison cells becomes an incremental cost to include in the analysis.

Economists tend to argue that all costs are incremental in the long run. While maintaining a prison which has already been purchased is a fixed cost, over a long enough time horizon, extra capacity might be built, or indeed, existing facilities might be moth-balled or sold off. It may be the case, where a prison is already at capacity, that in the short run the cost of incarcerating violent prisoners for a longer period (for example) is borne by society through a greater number of non-violent offenders who are not held in custody, but who would have been incarcerated had sufficient cells been free.

Therefore, although in principle including "only the costs (and benefits) that vary with the decision" (Cohen 2000) is an uncontentious rule, to implement this rule is often less than straightforward. Careful analysis of which costs and benefits vary with a decision is required.

Gathering data on inputs

There are different ways of gathering data on inputs, which is to say, the resources used by a programme or intervention. For the first three categories of cost described above, estimates are often developed through a review of financial reports; invoices and progress reports to funders; and interviews with key staff (Roman 2004). In some cases these might be supplemented by surveys, activity diaries or activity sampling exercises (Dhiri and Brand 1999).

For the fourth category of costs, a counterfactual is required to estimate the difference between the costs incurred by the intervention and costs which would have been incurred anyway. The counterfactual might take the form of comparing current budgets to the baseline (pre-intervention) level of resources (Dhiri and Brand 1999) or the cost of the next best approach to delivering the desired outcome.

If an intervention allows for variation in the way a service is delivered, it will be important to consider the distribution of costs. For example, an intervention with the aim of offender rehabilitation[2] might allow for variation in the intensity of service delivered to offenders with different needs or levels of risk. Alternatively, the costs incurred by other parts of the public sector may vary according to the types of support given to different groups of offenders. The needs of some might be addressed primarily by the new programme or intervention, while others might be referred to different parts of the public sector. In both of these circumstances, the distribution of costs will vary between different groups of offenders and between different parts of the public sector. Analysis of this distribution might provide insights as to the relative efficiency of working with different groups of offenders or working with offenders in different ways. Partly for this reason, it is common practice to identify both set-up and ongoing costs of an intervention.

It is important to consider the time period over which costs will be tracked (Drummond *et al.* 2005). One risk is that if costs are based on a short time period, they be influenced by atypical events or circumstances. Another risk is that if the costing period is early in the implementation phase of an intervention, resource use may be relatively inefficient as those implementing the intervention work out how to do so more efficiently. A third risk arises where a unit of treatment takes a long time to deliver (compare the length of time taken to deliver a heroin substitution intervention with the time taken to target-harden a residential property). In such a case, a short time period during which costs are captured might not take account of the full cost of implementation.

Valuing inputs

Once relevant costs have been identified, individual items must be measured and valued (Drummond *et al.* 2005). A general principle is that the economic cost of an input should be estimated. The economic cost of using a resource is the value of its next most valuable alternative use (Dhiri and Brand 1999). The economic cost of an input may differ from its financial cost (ibid.); however, generally, the market value of a resource is assumed to reflect its opportunity cost (ibid.).

While it may be relatively straightforward to estimate the market value of an office space used by staff delivering an intervention, even where this has not been the subject of a cash transaction, making such an estimation for some non-market items will be more difficult. For example, a mentoring project for young offenders where the mentoring is provided by volunteers may have a relatively small budget but, through the use of volunteers, might be deploying a substantial (if non-monetised) resource. The value given to this time will depend in part on the viewpoint adopted (see above). For example, if this is a project being run by the local authority, then from a local authority viewpoint, the cost of volunteers' time may be zero. But from a societal perspective, there is a value to this time – volunteers might use their time for other voluntary activities or paid employment. Different approaches to valuing volunteer time will be used in different studies and might be based on the cost of paying the market rate to a professional mentor, or (in the UK) the minimum wage. In addition to the viewpoint, the choice of estimate will be based in part on the type of person who volunteers, and whether the time they use for volunteering is time they would otherwise use for paid work or leisure.

Capital costs are the costs to purchase major assets required to deliver an intervention; generally equipment, buildings and land (Drummond *et al.* 2005). They represent an investment at a single point in time, often during the "set-up" phase of a project (see above). The benefit of the investment is then realised over time. Drummond *et al.* (2005) identify two components of a capital cost. First there is the opportunity cost of tying up funds in a capital asset, as these cannot then be invested in some other way, and second there is the depreciation over time of the asset itself. Drummond *et al.* (2005) suggest that the best method of measuring and valuing capital costs in an economic evaluation is to annuitise (that is, to distribute) the initial capital outlay over the useful life of the asset. They argue that this approach incorporates both the depreciation aspect and the opportunity cost aspect of the capital cost.

Discounting future benefits and costs

In an economic analysis, costs (and benefits) are generally paid or received at different points in time. Changes in price alter the buying power of a sum of money over time. The process of reducing a nominal future value to today's value (that is the say, the Present Value) is known as discounting; while the process of bringing up-to-date prices which were paid in the past is known as compounding. However, discounting is not simply a response to inflation. It extends beyond money transactions to goods and services (Drummond *et al.* 2005), and it recognises a more fundamental aspect of human nature: that people generally prefer to receive a benefit today rather than tomorrow. To put it another way, individuals require a greater benefit tomorrow to create an incentive to forgo consumption today. Alternatively, we might say that, where money is borrowed today, the principal plus interest must be repaid in the future.

For example, for the purposes of evaluation of interventions, the government generally uses a discount rate of 3.5 per cent. This implies that £103.5 in one year's time is discounted to £100 today.[3] By symmetry, £100 one year ago is equivalent to £103.50 today. Although the formulae used to discount may become somewhat complicated once (for example) discounting by parts of years or at different rates are included, in principle the concept is the same.

Discounting is used so that the Net Present Value of costs and benefits can be calculated. Net Present Value (NPV) is defined by the UK government in the Treasury Green Book as "The discounted value of a stream of either future costs or benefits" (Her Majesty's Treasury undated: 103). The "Net" in the "Net Present Value" implies that all costs have been factored out of the resulting total.

How might a cost analysis be used?

A piece of cost analysis is likely to present the average cost of the intervention being examined. The average cost provides a measure of the overall return to an intervention (Dhiri and Brand 1999). This is useful information on its own. It also forms one of the key building blocks for a cost-effectiveness or Cost Benefit Analysis.

The calculation of the average cost allows the evaluator to answer the question "What is the relative value for money of the intervention(s)?" (Dhiri and Brand 1999). However, another important question to answer is "What level of investment in an intervention yields the highest net benefit?" (Dhiri and Brand 1999). To answer this second question, the evaluator must calculate the marginal cost of the intervention. Marginal cost can be defined as the cost of producing one extra unit of output. As we have discussed above, when calculating the marginal cost, only those inputs which are required to achieve the extra unit of output are included. Fixed costs, such as premises or staff, are excluded unless they are required to achieve this extra unit (Dhiri and Brand 1999).

Fixed costs may be included, however, in the calculation of the average cost of the intervention. Drummond *et al.* suggest two reasons for the significance of the distinction between average cost and marginal cost:

> First, when making a comparison of two or more programmes it is worth asking independently of each, "What would be the costs (and consequences) of having a little more or a little less?" … Second, when examining the effects on (cost) of small changes in output, it is likely that these will differ from average costs.
>
> (Drummond *et al.* 2005, pp. 65–66)

To give an example, the marginal cost of keeping a prisoner in custody for one additional day might be less than the average daily cost of their whole stay in prison, because the average of their total stay includes the fixed cost of their incarceration in the first place. Similarly, the marginal cost of fitting one extra CCTV camera in a town centre might be less than the average cost per CCTV camera of the whole CCTV installation. Of course, sometimes the marginal cost might be higher than the average cost. In the limit, if a prison is at full capacity, taking one additional prisoner might necessitate building a further prison wing and recruiting more staff, in which case the marginal cost of accommodating that one extra prisoner will be far higher than the average cost per prisoner.

Cost analysis example: Dedicated Drug Courts

An evaluation of Dedicated Drug Courts, undertaken by The Matrix Knowledge Group (2008), included an economic analysis, the first stage of which was a cost analysis. Dedicated Drug Courts are specialist courts in the UK which exclusively handle cases relating to drug-misusing offenders, from conviction through sentence to completion (or breach) of a community order. Offenders are sentenced to a Drug Rehabilitation Requirement (DRR), which is then supervised by the court. This includes regular drug testing, probation supervision, and the offender returning to court regularly to report on their progress. The evaluation looked at two magistrates' courts that had been piloting the Dedicated Drug Courts, one in Leeds and one in West London (The Matrix Knowledge Group 2008).

Data for the cost analysis was gathered via interviews with practitioners and key stakeholders and a review of relevant documentation. The analysis of costs identified the extra resources when compared with what would have happened in the absence of the Dedicated Drug Court. This counterfactual was defined as delivery of a DRR in courts that comply with the minimum National Standards relating to a DRR, but that do not operate the DDC model.

The cost analysis distinguished between the costs of setting up Dedicated Drug Courts (for example, the costs of training magistrates) and ongoing running costs (for example, the costs of maintaining a steering group). The cost analysis also identified direct and indirect costs. Direct costs included the steering group, training, and judiciary rota administration. Indirect costs included the cost to the probation service of undertaking additional drug tests and writing and presenting additional reviews for the courts. By looking at the number of offenders processed by the Dedicated Drug Court, a unit cost (the cost per offender) was also calculated. These costs are set out in Table 6.1.

Table 6.1 First year direct costs of the Dedicated Drug Court pilots

		Leeds	*West London*
Set-up costs	Systems design	£22,013	£22,013
	Training	£3,744	£971
	Total first year set-up cost	**£25,757**	**£22,984**
Running costs	Steering group	£3,233	£2,567
	Magistrates' meetings	£3,518	–
	Communication	£4,564	–
	Rota administration	£852	–
	Total first year running cost	**£12,167**	**£2,567**
Total cost		**£37,924**	**£25,551**
Number of new offenders per annum		276	60
Cost per new offender		**£137**	**£426**

Source: based on the Matrix Knowledge Group 2008: Table 3.1.

Conclusions about cost analysis

It is important to recognise that for many interventions studied, the costs involved are extremely complex. Therefore, when gathering costs data there will normally be a trade-off made between the time and effort required to gather data and the magnitude of the costs involved in data collection.[4] As Drummond *et al.* note: "It is not worth investing a great deal of time and effort considering costs that, because they are small, are unlikely to make any difference to the study result" (Drummond *et al.* 2005: 57). In Justice Reinvestment programmes this complexity will pose particular challenges, because an understanding of the costs is likely to be critical to the overall delivery of the programme and to strategic choices that are made around changing the system.

Cost Benefit Analysis

In general, a cost analysis will only give one-half of an answer to the question of whether a new intervention should be implemented or an old one withdrawn. Often criminal justice interventions will be judged not only on the cost of their deployment, but also for the benefits they bring. Cost Benefit Analysis is the pre-eminent form of economic analysis for assessing the efficiency of interventions, and so we will examine in detail its use in the field of crime reduction and criminal justice.

Cost Benefit Analysis is concerned with measuring both the effectiveness of an intervention and whether an intervention is efficient in that the benefits of the intervention are greater than the costs (Dhiri and Brand 1999; Welsh and Farrington 2001). In a Cost Benefit Analysis, the effects – the outcomes of an intervention – are valued in standardised monetary units, such as the dollar or the pound, and compared with the costs of the interventions inputs. This approach creates a standardised measure which, in principle, allows for a direct comparison of two or more interventions, even if those interventions vary in their goals and objectives and target heterogeneous populations and outcomes.[5] However, it must also be recognised that "Benefit-cost analysis is an art that is built on many important assumptions" (Cohen 2000: 266). Some of these assumptions, such as the perspective taken or the analysis of intervention costs, we have already discussed in this chapter. Others will be discussed below.

A cost-effectiveness analysis is essentially a partial Cost Benefit Analysis and so, while there is no separate section in this chapter examining cost-effectiveness analysis, some key issues in relation to cost-effectiveness analysis can be imputed from this section.

Before we continue, a word on terminology. It is common in conversation for people to use the term Cost Benefit Analysis to refer, generally, to economic evaluation (Drummond *et al.* 2005). However, for economists, Cost Benefit Analysis has a specific meaning and is clearly distinguishable from other approaches to economic evaluation such as cost analysis or cost-effectiveness analysis. When we use the term Cost Benefit Analysis we are referring to its more technical meaning.

Stages in a Cost Benefit Analysis

There are a number of stages in a Cost Benefit Analysis (Welsh and Farrington 2001):

1 *Define the scope of the analysis* – Key issues to decide at this stage include the perspective to be taken in the analysis (for example, will the perspective be that of the state, the criminal justice system, or the whole of society?), what outcomes are to be measured, and the alternatives to be compared (for example, participation in a programme versus non-participation) (Welsh and Farrington 2001).
2 *Obtain estimates of programme effects* – There are different ways to measure programme effects, but most economists favour an outcome evaluation in which an experimental or quasi-experimental design has been used. This is a complex issue and we return to it below.
3 *Estimate the monetary value of costs and benefits* – We have discussed how the monetary value of costs is estimated in the section above on cost analysis. The defining feature of a Cost Benefit Analysis is that the effects of the intervention – the outcomes – are valued in standardised monetary units, such as the dollar or the pound. Thus the benefit of the intervention, expressed in monetary terms, can be compared directly with the costs of the intervention, also expressed in monetary terms.
4 *Calculate present value and assess efficiency* – As we discussed when looking at cost analysis (see above), if the monetary expressions of the costs and benefits of an intervention are to be compared directly, then it is important to recognise that not all of these costs and benefits accrue at the same point in time. Unless all of the costs and benefits accrue within the same year, it is important to account both for the effect of inflation and for the fact that people generally prefer to receive a benefit today rather than tomorrow (Welsh and Farrington 2001; Dhiri and Brand 1999). Therefore, a process of discounting is used to calculate the Net Present Value of all costs (see above for a more detailed discussion). Once the Net Present Value of costs and benefits has been calculated, then the intervention's efficiency can be calculated in the form of a benefit-cost ratio (benefits divided by costs) or net value (benefits minus costs) (Welsh and Farrington 2001).
5 *Describe the distribution of costs and benefits* – Describing the distribution of programme costs and benefits involves identifying who gained and lost from the intervention (Welsh and Farrington 2001). For example, in a Cost Benefit Analysis of a criminal justice intervention, it is common to find an analysis of efficiency from the perspective of the state and from the perspective of wider society.
6 *Conduct sensitivity analysis* – Once the intervention's efficiency has been calculated, it is important to check how sensitive the resulting figure is to variations in the estimates that have been used in the Cost Benefit Analysis. One approach to sensitivity analysis is the calculation of switching values,

in which analysis is undertaken to ascertain by how much a variable would have to fall (if it is a benefit) or rise (if it is a cost) to switch the calculation of efficiency from positive to negative or vice versa (Her Majesty's Treasury undated).

All of these stages are required for a Cost Benefit Analysis. For a cost-effectiveness analysis, the third and fifth steps are omitted (Welsh and Farrington 2001). Two aspects of a Cost Benefit Analysis are particularly challenging. Estimating the monetary value of costs and benefits is one. In the field of crime reduction and criminal justice, the benefits are often, but not always, a reduction in crime, and so a key issue for Cost Benefit Analysis in this field is how to place a value on different types of crime. Crimes give rise to tangible costs, such as repairing a car that has been broken into or replacing stolen property, but they also give rise to intangible costs such as the physical and psychological harm done to victims. A second challenge is obtaining estimates of programme effects. Most economists favour an outcome evaluation in which an experimental or quasi-experimental design has been used. This is critical to the success of a Cost Benefit Analysis and is also much contested within social science, and so the following section looks at this issue in more detail.

The pros and cons of Cost Benefit Analysis

Arguments in favourof Cost Benefit Analysis

As Marsh *et al.* (2009) note, economists make a number of arguments in favour of analysing the costs and benefits of criminal justice interventions.

First, even though an intervention may yield positive outcomes (such as desistance from crime and increases in pro-social behaviour such as getting a job), the cost of the intervention may outweigh the intervention's benefits; and an alternative intervention may achieve the same outcomes for a lower cost. Marsh *et al.* (2008) have illustrated the importance of Cost Benefit Analysis to decision-making in criminal justice. They demonstrate that the effect of a criminal justice intervention at reducing offending is only weakly related to net benefits in terms of savings to the Exchequer and/or wider society, and that in about a quarter of cases, considering both costs and benefits would produce different policy recommendations from those produced by analysing only changes in offending rates.

Second, whereas observational studies examine outcomes one at a time, Cost Benefit Analysis considers all outcomes jointly, using the standardised (monetised) estimates of costs and benefits as weights that generate a single measure of intervention effectiveness.

Third, Cost Benefit Analysis allows for the valuation of hard-to-observe outcomes, such as fear, pain and suffering. Fourth, Cost Benefit Analysis has the potential to account for externalities – outcomes for individuals not directly involved in the intervention, but who are nevertheless impacted by its results.

Finally, since public resources are scarce, it is incumbent upon policy-makers to choose the most efficient intervention, that is, the scheme where costs are minimised and benefits are maximised (Cohen 2000).

Arguments against Cost Benefit Analysis

There are also criticisms of the use of Cost Benefit Analysis in the fields of crime reduction and criminal justice. A good survey including a number of criticisms of Cost Benefit Analysis is provided by Cohen (2000).

First, it is argued that, on ethical or philosophical grounds, some things, such as safety, cannot or should not be valued. A related issue is that Cost Benefit Analysis assumes that economic efficiency is the goal, at the expense of other socially desirable goals such as equity or fairness (Cohen 2000). Answering criticisms of this type, Cohen argues that

> This is not a criticism of the methodology – only of those who want to impose benefit-cost analysis as the sole criteria for public decision making. Instead, when viewed as one policy tool available to policymakers, benefit-cost analysis has many benefits and only limited costs. Indeed, most texts on benefit-cost analysis include an analysis of the "incidence" of costs and benefits – i.e., who bears the costs and who reaps the benefits – as an integral part of benefit-cost analysis.
>
> (Cohen 2000: 280)

A second concern is that Cost Benefit Analysis presents "an aura of precision and objectivity that might not be justified" (Cohen 2000: 303). Consumers of Cost Benefit Analysis (policy-makers) often have little understanding of the methodology and of the assumptions underlying the analysis, and therefore are ill-equipped to make appropriate use of the results from such tools. Cohen argues that "Like any statistical tool, benefit-cost analysis is vulnerable to misapplication through carelessness, inexperience, or deception … The results can be no more precise than the assumptions and valuations that are employed" (Cohen 2000: 303).

A third criticism is that Cost Benefit Analysis and more straightforward valuation exercises incorporate inequities in society. This is not to say that economic tools discriminate on the basis of socio-economic status because, as Cohen (2000: 305) notes: "A $1,000 medical cost is valued at $1,000, regardless of whether the injured person is rich or poor. Thus, the tool is politically neutral and can (and will) be overridden when other policy goals come into conflict". The concern is a more subtle one (Cohen 2000): that the methodology itself may incorporate inequities in society. Cohen (2000) demonstrates this using the example of measuring wages lost by victims of crime. If those victims tend to be in the lower-income quartiles, the benefits of a crime prevention programme will be skewed downwards (Cohen 2000). A similar outcome might result from a contingent valuation survey of potential victims to determine their willingness to pay for crime reduction programmes, with the value likely to be highly dependent on their relative wealth or ability to pay. A wealthy man, for example, might be prepared to pay, and have the resources to pay, a great deal to reduce the threat of murder. A poorer man might not have the resources to pay such an amount. However, it is not clear we can therefore argue that the rich should enjoy greater protection under the law than do the poor. Cohen therefore concludes:

> [F]rom a public policy standpoint, benefit-cost analysis does indeed discriminate against society's less wealthy. If society deems this to be unfair, the analyst needs to make adjustments in the estimated costs and benefits to "neutralize" the effect of wealth on the estimated costs and benefits.
>
> (Cohen 2000: 305)

A fourth issue (examined in more detail below) is that the public's perception of the risk of crime may not be the same as the actual risk (Cohen 2000). The challenge for economists working in this field is that asking the public about their willingness to pay for reduced crime might be influenced by the public being misinformed about the risk and severity of crime (Cohen 2000).

For Cohen (2000), who is primarily interested in Cost Benefit Analysis, the key issue is therefore that the analyst is careful to set out the assumptions that have informed the analysis, the projected benefits, how those benefits are valued, and how alternative assumptions might affect results (sensitivity analysis). However, the same points could, in broad terms, be applied to all of the economic analyses considered in this chapter. When used in this way, one of the great strengths of economic analysis is that it forces analysts to be explicit about their assumptions and thus encourages "an open process where the issues can be debated on an informed basis" (Cohen 2000: 303).

Another key challenge to Cost Benefit Analysis comes from its reliance on the results of a robust outcome evaluation; as we saw in the last chapter, these suffer from numerous threats to validity (Farrington 2003, Roman 2004). Moreover, Roman (2004) suggests that, by taking the results of an outcome evaluation and then translating these programme effects into monetary values, the Cost Benefit Analysis introduces additional threats to validity that are not present in an outcome evaluation. The problem is that a traditional Cost Benefit Analysis cannot identify "externalities", whether positive or negative.

Externalities exist where part of the costs or benefits of any transaction are borne by individuals wo are not themselves party to the transaction (Roman 2004). So, for example, if a prison stay is averted because of a successful programme intervention, the outcome evaluation will capture data to show that, compared to the control group, a victimisation and a prison stay have both been averted, and a traditional Cost Benefit Analysis will place a value on these outcomes. But in doing so, most traditional Cost Benefit Analyses implicitly assume that the prison bed will go unused. In fact, it is likely that excess capacity in a prison will be taken up by another offender. Therefore, further victimisations will be averted due to that latter offender being incapacitated (Roman 2004). These externalities are not easily captured in a traditional Cost Benefit Analysis. Thus, Roman (2004) argues that a traditional Cost Benefit Analysis introduces two biases. In the above example, first, it overestimates programme benefits by assuming that the prison bed remains empty, and second, it underestimates programme benefits when incarceration of a different offender prevents other victimisation. Considering the utility of Cost Benefit Analysis (CBA) to policy-makers and the policy-making process leads Roman to argue that "A CBA that does not accurately describe the beneficiaries and the benefactors of programming will not assist in this policy-making process. CBAs that report benefits to administrators who cannot observe those differences will not benefit anyone" (Roman 2004: 270).

Roman suggests that while one response to this issue would be to tailor the Cost Benefit Analysis to meet the practical constraints of crime research, a better option is to choose policy questions that are more appropriately answered in an economic analysis.

> Generally, CBA researchers will test whether the program results in a change in net benefits from the programs, which implicitly focuses the research on individual participant outcomes. Instead, researchers could test a hypothesis about whether the intervention results in economic welfare changes (positive or negative) within the community it serves.
>
> (Roman 2004: 271)

Roman's suggestion is that one successful programme completion that diverts an offender from custody will simply make room for a further offender to enter prison (the benefits of whose incarceration are not included in the CBA). The point may, however, be made that, if an intervention succeeds in reducing the prison population by a large number, future (planned) capital investment might not be required. Thus there is what economists would call a non-linearity – the cost and benefit associated with 1,000 successful completions (for example) is not simply ten times as great as the saving made from 100 completions. This point is often overlooked in traditional CBA. Roman suggests that a range of studies be carried out for different effect sizes and different programme sizes to determine the trade-off.

A Cost Benefit Analysis example: the HighScope Perry Preschool Program

One of the most often quoted Cost Benefit Analyses in the field of crime reduction is the HighScope Perry Preschool Program. The results of this 40-year follow-up study have been reported in a number of publications over the years. This account draws principally on Belfield *et al.* (2006), who report analysis using data on individuals aged 40.

The programme involved an intensive pre-school intervention delivered to at-risk children in Michigan in the 1960s. The provision was composed of three parts: first, a centre-based programme for two-and-a-half hours per day for each weekday, with a child-to-teacher ratio of 5:1; second, home visiting for one-and-a-half hours per weekday; and third, group meetings of parents (Belfield *et al.* 2006).

The programme effect was evaluated using a social experiment. Of the sample of 123 children, 58 were randomly assigned to receive the programme and 65 to be in a control group. The children have been surveyed periodically since the programme.

Costs information was taken from school district budgets and the programme administration unit. Costs identified included both operating costs (instructional staff, administrative and support staff, overhead, supplies, and developmental screening) and capital costs (for classrooms and facilities). Using both individual-level data, on participants and the control group of non-participants, and national data sets, the advantages from programme participation are calculated in dollar amounts up to age 40 and projected forward to age 65. Belfield *et al.* (2006) report that these advantages are primarily gains in earnings, reductions in crime, and changes in welfare receipt, but there also are differences in schooling and adult-education costs. Benefits accrue to the individual, the general public, and to society, and so a number of separate Cost Benefit Analyses are necessary to cover each perspective (Belfield *et al.* 2006).

Programme costs are compared against treatment impacts on educational resources, earnings, criminal activity and welfare receipts. Net present values were calculated for participants, the general public, and society. Sensitivity analysis was also undertaken. The treatment group obtains significantly higher earnings. For the general public, higher tax revenues, lower criminal justice system expenditures, and lower welfare payments easily outweigh programme costs: they repay $12.90 for every $1 invested. However, programme gains come mainly from reduced crime by males (Belfield *et al.* 2006), as illustrated in Figure 6.1.

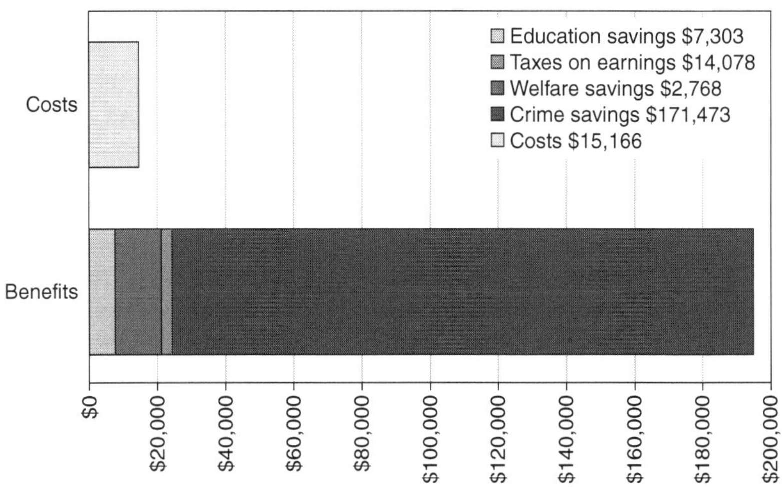

Figure 6.1 HighScope Perry Preschool Program public costs and benefits using data from the age-40 follow-up (source: Schweinhart [undated]: Table 3.1).

Note
Figures are per participant in 2000 constant dollars discounted 3% annually.

Conclusions about Cost Benefit Analysis

While Cost Benefit Analysis is potentially a powerful tool that can help policy-makers better understand the value or harm that might result from different interventions, it is not without its problems. Cost Benefit Analysis will involve assumptions and estimates that are not always apparent in the final result that is presented to decision-makers. If those decision-makers themselves have only a limited understanding of Cost Benefit Analysis, they may be ill-equipped to make appropriate use of the results (Cohen 2000). For Justice Reinvestment programmes, where a concern with the economics of a programme will often be to the fore, this could be problematic.

Modelling studies

It will be noted from the Cost Benefit Analysis example discussed above that the savings to society from the HighScope Perry Preschool Program fall into two broad categories: costs and benefits which are realised now, the values of which we may reasonably estimate from social service and education budgets; and costs and benefits which are speculative in nature, arising at a point in time after the study or intervention concludes. A large proportion of the savings identified from the HighScope Perry Preschool study result from "crimes which did not occur" among the intervention cohort compared to the control cohort. However, it is not clear how we can know the savings arising from "crimes which did not occur". In the HighScope Perry Preschool Program, the researchers were able to answer this question by undertaking an empirical study in which individuals were followed up for several decades and data on key outcomes collected. In many studies, however, there is no matched cohort, or we have no information stretching out forward into the future regarding costs which did not arise. How then can we address issues such as determining the saving from crimes which did not occur? Such questions are crucial in valuing criminal justice interventions.

Take, for example, the relatively simple choice of whether to send an offender to prison or not. Currently in England and Wales it costs society around £40,000 per prisoner per year of incarceration. Logically, society should only be prepared to bear such a cost if the benefits from the sentence (revenge, incapacitation, deterrence, rehabilitation) outweigh the costs. Focussing on incapacitation, the reduction in crime which comes from incapacitating an individual for, say, one year comes from the calculation of how much crime that offender *would have committed* had they not been in prison.

Similarly, the effect of deterrence comes from determining the amount of crime which *would have been* committed if prospective criminals knew for a fact that they would not be punished – or if the punishment had been less severe. The benefit of a rehabilitation programme comes from determining how much crime an individual *would commit* if they undergo rehabilitation compared to the amount they *would commit* if they do not engage with rehabilitation. The value of all of these is, as economists would say, an empirical matter – which is to say that they must be measured. However, the measuring process is by no means straightforward. Given the practical challenges and huge resource commitments to undertake long-term follow-up studies involving intervention and control groups, to say nothing of the long period of time that policy-makers will have to wait before they receive an answer, it is not surprising that economists often build models to capture these long-term effects.

The principles of modelling

The principles of modelling do not differ much in economics from those in the other sciences, but they may consider different effects. In essence, a model is intended to provide a reasonable and workable approximation to reality which will allow forecasts to be made about the results or outcomes of certain actions or changes in policy structures. Thus, models attempt a graphical and mathematical representation of a process which the intervention is designed to effect.

Many of the models economists use to represent the incentive structures which influence an individual's propensity to criminal activities are expressed mathematically: for example, the models of Becker (1968) and Ehrlich (1973), which we discuss in Chapter 8. For our purposes here, that is to say, to measure and value inputs and outputs, merely to model is not sufficient; we must parameterise the process. That is, once the basic structure of the model is calculated, the next step is to determine the values or weights which are given to the links and cells. For example, by how much will crime increase or decrease? What is the value of this change? etc.

An example: models of criminal justice and the decision to commit crime

In the context of evaluating criminal justice interventions, a useful illustration of the strength of the modelling approach is the calculation of the costs of a criminal career as discussed in the *Appraisal of Prisoner Resettlement Projects for Short-sentence Prisoners of the United Kingdom* (Ministry of Justice 2008). This insightful model has been used in a number of break-even analyses, both internally to the Ministry and externally (for example, Fox *et al.* 2010).

The Costs of Future Criminal Career model seeks to estimate the cost to society of an offender *after they have paid their debt to society for previous crimes*, and represents the average of lifetime crimes they are expected to commit weighted by the probability of their occurring. A feature of all such mathematical models is that they seek to simplify, through reasonable assumptions, the number of parameters. For example, MacLeod (Home Office 2003) looks first at the probability of re-conviction in the first year after release from prison[6] and assumes that this same probability applies irrespective of the number of previous convictions. In practice, this *probability* will be measured using the *proportion* of offenders who re-offend after their release. This follows because the proportion of the population with a particular attribute is equivalent to a probability of any one individual chosen at random having that attribute. If, for example, it is known that 10 per cent of the population are left-handed, the probability that any one individual is left-handed is 10 per cent (if they are chosen at random).

Clearly, when a cohort of prisoners is released from prison, a proportion[7] will be re-convicted in their first year after release, while the remainder will not. Of those who are not re-convicted in the first year, a lesser proportion[8] will be re-convicted in the second year after release. Of those who do not re-offend in the first two years, a lesser proportion[9] will be re-convicted in the third year after release, and so on.[10]

The Home Office (2003) model of future criminal career on release from custody thus implies that the proportion of released prisoners who continue without re-conviction is smaller and smaller as time goes on.[11] On the basis of this model, we may estimate the future probability of conviction based only on a single data point – the re-conviction rate in the first year after release. Having thus determined the probability of re-conviction, Ministry of Justice (2008) use the costs of crime, as calculated by Home Office (2005) and Brand and Price (2000), together with the observed proportions of crimes leading to re-conviction, to determine the expected cost to society of the future criminal career. Using this approach, Fox *et al.* (2010) determine the cost of the future criminal career as a function of the probability of re-offending, in order to monetise the benefits of interventions which reduce this probability.

Estimating the known unknowns – econometrics

In the example from Ministry of Justice (2008) discussed above, the parameters of the model – the probability of re-offending and the cost of each offence – are estimated directly by considering the outcomes of previous cohorts of prisoners. This straightforward technique is useful where outcomes or data occur independently, but is less useful when factors may be interrelated, and where effects cannot be taken as independent. In such situations, a more powerful technique, for example regression analysis, may be applied. Regression analysis, often called econometric analysis where economic data series are considered, requires the following:

- a set of variables supposedly related in some way;
- a partition of the variable set into those variables which are, broadly speaking, reactive, the caused or dependent variables, and those which are causes or explanatory variables;
- a mathematical representation of the suggested relationship;
- an appropriate technique by which the parameters of the relationship may be estimated; and
- a determination of the adequacy of the model and estimation process.

Variables

In general, the set of variables which we consider in an econometric analysis is determined by socio-economic theory, and/or by the factors which a study has been taxed with considering. An example is a recent Civitas report (Bandyopadhyay 2012) that sets out to determine how sentencing and detection, together with socio-economic factors, affect crime in England and Wales. The nature of the report's analysis suggests a set of variables which will be of interest: burglary, theft, robbery, and fraud, along with a set of possible control variables: detection; sentence length; the proportion of youth in the population; the level of unemployment; real earnings; and population density. Often we may wish to include transformations of the explanatory variables to capture non-linear effects. For example, Bandyopadhyay (2012) suggest that short sentences are associated with increased criminality, while longer sentences reduce criminality. To capture this effect, they use the square of sentence length as an explanatory factor. However, we have not yet addressed the issue of how we know which factors are "explanatory" (causes) and which are "explained" (caused).

Causation

Although the choice of variable set is often straightforward, as Bandyopadhyay notes, it cannot be taken for granted, even where a set of variables is related, that one of the variables is a causal factor in predicting the other. For example, suppose for some reasons the level of crime in the economy increases, following which the government, by way of response, increases the police budget and hence the rate of detection. Thus the data set might well give the impression that high crime is related with increased detection. However, this does not mean we can conclude that increasing detection rates will increase the rate of criminality. Similarly, Levitt (2001) and Raphael and Winter-Ebmer (2001), among others, postulate that increased crime rates might lead to increases in unemployment, as well as vice versa. The direction of causation is, so it is said, an empirical matter; in other words we need to consider data to be able to answer this. To economists, however, the question is framed in a particular way.

So as to avoid ambiguity, causality in econometric studies (or more precisely, Granger Causality, as explained in Granger 1980) is defined in the following way. Effect "A" Granger-causes effect "B" if taking "A" into account improves our forecast of "B", and if the reverse is not true; in other words, if changes in "A" occur before changes in "B", but not vice versa. It will be noted that this definition of causality, while unambiguous, differs from the general English usage. That is to say, we use the word "cause" in the sense of a predictor. This brings us to one of the weaknesses in the Granger Causality approach – if an event is easily forecast, or expected, we may take steps to prepare for it before the event occurs. Thus our pre-emptive measures may appear to be a Granger-cause, not a response to the actual event.

Another issue with Granger Causality is empirical (i.e. data-related). There will obviously be situations where one effect does indeed precede the other, but where the data is not collected with enough frequency for us to determine which does indeed come first. In quarterly data, for example, an increase in crime which is followed very quickly by an increase in the number of arrests will appear to be two simultaneous events. If the data indicate that the number of arrests increases at the same time as the crime rate, we might be tempted, erroneously, to conclude that it is arrests which are causing crime – leading to the conclusion (incorrect, one would hope) that, if we wish to reduce the crime rate, we might start by reducing the number of arrests. Thus we require data to be collected at a high frequency to be able to apply Granger Causality testing.

Spurious relationships

A further data issue which we must take into account when estimating econometric models is whether event "A" precedes event "B" not because it is a cause, but because some other event causes both. Similarly, where two series both increase or decrease quite independently over time, correlation or regression analysis gives misleading results. The reason why standard statistical procedures fail here is that the both series are changing consistently over time – whether increasing or decreasing. Thus it appears that the increases in one lead to increases or decreases in the other, when it is merely the passage of time which gives rise to this "pattern". In this case the "observed" relationship between the series is said to be spurious. To allow for this, researchers often specify model in rates of change of the data, and/or include a trend variable in the data set (as does Bandyopadhyay 2012). Similarly, where some other effect causes both "A" and "B", we must also include this in the data set.

The significance of insignificance and sensitivity

The calculations we may make from any modelling or regression estimation arise from random processes, in that they are calculated based on data from a sample – one of a potentially infinitely large number of possible samples. Thus we may be sure our estimates are not necessarily equal to the true parameter values. It is reasonable, therefore, to carry out some further analysis to determine what they do and do not tell us about the true parameter values.

Such further analysis often takes one of two forms: tests of the significance of our results – which is to say a mathematical calculation of the likelihood that we have arrived at our estimates from an unrepresentative sample; and sensitivity analysis – whereby we consider whether our conclusions might differ had we obtained a different set of data. It should be noted that, where an effect is considered to be insignificant in the statistical sense of the word, this does not mean that there is no effect, or that the effect might or might not be of practical significance; it merely means that we cannot rule out the possibility that our results have arisen by statistical chance.

By way of illustration, consider the analysis carried out by Levitt (2002), who determined to discover the effect of policing on criminality. The issue of simultaneity in the data is addressed in a clever and insightful way by Levitt, who begins by pointing out that "The challenge in estimating a causal impact of police on crime is to overcome simultaneity bias" (ibid.: 1244). Levitt considers that three studies have taken simultaneity bias seriously: Levitt (1997), Marvell and Moody (1996), and Corman and Mocan (2000). The latter two studies use monthly data in an attempt to eliminate simultaneity, arguing that it takes authorities more than one month to increase the size of the police force in response to increases in crime. Levitt (2002) suggests that this approach depends crucially on policy-makers being unable to forecast changes in the crime rate. If city fathers are aware that crime rates may increase, and increase police numbers as a precaution, the direction of causality will be confused.

To counter this problem, Levitt suggests using the budget for fire-fighters as an instrument to capture the way police budgets may be affected by issues other than the crime rate. Although police and fire-service budgets within USA cities are correlated, changing with, for example, the electoral cycle, Levitt suggests that the fire-service budget will not be directly related to crime. Thus we can determine the effect of a change in budgets unprompted by crime rates (technically, an exogenous change).[12]

In the case of property crime, Levitt's results are represented in Figure 6.2. The magnitude and significance of the effects estimated are represented in these graphs in the following way: along the horizontal axis are the suggested explanatory variables; the size of the estimated effect is shown on the vertical axis. Simple estimates of the effects are shown by dots or points, while the level of uncertainty is shown by vertical lines in each case.[13] If a point is at a level higher

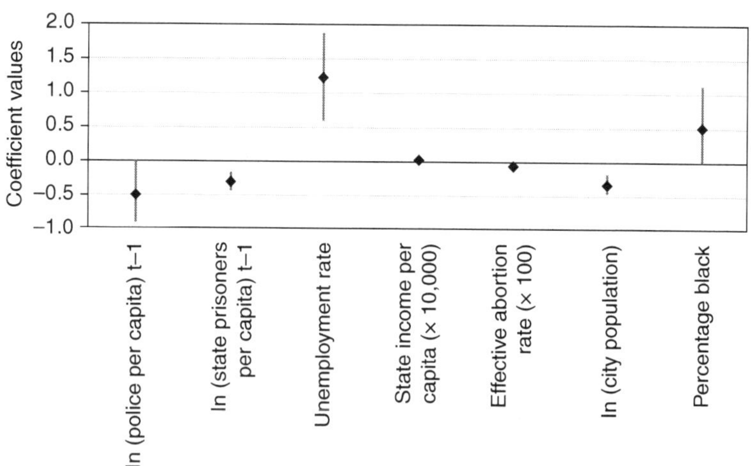

Figure 6.2 Property crime coefficient estimates (IV – city-fixed effects and year dummies included) and 95% confidence intervals (source: Levitt 2002).

than zero it implies the expected impact of the variable is positive. If, however, the uncertainty bars cross the zero line, it implies that we cannot be sure the effect does indeed differ from zero – the estimate might have resulted from a statistical fluke. Where we cannot be confident that an estimate differs from zero, we say the effect is not statistically significant.

Meta-analyses

Because of the variation in estimated effects from economic and econometric models of crime, analysts often consider analyses of analyses. That is to say, we might wish to consider, of the studies which have sought to parameterise the link between policing and crime, how many have shown a significant effect. Also, we may wish to consider how studies have been conducted – is it the more or the less rigorous studies which tend to show an effect? Such an analysis of analyses is known as a meta-analysis[14] and forms a core principle of the work of WSIPP, among others.

In an interview with the authors carried out in September 2011, Steve Aos of the WSIPP described the three-step process they use to suggest appropriate policy instruments to the state government. Initially, WSIPP researchers focus on a thorough review of the relevant literature using a meta-analytic approach. They are interested in studies that show which interventions work – and have been shown to work – and which do not. The goal at this point is to identify causal relationships between policy variables and hoped-for social outcomes – and the strength of the effects which might be expected. Thus a list of potential strategies is drawn up. A part of this process is judging how well the results will translate, as often studies include interventions which were undertaken in other states (than Washington) or in other nations.

Cost Benefit Analyses are undertaken by the WSIPP team for all chosen interventions. Examples of costs include personnel, while benefits would take account of how many crimes are likely to be averted, what kind of crimes and when they would have occurred, etc. Benefits are calculated in two forms, the savings made by the taxpayer and the savings (in reduced victimisation) which are enjoyed by society. These are monetised, and net present values, internal rates of return etc. are calculated.

A portfolio of interventions is drawn up to show which intervention is considered most likely to achieve what the policy-makers have stated as their goals – a list of the "best" and the "worst". A possible drawback of this approach is that, when social interventions are evaluated and reported in the economics or criminology literature, it is not common for them to be tried in combination with other things, whereas the portfolio approach which the WSIPP adopts means that interventions are employed in combinations. Therefore risk analysis must be carried out, along with a modelling of interaction effects to estimate the combined effects of several interventions.

Consider, by way of example, the WSIPP's model designed to assist states in identifying interventions which may reduce the costs of crime and criminal

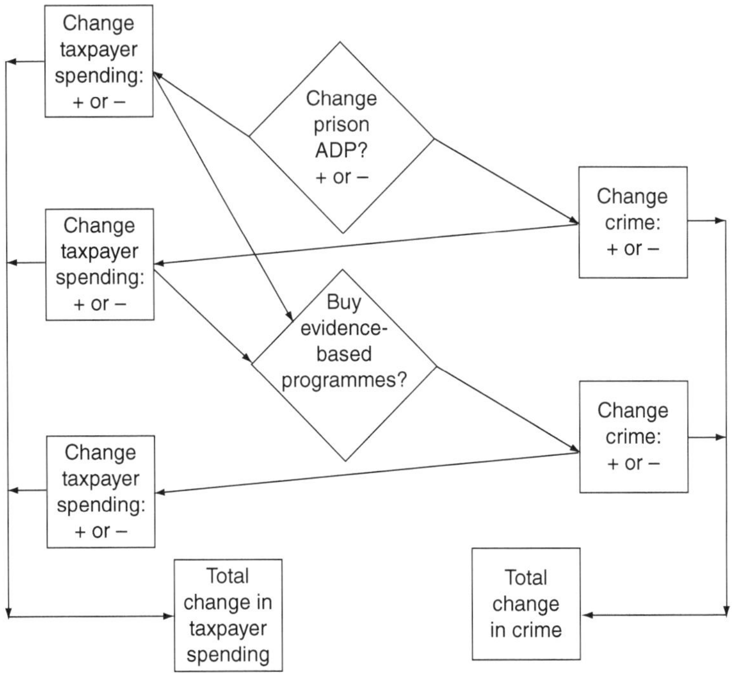

Figure 6.3 Structure of the WSIPP sentencing tool (based on Aos and Drake 2010).

justice (see Figure 6.3). The purpose of the model is to identify those interventions which are cost-effective in reducing the average daily population, ADP, of a prison. The intervention which might or might not be implemented is the "evidence-based programme", so called as its costs and benefits have been calculated through prior analysis. The flow chart gives the links which affect outcomes and intermediate outcomes.

On the basis of such analyses, the WSIPP is able to recommend and justify programmes which might require large initial outlay on the part of state governments.

Conclusion

Justice Reinvestment, by its very nature, represents a policy dilemma for governments and decision-makers. Investment in communities that is intended to reduce future crime must take place now, and the level of investment required must be currently budgeted. However, the return takes place in the future and the level of the return is not observable, as crimes forestalled are, by definition, unobservable. On the other hand, by a similar line of logic, not knowing exactly how many heart attacks might be forestalled does not prevent authorities advising on diet and lifestyle choice. It is merely a matter of appropriate analysis of available data.

Using the principles of economic modelling, reasonable and justifiable forecasts of what might result where no intervention is put in place may be compared with the likely results of such an intervention. By this means, investment in justice policy can be carried out on the same footing as investment in any other government infrastructure or social project.

7 Using evidence and negotiating politics

Justice Reinvestment is avowedly committed to the use of evidence in shaping criminal justice services, and this commitment affects its political pitch for investing in justice services. In this chapter we explore different conceptions of evidence and recognise that there is not a consensus on "what works" in preventing offending and reducing re-offending. In particular, it is clear that politics and sometimes politicians will play a role both in the interpretation of evidence, and more generally in the success or otherwise of Justice Reinvestment programmes. The chapter starts by looking at the orthodoxy of evidence-based policy, sketching out the implications of this approach for Justice Reinvestment, before looking at criticisms of such an approach. We argue that "evidence" is rarely as clear-cut or as objective as some might argue. We also recognise that policy-making itself does not always follow a rational and linear process. We look briefly at the process by which evidence is translated into policy and practice, and finish the chapter by discussing the role of national and local politics and politicians in Justice Reinvestment.

Introduction

Through the use of justice mapping, we may draw inferences about which areas are likely to benefit from a Justice Reinvestment project (see Chapter 5). Economic analysis and evaluation will help us judge the costs and benefits of different options (see Chapter 6). Justice Reinvestment programmes will also draw on existing evidence about "what works"; but what constitutes reliable evidence of the effect of a criminal justice intervention is contested. In this chapter we explore different conceptions of evidence and recognise that there is not a consensus on "what works" in preventing offending and reducing re-offending. In particular, it is clear that politics and sometimes politicians will play a role both in the interpretation of evidence, and more generally in the success or otherwise of Justice Reinvestment programmes. In this chapter we explore the roles of evidence and politics and the interface between the two.

Different approaches to the use of evidence in Justice Reinvestment

In their recent guide to implementing Justice Reinvestment (JR) at the local level in the USA, La Vigne *et al.* (2010) discuss what interventions should be implemented after justice mapping and other system analysis has been undertaken. They suggest a range of interventions that can be implemented at different stages of the criminal justice process (see Chapter 4 for a discussion of typical JR interventions). These interventions are recommended in part because they are ones that are likely to meet the needs of a JR strategy, but these interventions in particular have been selected because they "have been evaluated with varying degrees of rigor" (La Vigne *et al.* 2010: 32). The descriptions of potential interventions that La Vigne *et al.* put forward are interspersed with references to evaluations of those interventions.

Let us look in a bit more detail at one group of interventions: those suggested at the sentencing stage. La Vigne *et al.*, over three pages, set out a range of alternatives to imprisonment designed to lower the average length of incarceration in a locality and hence generate significant financial savings at the sentencing stage. We will look at just two of the many options La Vigne *et al.* cover. One of these is boot camps. Boot camps have been subject to many evaluations, and some of these evaluations, deemed to be the most methodologically rigorous, have been pulled together and "meta-analysed" in several Systematic Reviews (we discuss all of these terms in more detail later in this chapter). These Systematic Reviews suggest that boot camps are not effective (e.g. MacKenzie *et al.* 2001), and some suggest that boot camps actually increase recidivism and are therefore harmful. For example, Aos *et al.* (2001) found that boot camps increased recidivism for young offenders. La Vigne *et al.* (2010) also suggest that "drug courts" can be implemented to address the needs of substance-misusing offenders and thereby reduce recidivism among that population. Many evaluations of the effect drug courts have on recidivism have also been undertaken, and more than one Systematic Review has been completed. All of the ones that we are aware of show that drug courts are effective at reducing recidivism (e.g. Wilson *et al.* 2006). La Vigne *et al.* (2010) therefore seem to be on much more solid ground when putting forward drug courts as one possible intervention to consider at the sentencing stage.

Contrast the approach taken by La Vigne *et al.* (2010) with that taken by Aos *et al.* (2006). These researchers are part of the Washington State Institute for Public Policy. They were charged by the Washington State Legislature with studying the potential fiscal savings to state and local governments if evidence-based intervention, prevention, and sentencing alternatives were implemented in Washington State. Their approach[1] was to undertake an extensive Systematic Review of all research evidence they could locate, to identify what works in reducing crime. They found and analysed 571 rigorous comparison group evaluations of adult corrections, juvenile corrections, and prevention programmes. Their analysis included grouping together similar interventions: for example, they found 57 evaluations of drug courts and analysed these as a group, finding that they led, overall, to an 8 per cent reduction in crime.

In the UK a similar study, albeit on a smaller scale and not tied to a specific geographical location, was undertaken by researchers at the Matrix Knowledge Group (see Marsh and Fox 2008). They set out to test the hypothesis that prisons are an economically efficient means of reducing re-offending in the UK by examining alternatives to prison that included community-based interventions and prison-based interventions that add elements on to standard prison sentences. They started by undertaking a Rapid Evidence Assessment of studies of the effectiveness of such alternatives. A Rapid Evidence Assessment is a form of Systematic Review (see below for a more detailed discussion). This identified 121 methodologically rigorous studies that evaluated the change in re-offending resulting from moving an offender from a standard prison sentence to an alternative sentence. Meta-analysis of studies of similar interventions identified a number that reduce re-offending when compared with standard prison, including: residential drug treatment; surveillance in the community; offender behaviour interventions undertaken in prison; educational and vocational interventions undertaken in prison; sex offender treatment undertaken in prison; and drug treatment undertaken in prison (Marsh and Fox 2008).

Overview of the remainder of this chapter

These examples raise interesting questions for JR. To what extent are existing models of JR evidence-based, in the sense that they draw on existing evaluations of criminal justice interventions? To what extent can and should they be evidence-based? At first glance the reader might be tempted to reply to this latter question that "of course they should be evidence-based", and indeed we start our discussion below by setting out a model of "evidence-based" JR. However, as we shall see in the subsequent section, the debate around evidence-based policy and practice is not a straightforward one. What constitutes "evidence", and its actual and potential role in the policy-making process, is contested. Indeed, there are divergent views on what "policy-making" actually entails, and hence it is not necessarily straightforward to describe the role of evidence in JR, actual or potential.

As will become clear in our discussion of evidence-based policy and its possible application to JR, the role of politics in JR is clearly an important one. In the USA, JR has involved radical reforms to state and county criminal justice systems. Clearly these would not have been possible without a degree of political support and leadership. As we consider the political dimension of JR, we must also look briefly at the role public opinion and the media have played and could play.

An evidence-based approach to justice reinvestment

In this section we stick to what, increasingly, has become the orthodoxy of evidence-based policy and consider what an evidence-based approach to JR might look like.

What is "evidence-based policy"?

In the introduction to this chapter, we suggested that JR is an approach to designing criminal justice systems where evidence of "what works" is likely to be important, and we posed the question "to what extent can and should JR be evidence-based?" A useful starting point for thinking about the role of evidence in JR is to look, briefly, at the debate around evidence-based policy.

Defining evidence-based policy is not straightforward, and definitions are contested. The UK government has defined "evidence-based policy" thus:

> Policy makers' advice/decisions are based upon the best available evidence from a wide range of sources; all key stakeholders are involved at an early stage and throughout the policy's development. All relevant evidence, including that from specialists, is available in an accessible and meaningful form to policy makers.
>
> (Cabinet Office 1999: 73)

Davies suggests that the evidence-based approach "helps people make well informed decisions about policies, programmes and projects by putting the best available evidence from research at the heart of policy development and implementation" (Davies 1999, quoted in Davies 2004: 4), and contrasts it with opinion-based policy, which "relies heavily on either the selective use of evidence (e.g. on single studies irrespective of quality) or on the untested views of individuals or groups, often inspired by ideological standpoints, prejudices, or speculative conjecture" (Davies 2004).

However, it is widely recognised that the relationship between policy-making and evidence is more complex than the "rational" model of policy-making would suggest, and this is an issue we return to later. Before we consider the limitations of evidence-based policy, it will be helpful to look in more detail at what is meant by "evidence", and so for the time being we will accept the rational policy-making model and look in more detail at what it entails.

The case for experimental criminology

As we noted above, the orthodox model of evidence-based policy tends to be grounded in a positivist understanding of research and the interplay between research and policy (Pawson 2002). This approach is characterised by Young thus:

> [S]cience produces information that is free of personal prejudices and manipulation, and only information that possesses such objectivity can properly be labelled "evidence" (or so it was/is argued). In turn, evidence is understood to offer a foundation for decision-making that avoids the distracting partisan considerations that often undermine the generation of effective and efficient public policy.
>
> (Young 2011: 20)

In this model, experiments are the gold standard of evaluation; to some extent, the term "evidence-based policy" has become understood to mean experimental-based policy (Sampson 2010). There is certainly some evidence to support this assertion. Take the UK government as an example. The Cabinet Office (the government department that, according to its website,[2] has the purpose of making government work better through supporting the effective development, coordination and implementation of policy and operations across all government departments) has promoted the greater use of experiments (Government Social Research Unit 2007a) and in recent guidance on "Developing Policy with Randomised Controlled Trials" argued that "Randomised controlled trials (RCTs) are the best way of determining whether a policy is working" (Haynes *et al.* 2012: 4). Social experiments test whether a programme or policy has led to change in the outcomes that the programme or policy was designed to affect, over and above that which would have occurred in the absence of the programme or policy (Government Social Research Unit 2007a). Central to a social experiment is the concept of random allocation, alternatively referred to as random assignment or randomisation, as illustrated in Figure 7.1.

The units in a social experiment can be individuals, institutions or areas, and the control group is the "counterfactual" (Government Social Research Unit 2007a). This group represents what would have happened in the absence of the new intervention, and as such normally receives either the next best treatment or treatment as usual (Government Social Research Unit 2007a). Welsh and Farrington (2001) note that a social experiment is a convincing method of evaluation only if a sufficiently large number of units is randomly assigned to ensure that the programme group is equivalent to the control group on all possible extraneous variables. As a rule of thumb, they suggest that at least 50 units in each category are needed.

Arguments for the superiority of RCTs are often found in the social and behavioural sciences (Weisburd *et al.* 2001; Lum and Yang 2005). Advocates of experiments point to their potential to deliver unbiased estimates of the programme or policy being evaluated (Government Social Research Unit 2007a). This is because, if implemented properly, they have the highest possible level of internal validity. Internal validity refers to "the correctness of the key question about whether the intervention really did cause a change in the outcome"

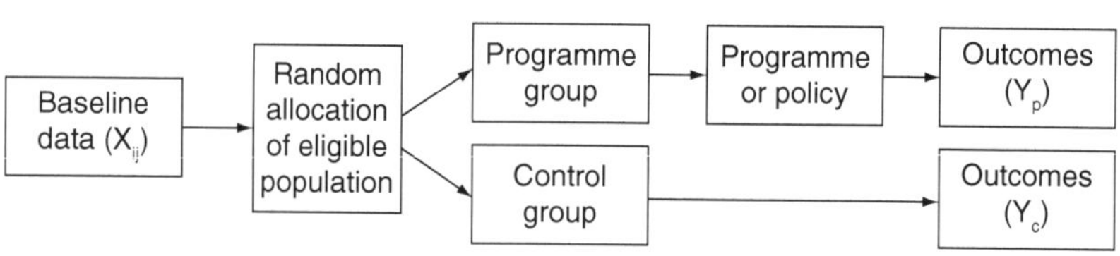

Figure 7.1 Design for a social experiment (source: Government Social Research Unit 2007a: Figure 7.2).

(Farrington 2003: 52). The main threats to validity, as set out by Shadish, Cook, and Campbell (2002: 55) and reproduced in Farrington (2003: 53), are:

1 *Selection* – the effect may reflect pre-existing differences between experimental and control conditions. In other words, the allocation to the experimental and control groups is not in fact random.
2 *History* – the effect may be caused by some other event occurring at the same time as the intervention. A suitably specified control group should allow the researcher to determine whether this is indeed the case.
3 *Maturation* – the effect may reflect a continuation of pre-existing trends, for example, in normal human development. It is known, for example, that a proportion of offenders naturally desist from criminal activity as they mature. Thus any intervention running over a period of years might be expected to show some (natural) desistance. Again, examination of the outcomes of the control group should allow the researcher to allow for such effects
4 *Instrumentation* – the (observed) effect may be caused by a change in the method of measuring the outcome.
5 *Testing* – the pre-test measurement may cause a change in the post-test measure.
6 *Regression to the mean* – where an intervention is implemented on units with unusually high scores (e.g., areas with high crime rates), natural fluctuation will cause a decrease in these scores on the post-test, which may be mistakenly interpreted as an effect of the intervention. The opposite (an increase) happens when interventions are applied to low-crime areas or low-scoring people.
7 *Differential attrition* – the effect may be is caused by differential loss of units (e.g., people) from experimental compared to control conditions.
8 *Causal order* – it may be unclear whether the intervention preceded the outcome.

Over recent years, the number of experiments undertaken within the criminal justice sector has been rising. For example, the number of experiments with offending outcomes published between 1982 and 2004, while still relatively small at 83, was a substantial increase on the 35 published between 1957 and 1981 (Farrington and Welsh 2005, Farrington 1983).[3]

It is not always possible or desirable to implement a social experiment (for a discussion of some of main critiques of social experiments see below), and this is why economists often favour the use of a robust quasi-experiment. These are:

> Experiments that have treatments, outcome measures, and experimental units, but do not use random assignment to create the comparisons from which treatment-caused change is inferred. Instead, the comparisons depend on non-equivalent groups that differ from each other in many ways other than the presence of the treatment whose effects are being tested.
>
> (Cook and Campbell 1979: 6)

In essence, the further away the design moves from the "gold standard" of a social experiment, the less strong the internal validity assured by the design becomes, and the less certainty there is that any effects observed can be attributed to the intervention being studied.

The case for Systematic Review and meta-analysis in the criminal justice system

Experimental criminology provides an approach to evaluation that, it is claimed, will provide policy-makers and practitioners with reliable evidence about what works. However, in reality, "Evaluation research is tortured by time constraints. The policy cycle revolves quicker than the research cycle, with the result that 'real time' evaluations often have little influence on policy making" (Pawson 2002: 157). Thus, policy-makers with an interest in evidence-based decision-making have turned increasingly to Systematic Reviews of the results of previous inquiries in the relevant policy domain (Pawson 2002).

To some extent, the "present fascination" with evidence-based policy was a response to contemporary interest in evidence-based medicine (Young 2011). In medicine, the Systematic Review has become a vital tool for policy-makers and practitioners and the creation of Systematic Reviews an important element of medical research, policy and practice. The scale and reach of this endeavour is perhaps clearest when one considers the Cochrane Collaboration – an international collaboration of more than 28,000 people across over 100 countries which has so far published over 5,000 Systematic Reviews (Cochrane Reviews) in an open-access, online library.[4]

Systematic Reviews are overviews of the existing research literature on a topic, based on

- comprehensive searching of print, electronic, and unpublished sources;
- explicit search procedures for identifying the available literature;
- explicit criteria for distinguishing the quality of research studies;
- presenting available evidence in a way that makes the quality of the evidence upon which the review is based transparent (Government Social Research Unit 2007b).

This systematic approach to reviewing the existing evidence is intended to overcome some of the problems inherent in traditional, "narrative" literature reviews, which typically suffer from several limitations. They are often opportunistic, only reviewing literature and evidence that is readily available to the researcher, and such "selection bias" is a limiting factor (Government Social Research Unit 2007b). They also risk being subject to "publication bias", because some journals disproportionately report studies with positive outcomes, while some other sources disproportionately report studies with negative outcomes (ibid.). Narrative reviews often provide few details of the procedures by which the reviewed literature has been identified and appraised; moreover, they are often unclear as to how their conclusions follow from the evidence presented (ibid.).

Within the field of criminology and criminal justice, Systematic Reviews have become increasingly important. In the field of crime prevention, a milestone was the publication by Sherman *et al.* (1998b) of *Preventing Crime: What Works, What Doesn't, What's Promising*. This extensive review of the evidence base for preventing crime was commissioned by the US Justice Department. Sherman and colleagues at the University of Maryland reviewed 500 evaluations that reported evidence of a programme's impact upon crime. It was not a Systematic Review; Welsh and Farrington (2006) class it as a "Vote-Count Review Method", albeit a relatively sophisticated one. In addition to counting up the number of studies with statistically significant findings in favour of, and contrary to, a particular intervention, Sherman and colleagues also developed the Scientific Methods Scale, in which evaluation designs are ranked according to their level of internal validity (ibid.). Randomised control trials are identified as the most rigorous evaluation design, and quasi-experiments in which a comparison group is used are identified as the "next best thing". The full scale is as follows:

> Level 1. Correlation between a crime prevention program and a measure of crime or crime risk factors at a single point in time.
>
> Level 2. Temporal sequence between the program and the crime or risk outcome clearly observed, or the presence of a comparison group without demonstrated comparability to the treatment group.
>
> Level 3. A comparison between two or more comparable units of analysis, one with and one without the program.
>
> Level 4. Comparison between multiple units with and without the program, controlling for other factors, or using comparison units that evidence only minor differences.
>
> Level 5. Random assignment and analysis of comparable units to program and comparison groups.
>
> (Sherman *et al.* 1998b: 5–6)

For a programme to be classed as "working" by Sherman and colleagues, it had to have at least two Level 3 evaluations and the preponderance of all available evidence showing effectiveness. On the basis of this assessment, Sherman *et al.* (1998b) identified 15 programmes that worked, 23 that didn't and 30 that were promising. A similar approach has been used by the University of Colorado's Centre for the Study and Prevention of Violence, which is funded by the US Health Department. To date[5] more than 800 programmes designed to reduce violence have been assessed. The assessment criteria are more conservative than those adopted by Sherman *et al.* (1998a and b). For inclusion as a "Blueprint for

Violence Prevention", studies must be based on an experimental design; provide evidence of a statistically significant (or marginal) deterrent effect; be replicated at multiple sites with demonstrated effects; and provide evidence that the deterrent effect was sustained for at least one year post-treatment. On the basis of these criteria, 11 programmes have so far been identified that meet these criteria, and 19 are designated as promising.

Many Systematic Reviews have been undertaken in the fields of crime reduction and criminal justice. Particularly well-known and widely used include: Petrosino *et al.*'s (2000) review of Scared Straight; Welsh and Farrington's (2001) review of the costs and benefits of crime prevention; Lipsey *et al.*'s (2001) review of Cognitive Behavioural Therapy for offenders; Losel and Schmucker's (2005) review of treatment for sex offenders; and Wilson *et al.*'s (2006) review of drug courts. The Cochrane Collaboration was established in 1993 (Welsh and Farrington 2006). In 2000, the Campbell Collaboration was formed to draw together and promote the use of Systematic Reviews in a number of social policy areas including "Crime and Criminal Justice". At the time of writing, the Crime and Criminal Justice Group listed 34 Systematic Reviews that had been published by Campbell.[6]

Particularly influential in criminology and criminal justice, as in other sectors such as health care, are the results derived from meta-analysis. Meta-analysis is a statistical method for combining and summarising the results of studies in a systematic review (Lipsey and Wilson 2001). Relevant studies are identified and grouped together according to similar intervention characteristics. For each study, outcomes are identified and effect sizes computed. Corrections are applied for small sample sizes, and the mean effect of each class of intervention is calculated (Government Social Research Unit 2007b).

Justice Reinvestment as evidence-based policy

Thus far, we have a clear sense of how JR might proceed as an application of evidence-based policy.

A good example of the use of meta-analysis in criminology and criminal justice is to be found in the Risk-Need-Responsivity model (see, for instance, Andrews *et al.* 1990, Andrews and Bonta 2006, Andrews and Bonta 2007), the dominant paradigm in offender rehabilitation on both sides of the Atlantic. This model of offender rehabilitation is clearly underpinned by a strong rational empiricism (Ward and Maruna 2007). Its proponents prefer evidence from experiments and, where these are not possible, quasi-experiments (e.g. Lipsey and Cullen 2007) and place great emphasis on meta-analysis of available robust evaluations. The result is a paradigm of offender rehabilitation that has a strong evidence base that suggests that reducing re-offending is possible. There are hundreds of robust evaluations of rehabilitative interventions that show that such interventions can be effective. A series of influential Systematic Reviews and latterly "reviews of reviews" (e.g. Lipsey and Cullen 2007) show that effective treatment is cognitive-behavioural in its orientation and highly structured in its delivery (Andrews and Bonta 2006). Thus the Risk-Need-Responsivity model is a good example of evidence-based policy in practice.

Another model of JR very much in the evidence-based policy vein is that developed by the Washington State Institute for Public Policy (WSIPP) and described in more detail in Chapter 6. To recap, WSIPP researchers focus on a thorough review of the relevant literature, identifying studies that meet predefined evidential criteria and then using a meta-analytic approach to combine findings from individual studies into an overall estimate of effect. The goal is to identify causal relationships between policy variables and hoped-for social outcomes – and the strength of the effects which might be expected.

In the UK criminal justice system, evidence of a move towards more evidence-based policy-making can be seen in the changing approach used by the Home Office to identify and assess the quality of existing evidence. For example, Home Office Research Study 187 (Goldblatt and Lewis 1998) was clearly influenced by existing reviews of evidence such as the then recently published *Preventing Crime: What Works, What Doesn't, What's Promising* (Sherman *et al.* 1998a). However, Home Office Research Study 187 was not itself a Systematic Review. By 2005, when Harper and Chitty published *The Impact of Corrections on Re-offending: A Review of "What Works"*, a more systematic review methodology had been adopted and the Scientific Methods Scale developed by Sherman *et al.* (1998a) had been adapted for re-conviction studies (see Harper and Chitty 2005: Table 1.2). More recently, summaries of the evidence on reducing different types of re-offending published by the National Offender Management Service (NOMS) in 2010 draw primarily on the Systematic Reviews produced by researchers closely associated with the Risk-Need-Responsivity model.

Justice reinvestment in the real world

In this section we start to question the philosophical, methodological and practical implications of evidence-based policy and consider the implications for the use of evidence in JR. This will take us on to a consideration of politics and public opinion in the following section.

The use of experiments, quasi-experiments and meta-analysis to underpin evidence-based policy is contested. Here, following in part Marsh and Fox (forthcoming), we outline a number of broad criticisms.

Experiments and quasi-experiments are difficult to implement in the criminal justice system

Despite the apparent methodological advantages of randomised controlled trials (RCTs), relatively few have been carried out in criminology. As noted above, Farrington and Welsh's (2005) review of RCTs performed in criminology identified 83 experiments with outcomes related to offending in the last two decades. However, few of these were performed outside the US: four in Australia, three in Canada, one in Germany, one in Switzerland and one in Hong Kong. Sherman *et al.* (1998a), the most comprehensive collection of data on criminal justice evaluations in the USA – identifying 657 evaluations – found that only 16 per cent of evaluations employed random allocation. This dearth of randomised experiments caused the Campbell Collaboration Crime and Justice Coordinating Group to conclude that it is unrealistic to restrict Systematic Reviews on the effects of interventions relevant to crime and justice to experimental studies that employed random allocation (Weisburd *et al.* 2001). The UK Home Office also noted a similar lack of randomised experiments in the evaluation of UK criminal justice intervention. They conclude that to assess the impact of interventions on re-offending there is a need to develop randomised experiments in the correctional services (Harper and Chitty 2005).

As Marsh and Fox (forthcoming) note, the limited number of RCTs completed is, in part, a product of concerns are raised about the practicality and ethics of RCTs. Experiments are seen as difficult to conduct in non-clinical settings due to implementation issues, such as difficulties in convincing practitioners to participate, ethical concerns about treating some individuals and not others based on random allocation, or a lack of relevant training among criminologists (Farrington and Jolliffe 2002; Lum and Yang 2005; Hollin 2008). Ethical concerns include the argument that individuals allocated to the control group are discriminated against because they are not receiving an intervention given to the treatment group. For instance, random allocation may require passing sentences that would randomly assign offenders to programmes, or giving researchers power of "sentence-override". Withholding treatment on the basis of random allocation may result in legal challenges and political ramifications. However, a counter argument is that until a social experiment is completed we do not know that intervention is beneficial (Government Social Research Unit 2007a, Sherman 2009).

Heckman and Smith (1995) point out that RCTs face a number of institutional limitations that restrict the researcher's ability to control the interventions received by the treatment and control groups, causing randomisation to occur at a sub-optimal point in the process of policy implementation.

Experiments do not provide the clear-cut results their advocates suggest

Moving away from practical and ethical concerns, other authors have raised concerns about the theoretical claims made by those advocating the use of experiments in the social sciences (Marsh and Fox forthcoming). For instance, Sampson (2010) queries the claims made for RCTs' ability to solve the causal inference problem. He points to three concerns with the claim that RCTs provide a better assessment of the causal impact of interventions. First, random allocation to intervention and treatment is often emphasised at the expense of random selection of participants into the sample being studied, undermining the assumptions made when implementing RCTs. This problem is exacerbated if treatment effects are not homogenous across people or settings, which is often the case.

Second, compliance with experimental treatments is often low. Third, causal explanation requires a theory of the unobserved mechanisms and social processes involved in the generation of effects, something that is often overlooked by those conducting RCTs. As Marsh and Fox (forthcoming) demonstrate, the questionable superiority of RCTs is also reflected in an inconsistent impact of RCTs on assessments of the effect of criminal justice interventions when compared with quasi-experimental designs (QEDs).

- Lipsey (1993) examined the effect of methodological variables in a meta-analysis of offender treatment studies. He found that the key determinant of outcome was not whether allocation to treatment and control was random or not, but "the presence or absence of specific areas of non-equivalence – for example sex differences – whether they occurred in a randomised design or not" (ibid.:120).
- Lipsey and Wilson (1993) tested the hypothesis that lower-quality research designs introduce a positive bias into effect size measurement. Based on a meta-analysis, Lipsey and Wilson found that the mean measured effect size for QEDs was slightly smaller than for RCTs.
- Shadish and Heinsman (1997) found that RCTs on two interventions – drug use prevention and ability-grouping children in classrooms – produced higher measured effect sizes than QEDs. However, they found no difference in effect size estimates between RCTs and QEDs when applied to two other interventions – SAT coaching or pre-surgical psycho-educational interventions.
- Weisburd *et al.* (2001) reviewed the research on crime and justice interventions identified in the Maryland Report – *Preventing Crime: What Works, What Doesn't, What's Promising* (Sherman *et al.* 1998a). They concluded that RCTs tended to produce smaller estimates of effect than other research designs.
- Babcock *et al.* (2004) undertook a meta-analysis of treatment outcomes for men who had committed domestic violence. They found that there was no difference in the measured effect size according to type of design.
- Wilson *et al.* (2005) analysed the results of studies of treatment programmes for offenders. They found that both high-quality RCTs and QEDs produce broadly similar findings.
- Losel and Schmucker (2005) reviewed studies of treatment for sex offenders and found that the results from RCTs and QEDs were not significantly different.
- Mitchell *et al.* (2006) reviewed studies of incarceration-based drug treatment and found that studies that randomly assigned offenders to conditions tended to produce higher estimates of effect.
- Lipsey and Cullen (2007) undertook a review of Systematic Reviews in order to summarise the available evidence about the effects of correctional interventions on recidivism. They undertook analysis to find out whether larger effect estimates were found for the studies with stronger designs. Overall they found "little indication of a consistent bias" (ibid.: 305).

Philosophical objections to the use of experiments in criminal justice

More fundamentally, social scientists and evaluators arguing from different paradigms question philosophical assumptions upon which social experiments are based.

Heckman and Smith (1995) argue that the "black-box" of such experiments only allow researchers to answer the question of the mean effect of an intervention, while policy-makers are also interested in how effects vary between groups or which factors impact participation in the programme. That is, randomised experiments do not tell us why interventions succeed or fail. Furthermore, this lack of attention to theory may have implications for the generalizability of the findings of a RCT to other settings, populations, and points in time.

To take this idea a little further, social processes may not only undermine the generalizability of the findings generated by RCTs, but they may also undermine the assumptions required to implement RCTs. Sampson (2010) identifies the requirement for RCTs to assume that outcomes are independent of treatment assignment; an assumption that he points out may be undermined by social processes. That is, contagion, information diffusion, jealousy and learning are all social processes that may invalidate statistical interference as they violate the "stable unit treatment value assumption" (SUTVA). He illustrates this with the example of housing vouchers designed to support people to move away from poor areas. The way in which people use these vouchers will be impacted by the experience of others in receipt of vouchers if they know others in the treatment group. That is, outcomes are not independent of treatment assignment. These critiques alert us to a more fundamental criticism of the positivist paradigm that underpins much of the evidence-based policy movement.

One of the most widely discussed critiques of recent years has come from Pawson and Tilley (1997), who argue that:

> For us, the experimental paradigm constitutes a heroic failure, promising so much and yet ending up in ironic anticlimax. The underlying logic … seems meticulous, clear-headed and militarily precise, and yet findings seem to emerge in a typically non-cumulative, low impact, prone-to-equivocation sort of way.
>
> (Pawson and Tilley 1997, 8)

Pawson and Tilly argue that instead, of undertaking experiments and quasi-experiments, researchers should investigate context–mechanism–outcome configurations: "Programs work (have successful outcomes) only in so far as they introduce the appropriate ideas and opportunities (mechanisms) to groups in the appropriate social and cultural conditions (contexts)" (Pawson and Tilley 1997, 57).

Meta-analysis is also a contested methodology. For example, Pawson (2002) puts forward a number of objections. Specifically, his arguments concentrate on the melding of programme mechanisms (the danger of grouping together interventions which are dissimilar), oversimplifying programme outcomes (the outputs of a meta-analysis are expected outcomes of averages of means) and the concealment of programme contexts (the danger of not taking sufficient account of subjects and situations) (Pawson 2002). In response to these concerns, a number of methods have been developed for reviewing and synthesising qualitative studies (see for instance Barnett-Page and Thomas 2009), but to date there is no widely agreed strategy for bringing together the output from these qualitative syntheses with those from traditional, quantitative reviews and meta-analyses.

How rational is the policy-making process?

JR programmes will involve not just the implementation of new policy, but, as we have discussed above, a different approach to policy-making in which data analysis, economic analysis and the use of research evidence will all be important. In broad terms, this amounts to an assertion of the importance of evidence-based policy-making in the criminal justice system, and we have described (above) the basic assumptions that underpin evidence-based policy-making. However, we have then questioned whether the evidence that underpins evidence-based policy-making is as clear-cut and objective as it might at first appear. The critique of evidence-based policy is not just based on concerns about the methodology (and underlying epistemology) involved in the generation of evidence. Many also question the rational model of policy-making.

The rational model suggests a logical and ordered sequence of policy-making phases (Stone *et al.* 2001), in which policy-making is a linear process and knowledge is apolitical and neutral (ibid.). The underlying model of science hints strongly of positivism (Stone *et al.* 2001, Pawson 2002). However, many would argue that the reality of policy-making is more complicated.

Clearly, policy-makers do not just rely on evidence generated from robust evaluations. They bring their own experience, expertise and judgement to the process (Davies 2004). Policy-making takes place within the context of finite resources, and this influences decisions (ibid.). Policy-makers are also influenced by values (their own, that of politicians and of institutions) as well as the habits and traditions of institutions such as Parliament, civil servants and the judiciary (ibid.). Outside forces such as lobby groups, pressure groups and consultants are able to influence the policy-making process, and the whole process is subject to pragmatics and contingencies such as parliamentary terms and timetables and the capacities of institutions (ibid.). Thus, many commentators prefer the phrase "evidence-informed policy" (e.g. Treadwell Shine and Bartley 2011).

However, some would go further and question the extent to which evidence-based policy-making actually takes place at all. Stone *et al.* (2001) set out alternative models of policy-making where the role of evidence and of evaluators is either marginal (for example in a "muddling through" model of policy-making premised on the notions of "bounded rationality" and "satisficing") or only influential at certain stages in the development of a "policy paradigm". A recent ethnographic study by Stevens describes civil servants in the UK government using evidence selectively to build convincing narratives or "create persuasive policy stories" (Stevens 2011: 237) and concludes that the very use of evidence is "ideological in that it supports systematically asymmetrical relations of power" (Stevens 2011: 237).

Steven's view is in part supported by Boden and Epstein's (2006) conclusions on "policy based evidence making":

> This need [for evidence] has been reified in the UK and elsewhere, as routines of "evidence-based policy-making" have been hardwired into the business of Government. Intuitively, basing policies that affect people's lives and the economy on rigorous academic research sounds rational and desirable. However, such approaches are fundamentally flawed by virtue of the fact that Government, in its broadest sense, seeks to capture and control the knowledge producing processes to the point where this type of "research" might best be described as "policy-based evidence".
>
> (Boden and Epstein 2006: 226)

This was something that was acknowledged by the report by the UK House of Commons Select Committee on Science and Technology into Scientific Advice, Risk and Evidence Based Policy Making issued in October 2006. The committee stated:

> [Ministers] should certainly not seek selectively to pick pieces of evidence which support an already agreed policy, or even commission research in order to produce a justification for policy: so-called "policy-based evidence making" (see paragraphs 95–6). Where there is an absence of evidence, or even when the Government is knowingly contradicting the evidence – maybe for very good reason – this should be openly acknowledged.
>
> (House of Commons Science and Technology Committee 2006: para.89)

Getting the evidence into policy and practice

A related range of issues concerns the potential for interventions that are ineffective, or even harmful, to be continued despite ample evidence of their failings. This in turn raises questions about the politics of JR, which we move on to later in this chapter.

Interventions can have iatrogenic (i.e. adverse) effects, and yet agencies may continue to deliver and promote them regardless. The most striking example of this is Petrosino's Systematic Review of Scared Straight programmes (Petrosino *et al.* 2000), perhaps one of the most widely known Systematic Reviews of criminal justice interventions. Despite the review indicating that children and young people were harmed by Scared Straight, this has not dampened enthusiasm for implementing similar programmes in the UK or the USA.

In the UK, the "Prison Me – No Way" programmes, conducted by prison officers and organised by the No Way Trust, have been running since 1995. Their claim is that the way in which their programme is delivered does not replicate the iatrogenic impacts found by Petrosino *et al.* (Prison Me – No Way 2012[7]). In the USA, Scared Straight has been recently been turned into a reality TV series – Beyond Scared Straight. This has generated public debate about the reliability of the evidence. In Schill's report (2011: unnumbered) on the controversy, Anthony Petrosino, who co-authored the Systematic Review, commented: "What these studies show is that in the aggregate, more kids were hurt by Scared Straight than helped by it" (ibid.: unnumbered). In the same report, Petrosino's review and a further review by the Washington State Institute for Public Policy was dismissed by the TV series' producer Arnold Shapiro. He defended the programme, commenting "Academic studies don't work. It's all about follow up. I've done more follow up than anyone. Scared Straight: 20 Years Later is the longest study ever done" (ibid.: unnumbered). In Schill's report, another critic of Scared Straight, Tara Andrews from the Washington-based Coalition for Juvenile Justice, commented:

> There is a concern because states are in a pinch for money right now and they are looking for low-cost solutions, even if they have a low impact. Scared Straight programs feel intuitively good but the research doesn't bear that out.
>
> (Quoted in Schill 2011: unnumbered)

Andrews' last point illustrates the problem of using evidence and research findings which may run counter to what individuals intuitively believe, be they politicians, commissioners of services, operational managers or front line staff. Research evidence may carry insufficient credibility to deter individuals from ceasing to deliver such interventions and/or change practice.

However, sometimes individuals have good reasons to continue to deliver interventions where, prima facie, the evidence would suggest otherwise. An example cited by Berman and Fox (2010) is the schools-based Drug Abuse Resistance Education (D.A.R.E.) programme, which as they note has been shown in numerous studies to be ineffective: "The scholarly record on D.A.R.E. is clear. In the past 15 years, no fewer than 30 studies have taken aim at the idea that D.A.R.E effectively prevents drug use among young people" (Berman and Fox 2010: 99). And yet, despite the evidence, the programme is still widely used and has many supporters among local politicians and practitioners. However, a study by Weiss *et al.* (2008) showed that those implementing D.A.R.E were aware of the evidence of its ineffectiveness. They were neither uninformed nor ignoring the research (Berman and Fox 2010). Weiss, in an interview given to Berman and Fox (2010), suggested that local decision-makers had relatively sophisticated reasons for sticking with D.A.R.E.:

> Local officials thought scholars had erred by focusing almost exclusively on the program's official goal of reducing drug use. Instead, they cited a number of secondary reasons to support the program, starting with the positive relationships it fostered among police officers, students and educators.
>
> (Berman and Fox 2010: 106)

In an interview for this book, a policy manager involved in the implementation of the Transforming Justice Programme in Greater Manchester (a Ministry of Justice Local Reinvestment Pilot) reported that local agencies had reviewed the evidence on interventions that were being considered for the programme. They found that there was limited experimental evidence which showed that interventions work. She suggested it was decided locally that basing decisions purely on this type of experimental evidence was a flawed approach. Instead they adopted an approach based on determining the confidence that interventions have got the ingredients to make them work, determining what was "good enough", capturing a "flavour of all the things in the programme" and looking to see if there was a national evidence base, local evidence and/or whether or not some interventions were worth evaluating, and therefore investing resources in this.

The politics of Justice Reinvestment

Clearly, we are now moving from the role of evidence in informing JR into the role of politics, and in this section we explore the political dimensions in more depth. We start by looking at the role of national party politics in JR and then move on to look at the role of local politics.

National party politics

In the USA, a defining feature of successful JR projects has been their bipartisan nature. Indeed, the Justice Center at the Council of State Governments, an organisation that has supported JR strategies in a number of states, has only done so where politicians have signed up to a bipartisan approach.

A bipartisan approach may be aided by the fact that JR, perhaps in part because of its economic underpinnings, transcends traditional political demarcations. So, as Skolnick (2011) points out, it is noticeable that, in the USA, "progressive re-entry initiatives" are often championed by "conservative states with conservative leaders". Thus: "It's all very warm and fuzzy, yet such policies have been championed by the likes of Newt Gingrich and Louisiana governor Bobby Jindal" (Skolnick 2011: unnumbered). The same is true to some extent in the UK where, in the run-up to the 2010 national election, the Conservative Party (2009), which might not be thought of as a progressive party on issues of law and order, enthusiastically endorsed the work on justice undertaken by the Washington State Institute for Public Policy, arguably one model of JR (see Chapter 3).

The potential for a bipartisan or at least de-politicised approach to JR in the UK remains to be seen. Many recognise the need for such an approach. For instance, the cross-party Justice Committee argued that:

> One important element in any solution to the seemingly inexorable rise in prison numbers is the reduction of the heat in political debate and to

> introduce some more light in this area with the aim of building a party political consensus on the ideal direction of policy.
>
> (Justice Committee 2009: 102)

The Committee went on to argue that "There appears to be most potential for consensus around two issues: first 'what works' (evidence-based practice) in order to reduce crime and re-offending; and secondly, the most effective use of limited resources to achieve this" (Justice Committee 2009: 103). As we have seen in this chapter, while evidence-based policy and practice offers much, it may not always provide such clear-cut advice as politicians would hope for. Perhaps more promising is the emerging economic agenda around justice. This seems to provide opportunities for a political consensus to emerge, especially given that all of the mainstream political parties embrace, to a greater or lesser extent, the need for fiscal restraint and the need for a mixed economy of provision. Thus the Justice Committee suggested that:

> In basing arguments for reform on the best use of taxpayers' money, the political argument could be shifted away from notions about which party is "harder" or "softer" on crime and criminals to questions about the most effective use of scarce resources to reduce offending and re-offending.
>
> (Justice Committee 2009: 103)

However, as events of the last few years have shown, economists are not infallible. Similarly, economic theories do not always provide adequate accounts of the real world. If JR is to be grounded in economic thinking, there is work to do to elaborate that theory in the context of the justice system, a topic we return to in Chapter 8.

Continuity

Even if a degree of bipartisanship can be negotiated, policy continuity is likely to remain a significant political challenge to JR. JR takes time to realise benefits. The long-run economic modelling of JR portfolios (the description indicates the scale of the challenge) undertaken by Aos *et al.* (2006) showed a break-even scenario four years after implementation, and forecast five years before the benefits started to outweigh the costs. As noted by Leeson (2004: 27), political cycles of four or five years (generated by elections) "work against the formulation of any long-term solutions", with new political administrations overturning policies from previous incumbents.

Policy changes within political administrations are just as likely to occur, as indicated by the rise in prison numbers in the UK following the change from Kenneth Clarke to Michael Howard as Home Secretary during the period of Conservative government from 1992 to 1997.

The issue of continuity is illustrated by the recent changes of political leadership in the UK Ministry of Justice, which have taken place within the lifetime of one administration. When Clarke regained part of the Justice portfolio[8] as Justice Minister in the Conservative and Liberal Democrat Coalition government in 2010, he stated his intention to "stem the unsustainable rise in the prison population" – an approach endorsed by the Treasury (Travis and Hirsch 2010). This was an approach which "angered Lord Howard, the former Tory home secretary, and other Tory Rightwingers" (Whitehead 2010).

Clarke's replacement, during the cabinet re-shuffle of September 2012, by Chris Grayling, described by the Independent's Wesley Johnson as being on the "right of the Conservative Party" (Johnson 2012), has prompted some concerns from commentators about what this might mean for the future direction of criminal justice policy in England and Wales. For example, at the 2012 Conservative Party Conference, Grayling announced "We're today putting punishment back into community sentencing" (Ministry of Justice 2012c). Yet the Ministry of Justice itself has warned that re-offending may increase as a result of increasing the punitive nature of community sentences (*The Guardian* 2012a). Regardless of whether or not Grayling will continue with Clarke's policies on rehabilitation and checking prison growth, his previous conduct raises concerns about his use of data in informing policy-making. In 2010, as Shadow Home Secretary, he was rebuked by Sir Michael Scholar, the head of the Office for National Statistics, who accused Grayling of "damaging trust in official statistics" by drawing comparisons between different sets of violent crime figures (ibid.). More recently he has been criticised again by the Office for National Statistics along with other ministers for "rushing out figures showing 371,000 immigrants were on benefits with insufficient regard for 'weaknesses' in the data" (ibid.). Grayling himself is on record as holding the point of view that government ministers may be " 'evasive, difficult, or downright disingenuous' but should not lie" (BBC 2005).

Localism

According to the Commission on English Prisons Today (2009), localism in criminal justice policy would confront public alienation from the criminal justice system and, through devolved spending, open up policy choices that should lead to less expenditure on process and more on actions which produce beneficial outcomes for communities. However, gaining public support cannot be left to chance. While 74 per cent of the public would like more prisons built (Duffy *et al.* 2007), a poll for Rethinking Crime and Punishment found that, when given options, five times more people favoured better parenting (57 per cent) than more offenders in prison (11 per cent) as the best way to reduce crime. Over half thought residential drug treatment and tougher community punishments were the way forward. Perhaps the most telling statistic on public perception is their view that the most important feature of sentencing is public protection – 95 per cent identify this of high importance. This can be interpreted as protecting the public from further offences (Hough *et al.* 2009). Of particular relevance to JR is that surveys show that the public has more confidence in the criminal justice system as it operates in their area than as it operates nationally (Page *et al.* 2004, Thorpe and Hall 2009).[9]

What these survey results do not demonstrate, however, is the public's willingness and capacity to engage in a more complicated and nuanced debate about the use of evidence in determining which criminal justice interventions should or should not be used. The options offered in the surveys are arguably ones that the public is able to recognise and may understand as "intuitively" effective. A recent study by Meadows *et al.* (2012) suggested that both for the public and for practitioners, awareness and acceptance of the effectiveness of innovations in the criminal justice system, in this case restorative justice delivered by police officers, varied based on direct experience.

> Positive opinions were significantly more strongly held amongst those police officers who had had experience of RJ [restorative justice] when compared to those staff who had not. This to some extent mirrored the differences between the views of victims who had direct experience, and generally more positive views, than communities who had not experienced RJ. This suggests that communication of the benefits is not as effective as direct experience in shaping positive perceptions of RJ.
>
> (Meadows *et al.* 2012: 47)

This has significant implications for the way in which JR approaches, and the use of evidence to determine which interventions to invest in and which interventions to divest from, are communicated to both practitioners and the public.

In an interview for this book, Rob Allen suggested that there was a tension between localism as practised by practitioners on the ground, responding to local demands from the community, and adopting a scientific approach to the use of evidence. He cited the example of the different ways in which anti-social behaviour was addressed by local areas in the UK following the introduction of Anti-Social Behavour Orders (ASBOs) in the Crime and Disorder Act 1998. Across the three police force areas in Wales, North Wales (a predominantly rural area with relatively low levels of crime and anti-social behaviour) had the highest number of ASBOs – 415 compared with South Wales (a more urban, densely populated area with higher levels of crime and anti-social behaviour), where there were 360 over the same period (Hickey 2011). Such differences indicate a postcode lottery in the delivery of justice, something also indicated by the variation in sentencing outcomes for the same or similar offences from area to area:

> Variations in sentencing practice may be the result of "local justice" or the "human factor", defined as the need to establish and maintain consistent policy in individual courts, which may have taken priority over maintaining consistency at a national level.
>
> (Mason *et al.* 2007: 3)

It has been argued that community support will be key to overcoming the some of the political challenges to JR (Justice Committee 2009). The public view of crime is complex and contradictory. The previous UK government proposed a number of ways to increase public involvement in the criminal justice system, focussing mainly on prosecution and punishment. These included local crime data and monthly police beat meetings. In the Participatory Budgets pilot being undertaken by some Community Safety Partnerships, communities are given some powers over their local budget (Ministry of Justice 2010c). However, such community involvement approaches are only ever likely to impact on a small segment of the population. Moreover, in the case of community engagement by the police, the criminal justice agency with the longest track record of such activity, formal engagements through consultative forums "tend to be unrepresentative, insufficiently independent and unsuccessful" (Lloyd and Foster 2009: 25).

The Justice Committee (2009) received a variety of evidence about the likely effectiveness of different ways of engaging the public in a debate about the criminal justice system and effectiveness of the system. They proposed that the way to tackle this was to link effectiveness to cost and affordability. Taking a whole-population approach, they recommended that:

> Public information campaigns should seek to promote understanding of the cost of the criminal justice system to the public purse and where the costs of the failure of current initiatives fall. The Government should use this to gauge public reaction to the costs of the system.
>
> (Justice Committee 2009: 160)

Conclusion

Evidence-based Justice Reinvestment

The debate on evidence-based policy in criminology and criminal justice raises interesting questions about JR:

How should proponents of JR select interventions? One option is to favour evidence generated through (quasi) experiments and synthesised in Systematic Reviews. However, such an approach runs the risk of missing the very essence of what makes a social intervention "work". The various criticisms of Systematic Review methodologies are particularly pertinent when we consider the application of JR approaches in the UK, because the majority of studies identified in Systematic Reviews relevant to JR took place in the USA. A particular challenge in evaluating interventions in the UK is the range and complexity of governance arrangements in place. This complexity profoundly shapes the context for "realistic evaluation" (Pawson and Tilley 1997). Thus there are concerns about whether or not US findings can be transferred to a UK context. For example, Villetaz *et al.* (2006) looked in particular at studies which test the effects of custodial versus non-custodial sentences on re-offending. Their extensive Systematic Review identified only 23 relevant and methodologically robust studies. None were from the UK.

What should the JR movement do in response to these issues? At this point we make two suggestions. First, we suggest that when thinking about the generation and use of evidence to inform policy, JR cannot be located within the positivist paradigm. Second, we highlight the importance of a strong theoretical framework within which to locate JR. We will say a little about these two issues by way of conclusion, and will return to them in the next two chapters.

The problem with positivism

Experimental criminology and the "traditional" approach to Systematic Review sits in the positivist paradigm.[10] Positivism is based on a belief in a unified scientific method that can explain both the natural and social worlds. In other words, it is assumed that man is a part of nature (albeit a particularly complex part). Hence the same form of scientific method can be used to explain man as is used to explain everything else in the natural world. Human behaviour is assumed to be determined, in the sense that it always has a causal explanation (Hollis 1977). Thus, for the positivist operating within the social sciences, the key to discovering "statements of a law-like character" is the measurement and quantification of human behaviour.

The scientific method advocated by positivism is based on the Empiricists' conviction that all true knowledge is grounded in empirical observation of the external world. The social scientist's suggested "law" or initial hypothesis emerges from empirical observations and it is then verified by empirically testing the accuracy of its predictions against empirical experience. As hypotheses are validated, a theory emerges. Thus, positivism provides a method of science which allows for the objective and neutral validation of theories.[11] Empirical observation is therefore the ultimate and objective arbitrator of the validity of a theory (Hollis 1977).

Clearly, the claim to objectivity is attractive to policy-makers and practitioners (to say nothing of the public) looking for definitive statements about "what works". It will be particularly attractive in any approach to JR in which understanding the costs and benefits of different options to reduce offending and re-offending plays a part.

However, the claim to objectivity has been under sustained attack for a very long time. The key to the positivist claim to be able to produce objective, scientific knowledge is the assumption that hypotheses – and hence theories – are based upon objective, empirical observations rather than the scientist's particular views and prejudices. This approach has been criticised as being not so objective as is supposed. For instance, Popper (1972) argues that:

> The belief that we can start with pure observations alone, without anything in the nature of a theory, is absurd.... Observation is always selective. It needs a chosen object, a definite task, an interest, a point of view, a problem. And its description presupposes a descriptive language, with property words; it presupposes similarity and classification, which in turn presupposes interests, points of view and problems.
>
> (Popper 1972: 46–47)

If, however, we accept that observation is never theory-neutral and that any examination of the social world involves interpretation, this undermines the positivist claim to be able to produce objective knowledge. For JR a key question will be whether an interpretive approach can also provide a degree of objectivity.

The need for theory

To move out of the positivist paradigm does not necessarily mean rejecting (quasi) experimental methods outright (see, for instance, Pawson and Tilley 1997). It is possible to recognise that while experiments and Systematic Reviews have a place, the range of evidence we consider and the understanding of the social world that underpins it needs to be formulated based on a different set of assumptions. Hough (2010), focussing particularly on the evidence base for interventions which reduce re-offending, is concerned that "traditional" Systematic Reviews fail to recognise that "work with offenders is a highly reflexive process in the sense that the meanings attributed to the process by those involved in it will affect the outcomes" (Hough 2010: 14). Systematic Reviews that look for "'clinching evidence' based on Randomised Control Trials (RCTs) and similar evaluative methods can result in an accumulation of generalisable hard knowledge about what works in reducing reoffending" (ibid.) but fail to recognise that the effectiveness of interventions will be highly context-specific. Thus: "What is missing from systematic reviews in this field – as currently practised – is the development of 'middle level theories' to explain why some things work and others don't" (ibid.: 14). It is to this issue that we turn in the next chapter.

The political dimension

Overlaying the debate about what evidence to use and how to generate it is the "politicisation" of evidence. Regardless of the efforts of the research community to devise approaches which offer the best evidence available, the impartial use of such evidence cannot be guaranteed. JR relies on gaining the assent and support of multiple stakeholders: policy-makers, both politicians and civil servants; senior managers of local agencies, including local authorities, probation services and the police; middle managers, operational managers and front line staff from public, private, voluntary and community sector agencies; and the public. Negotiating the multiple and sometimes conflicting interests that these stakeholders represent is far from simple. Commenting on the reliance on evidence to formulate policy, Walker (2004: 40) suggested that "we have gone from nothing works to everything works".

In the UK, the experience of current efforts to implement JR based on establishing an evidence base for interventions suggests that "some things may work" – but the level of trust that stakeholders are willing to place in the evidence is uneven. Aside from individual and organisational reluctance to accept evidence that may be counter-intuitive and/or counter to their interests, the unwillingness to accept evidence and act on it appears to be due to a desire for cast-iron certainty. Politicians, policy-makers and commissioners of services don't want to be wrong; they fear blame and criticism for poor use of public funds, especially in a time of public sector spending cuts.

Ironically, perhaps, the fact that there is more evidence available, however contradictory or disappointing some of it may be, appears to have made the task of decision-making more difficult – inducing an "analysis paralysis" that wasn't present when there was little or no evidence. Perhaps all stakeholders in criminal justice need to be reminded that they have inherited a criminal justice system with prison as a mainstay intervention from a time when no-one had examined any evidence about whether or not it worked.

8 Towards a new theory of Justice Reinvestment

The economic dimension

Justice Reinvestment introduces an explicitly "economic" approach to developing criminal justice policy. This chapter explores economic conceptions of crime and criminal justice and demonstrates how these might relate to broader issues of social justice and economic well-being. We discuss how economists have used Rational Choice theory to theorise crime and criminality. Understanding crime and criminal justice starting from the premise of instrumentally rational individuals provides us with some useful insights into offending behaviour. Ultimately, however, pure Rational Choice theory falls short of explaining the relationship between offenders and the communities in which they live or describing the process of desistance from offending.

We argue that a different conception of rationality is needed for this, and we turn to concepts of substantive rationality and procedural rationality. Employing the concept of substantive rationality allows us to develop a model of social action in which reciprocal rights are central to explaining how rational actions may be constrained by social norms. This model seems to provide a much more appropriate basis for developing a theory of Justice Reinvestment. Thus, a more realistic and subtle model of decision-making is presented, one which is more in accord with the complex interactions between humans and the societies in which we live – societies which introduce and reinforce norms and provide the context and constraints for individuals' decisions. This approach provides the foundations for developing a theory of Justice Reinvestment in which delivering social justice is central. We also note that there are many points of similarity with the Good Lives model (see for example Ward and Maruna 2007) and suggest that that model of offender rehabilitation might sit comfortably within a broader theory of Justice Reinvestment.

In summary, then, this is a theory of Justice Reinvestment in which the delivery of social justice is central and in which interventions to prevent offending and re-offending must necessarily involve interventions with "at risk" individuals *and* the communities in which they live.

Introduction

Although early work on Justice Reinvestment (JR) envisaged a radical rethinking of criminal justice, the model that has emerged on both sides of the Atlantic in latter years is more limited in its aspirations. It is a model based on redesigning the criminal justice system to make it more cost-effective. It therefore concentrates on traditional criminal justice agencies: the police, the courts. prison and probation services. It has a more "closed" view of the criminal justice system than the original vision of Tucker and Cadora (2003) and tends to promote a dual strategy of diversion from the criminal justice system for lower-risk, lower-need offenders and reducing re-offending for higher-risk, higher-need offenders. It is less directed toward reducing the inclination to offend in the first place.

Under the currently prevailing framework, JR interventions are predominantly either located within traditional criminal justice agencies or, in the UK in particular, to do with out-sourcing (via so-called Payment by Results) traditional criminal justice tasks such as probation or prison services. Allocation of offenders to interventions is often based on data-driven analyses of their risk of re-offending and criminogenic need, coupled with new analysis of the cost-drivers of the criminal justice system and "flows" of people through the system. As we have noted above, these methods are rooted in a positivist approach to social science and it is also one that neglects to provide a clear etiology of an individual's turning to crime or a clear vision for the role of different criminal justice and wider social institutions in reducing offending and re-offending. Cost savings from this narrow adoption of JR are generally not invested but go to reducing government deficits (Herbert 2010).

In this chapter and the next we return to the original conception of JR sketched out by Tucker and Cadora (2003). We develop this further into a more complete theory of JR which takes account of all aspects of the (potential) offender's career. This encompassing model of JR will start from the premise that interventions designed to prevent offending and reduce re-offending must be founded on the clear understanding of the interaction between individual offenders, their communities and the criminal justice system. Such interventions should consider a redesign of the criminal justice system that achieves greater social justice and builds social capacity. This broader model recognises the importance of diverting offenders from the criminal justice system, by placing greater emphasis on preventing offending altogether. Where this is not possible, the model allows a more holistic approach to reducing re-offending.

The implication for crime reduction is that investment in prevention will include measures which build community and individual resilience. The implication for reducing re-offending is that while there is a need to manage risk and address criminogenic needs, changing an offender's thinking and behaviour needs to include an offer to offenders of the opportunity to become good citizens and live a Good Life.

In this more radical version of JR, (potential) offenders are assumed to have a degree of agency. Thus some responsibility is placed on offenders for co-producing their own rehabilitation. At the same time, it is recognised that individual offenders should be supported in a positive way that includes identifying and working with their "assets" (their skills and experience), rather than concentrating on their deficits (criminogenic needs). Communities have a role, and building and mobilising community capacity to help reduce re-offending should be a key strategy. Compared with the narrower view of JR, this model places greater emphasis on the important role non-criminal-justice agencies play in preventing offending and reducing re-offending. Finally, implicit within this model is a mixed economy of criminal justice provision and an approach to commissioning that supports local communities.

As in Chapter 4, we will adopt the framework of Ward and Maruna (2007) for structuring the theory. We begin by outlining some general principles for this new theory of JR and discuss the etiology of crime before suggesting a range of interventions that might be most closely associated with the model. One additional dimension to our model of JR, not included by Ward and Maruna in their framework for theorising offender rehabilitation, is a dimension for commissioning and service delivery. We argue that this dimension is essential to a fully-rounded model, because the type of commissioning model adopted will influence the types of interventions adopted.

The strategy for this chapter

Our starting point is that JR is an approach that, to some extent, is grounded in an economic conception of criminal justice. We therefore begin our discussion of general principles and etiology by reference to relevant economic concepts and theory. However, while we take some elements from the traditional neo-liberal approach to economics, we also recognise the limitations of this paradigm and base our analysis on a more humanistic set of economic principles, in which the concept of social justice is central.

In the following chapter, Chapter 9, we discuss the types of interventions and the approach to commissioning them implied by this new theory of JR.

How the remainder of this chapter is organised

Justice Reinvestment introduces a much more explicitly "economic" approach to developing criminal justice policy. This chapter explores economic conceptions of crime and criminal justice and demonstrates how these might relate to broader issues of social justice and economic well-being. We discuss how economists have conceived of crime and how they have built a model of criminal behaviour and criminal justice built on individual rationality and market solutions. We accept this as an initial approximation; however, we identify the limitations of such a model and argue that it is not a sufficient basis for developing a theory of JR, in which criminal justice policy is inextricably linked to broader concepts of social justice and economic well-being. We adopt a different concept of rationality that is able to accommodate a theory of social justice in which individuals have reciprocal rights, and we explore the role of the market in delivering such a model, concluding that, while the market has a role, JR can only be delivered in a mixed economy where the public, not-for-profit and private sectors all play roles.

Economic modelling of crime and criminal justice

Most economists who consider crime and criminal justice adopt the micro-economic view of agents as individually rational actors weighing their options and deciding, given the prevailing criminal justice framework, which actions are in their own best interests. For the first part of this chapter, we will accept these assumptions and explore whether they are sufficient to allow us to develop a theory of JR. In this section we consider the theoretical basis of such a system, beginning with the seminal work of Becker (1968), who determines the optimal societal response to the potential of criminality. Becker's work has been expanded upon by Ehrlich (1973, 1996), who determines the optimal response of the potential criminal. As we shall see, however, while it is certainly true that societies are made up of individuals, it is no less true that prevailing societal norms and sub-cultural norms impact on the individual. Hence social responses to crime which consider only the individual are likely to be inefficient and insufficient. A broader suite of interventions to discourage criminality is required.

Beginning with Becker

In 1968 Gary Becker's seminal work on the economic analysis of crime was published. Becker (1968) took the supply of offences as a given and develops the proper societal response. His analysis considers a particular activity, denoted O, which, for some level of supply, causes a net cost to society. There is, however, a benefit to the individual of perpetrating O. Society is assumed to respond with a measured combination of detection – the probability of having the crime successfully detected and the perpetrator convicted Becker denotes p – and the level of punishment, f. All members of society are assumed to be potential offenders and to respond to p and f in a manner summarised by a Cobb-Douglas-style aggregate production function.[1]

Becker's model considers the trade-off between the harm the activity O does to society and the costs of detection, conviction and punishment. Becker assumes: (1) declining marginal efficacy of p and f; and non-decreasing marginal costs of p and f – these assumptions together imply that, as p and f increase, further increases become less cost-effective; and (2) increasing marginal damage to society from increasing O – this implies that, as O declines, a further marginal decline brings less cost savings. There will, therefore, be a point at which further increases in the policy variables, p and f, become uneconomic in the sense that they will increase societal costs by a greater amount than society saves by the reduction in O. This is the optimal level of criminal justice policy, represented in Figure 8.1. The dark curve represents the total cost of activity O – this is made

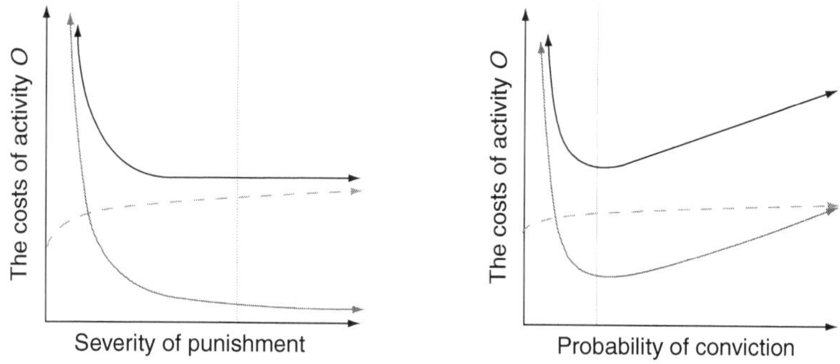

Figure 8.1 The optimal level of deterrence (source: Albertson and Fox 2012).

up of the harm done by *O* and the cost of apprehension and conviction, represented by the lower solid curve, and the cost of punishment, represented by the dashed curve.

In brief, Becker concludes that, for the most part, society cannot win the war on crime. That is, the optimal level is greater than zero – it is simply too expensive to eliminate criminality completely through the use of incarceration. The analysis suggests, however, those crimes with the most serious consequences for society should receive the main part of society's censure, with a higher rate of detection and heavier punishments imposed on those found guilty. Where it is possible to punish perpetrators with a cheaper alternative to incarceration (for example, community service or, where appropriate, a fine), this will reduce costs. In turn, this may lead to a more socially optimal solution. Society can move to an optimal point with less crime and reduced costs of punishment compared to a reliance on incarceration only.

Becker's model is intuitively appealing and has obvious and unequivocal policy implications. There are, notwithstanding, two main drawbacks: first, it merely describes a societal response to crime – it does not seek to explain in any way how potential perpetrators weigh up the decision whether to commit crime or not other than their response to deterrence; and second, it casts society in the role of reactive to crime (through punishment), not pro-active in reducing the incidence of crime and criminality. Thus, Becker's model is too narrowly constituted to form the basis of a theory of JR.

Becker envisages a society of people who, while individually desiring to commit criminal acts, organise as a state to protect themselves from each other. As a consequence of this, each agent may hold themselves in check through nothing other than fear of being found out and fear of the subsequent punishment. This represents a somewhat cynical view, it might be suggested, of the human condition, albeit in keeping with social contract theorists such as Hobbes (1943), writing in general terms about the human condition, and Beccaria (1764), writing specifically with the criminal justice system in mind.

Extensions with Ehrlich

Becker's model is substantially improved by Ehrlich (1973, 1996), whose model of crime and criminal justice seems, on the face of it, to offer a rather more promising foundation to a theory of JR. Ehrlich seeks to address the question of criminality from the other side, that is to say, not from the point of view of society's response to crime, but from the point of view of the agent considering a criminal act. In Ehrlich's model, the potential criminal weighs up the choice of how to spend their time in a way which will bring about the greatest expected net return to them. The agent considers: the return on the activity, denoted a; the cost of the activity, c; the opportunity cost (that is, the expected return on the licit activity which will be foregone if illicit activity occupies the agent's time), w; the probability of detection and the level of punishment, p and f; and the general distaste for crime, t. According to the model, a crime will be committed if

$$a - c - w - pf > t$$

It will be noted p and f are the same policy variables which Becker considers in his earlier model. There are, however, more subtle policy variables which society may choose to exploit so as to influence the agent's decision.

The benefits and costs of crime

The implication of Erlich's model is that one obvious way in which society might seek to influence the choice of an agent whether or not to commit crime is through modifying the return from the activity, a. It is in this context that (criminal) asset confiscation policies and denying the rewards of the activity are promoted. For a good example of the former, we may consider the provisions of the (UK) Proceeds of Crime Act 2002.[2] Assets which are able to be identified as arising from criminal activities may be recovered by the Serious and Organised Crime Agency (SOCA). In the USA, the FBI undertakes similar activities. Examples of actions which deny the rewards of the criminal activity include marking and registering property on, for example, the immobilise website, www.imobilise.com. The rewards from crime may also be reduced by denying access to a sell-on market for stolen goods. To the potential thief, there is little point in stealing goods which may not readily be turned into cash.

Society may also seek to increase the costs of the criminal activity, c. Examples of this include hardening targets, for example, with more secure locks, and increasing the risks of the activity.[3]

The opportunity costs of crime

A third way society may influence the choice of whether or not to commit crime is through the opportunity cost of the criminal activity, w. It is clear that, where well-paid and legitimate work is easily available, the potential criminal must weigh up the legal income which must be foregone if they invest their time in criminality. Similarly, the rational actor may weigh up the impact on their chances of future licit activity if they commit a crime and are caught, convicted and stigmatised. Once having been convicted, it seems reasonable to assume that further convictions will generate less impact on future employment. This implies there will be extra consideration given to criminality before the first conviction. There are, then, two elements which society might influence here: the availability of legal employment and the returns from legal employment. As the likelihood of employment increases, Ehrlich's analysis suggests criminality will decrease.

Society has indeed invested resources into trying to increase the return on legitimate work, and the likelihood of finding it – not just, of course, for the purpose of reducing criminality – through education. Universal education is a right and a requirement in western nations, as education has significant positive externalities for society.

In our context, as the level of education increases, the likelihood of finding, and the returns from, licit activity increase. Ehrlich's analysis suggests this will lead to a reduction in criminality. This is supported by the work of Levitt and Lochner (2001), Lochner (2004), and Lochner and Moretti (2004), among others.

Levitt and Lochner (2001) suggest that males who study mathematics are (statistically) significantly less likely to commit crime; for females, English is the significant discipline. Notwithstanding, in the UK at least, there is evidence that a perverse incentive structure at high school level has actually discouraged young students from these very subjects (Wolf 2011).

Although the beneficial effects of education are well established at an individual level, it is important to consider that some individuals are unable to benefit from an increasing emphasis on academic prowess. The labour markets in both the UK and the USA have recently seen an increasing "professionalisation" of employment. That is, work requiring lower levels of skills is increasingly difficult to find (Cappelli 1993). As an increasing proportion of the population have access to higher and further education, those who are less academically inclined are increasingly shut out of the employment market (Barrett 2010). This phenomenon may place them at increasing at risk of falling into criminal lifestyles.

The effect of the level of the wage that actors may receive for licit activities is unambiguous in Ehrlich's analysis; lower wages lead to increased criminality (other things being equal). There is a substantial body of evidence which supports his conclusion (for example Grogger 1998, Machin and Meghir 2004). Similarly, Hansen and Machin (2002) show that increases in the UK national minimum wage significantly reduced the incidence of crime.

Notwithstanding, as Ehrlich (1973) makes clear, it is not the case that increases in income per se will reduce criminality – it must be a source of licit income which is available to the potential criminal. Increases in national income from which some (many) are excluded may increase criminality. Where the income of some increases, their stock of valuable possessions increases, and so the return from property crime increases for those "left behind" by income growth. If the potential criminal's income from licit activities is unchanged, this will increase the equilibrium level of crime. It is well established that in the USA, the real income of the bottom four quintiles of the male workforce has declined since the 1980s (Burtless 1999). The labour market in the UK has also seen declining real incomes for all but the most well off in recent years (Brewer *et al.* 2007). Ehrlich's analysis therefore suggests that increasing inequality *ceteris paribus* is likely to lead to increases in crime.

While society may address criminality indirectly through, for example, extra training for work and educational support of those most at risk of a life of crime, such interventions will have limited impact where legitimate work is not readily available. Indeed, such interventions may well have a perverse effect. If an agent in danger of adopting a criminal lifestyle undertakes a programme of education on the understanding that legitimate work will be subsequently be made available, yet no work is forthcoming, this will reduce their expectation of future employment and skew the licit/illicit activity choice further towards criminal and/or anti-social behaviour.

The structure of employment opportunities also matters. In the UK and the USA there has been an increasing move to part-time work. The Ehrlich (1973, 1996) model would suggest this will give rise to increasing opportunities to commit crime. It is clear that flexible employment hours may allow an individual the scope to engage in both licit and illicit activities – whereas a full-time 40-hour-a-week job allows less flexibility.

Erlich's model is certainly more promising than Becker's in providing a foundation from which to build a model of JR. Within Erlich's work we can start to see how a more holistic response to the problem of crime might be constructed. But before we start this process we should look at some of the criticisms of this type of economic theory.

Limitations to the "traditional" economic model of crime and criminal justice

Becker and Erlich's models have, as their starting point, the economist's conception of Rational Choice theory, which assumes that individuals have fully ordered preferences, complete information and a perfect internal computer (compare Hollis 1994). There are many criticisms of Rational Choice theory and we examine some of these here. In the first instance, there are two issues which pose challenges to the theory as it is generally formulated, but which can be overcome without discarding it: the impossibility of obtaining perfect information; and the importance of intrinsic rewards. However, a third challenge, that of non-consensual games, requires a more fundamental re-working of the basic tenets of Rational Choice theory. One possible solution is to recognise the possibility of meta-preferences, and we consider whether the introduction of meta-preferences saves the theory or further illustrates its limitations.

Satisficing vs. optimising

The fully rational individual, it is postulated, makes use of all available information in reaching the decision rule which will optimise their objective. However, in practice, this is not feasible. In the first instance, not all information is available to all (or indeed any) individuals. This does not in itself pose a problem to strict rationality. What is more difficult is that some information may be available, and be known to be available, but be too costly (in time or resources) to acquire. In the interests of efficiency, for example, we do not research the relative benefits of types of chocolate bars so assiduously as we do the relative merits of cars or mortgages. The reason is because the savings to be made from accessing more information are less than the costs of acquiring the information. Extra information will be sought only if the expected benefits of the information outweigh the expected costs of its access.

This, of course, leads to a further question, noted by Hargreaves Heap *et al.* (1992): If the individual will acquire information up to the point at which the marginal benefit of additional information (in terms of additional utility) exactly matches the marginal cost of acquiring the information (in terms of utility foregone in other activities which might have been pursued), how is the individual to know what marginal benefits are to be had without knowing all the information? Thus individuals do not fully maximise their behaviour; they choose actions which "satisfice" (see Simon 1956). "Satisficing" allows the individual to overcome the availability of information problem by using rules of thumb to guide their action. Satisficing offers a solution to the problem of imperfect information, because whereas a maximiser only succeeds by arriving at the correct solution, a "satisficer" is content with a good enough one (Hollis 1987).

If the concept of instrumental rationality is to be preserved, then satisficing procedures must amount to nothing more than short-cut devices for decision-making which economise on the brain's limited computational capacity. Individuals will still be motivated by the desire to satisfy their objectives, but their rationality is "bounded" because they are not fully informed (Hargreaves Heap *et al.* 1992: 17–18). If it is conceived too broadly, bounded (or procedural) rationality can undermine Rational Choice theory by suggesting that every action is ultimately rule-bound and inextricably linked to its social context. This would undermine the fundamental individualism of Rational Choice theory (ibid.: 18). In practice it would appear humans act out of a combination of fully rational, bounded rational and satisficing decisions.[4]

The importance of intrinsic as well as extrinsic rewards

A theory of JR must assume cooperation between individuals. In any successful application of the theory, offenders will need to change their attitudes and behaviours and, in return, people living in the communities to which offenders are resettled will need to offer support and a degree of tolerance and trust. Staff in criminal justice agencies can be paid to offer support, but JR, in its more holistic sense, implies a degree of reciprocity between offenders and communities which goes beyond the relationship between offenders and staff in criminal justice agencies. It is not clear, from the point of self-interest, why people not paid to do so should provide support and understanding of offenders. Traditionally, economists posit that rational agents are motivated purely by extrinsic rewards (often, monetised) – see Persky (1995) and further references therein. However, there is a good deal of evidence that typical economic agents (other than economists – see Frank *et al.* 1993) are also guided by altruism – that is; they also consider fairness in addition to material profits.

To determine whether altruism is a motivator of actions, Henrich *et al.* (2001) carried out a series of behaviour experiments in a wide variety of societies – 15 in total – and found that in none of these were the hypotheses suggested by the purely rational agent supported. It is clear that the behaviour of typical human beings cannot be predicted by considering only extrinsic motivation.

In general, human beings are "programmed" to behave in an altruistic fashion as well as an extrinsically motivated (self-interested) fashion. We reward ourselves for our own regard for justice and fellow-feeling. As Adam Smith notes:

> Man naturally desires, not only to be loved, but to be lovely; or to be that thing which is the natural and proper object of love. He naturally dreads, not only to be hated, but to be hateful; or to be that thing which is the natural and proper object of hatred. He desires, not only praise, but praiseworthiness; or to be that thing which, though it should be praised by nobody, is, however, the natural and proper object of praise. He dreads, not only blame, but blame-worthiness; or to be that thing which, though it should be blamed by nobody, is, however, the natural and proper object of blame.
>
> (Smith 1759: III:II)

People, in other words, respond to intrinsic rewards. Recent neuro-scientific evidence supports this claim. The dorsal striatum area of the brain, which is activated when an individual receives monetary or external rewards, is also activated when individuals cooperate – or (rather more darkly) when they punish those who will not cooperate (O'Doherty 2004, De Quervain *et al.* 2004, Rilling *et al.* 2002, 2004). Self-satisfaction, then, is rather like cake, in the sense of the internal reward the individual gets from its presence. Sadly, however, as Mazar and Ariely (2006) and Mazar *et al.* (2008) show, individuals like to have their cake and eat it too; we are quick to find excuses for our failings.

To demonstrate this result, Mazar *et al.* (2008) supposedly tested their subjects' abilities in a simple "search" task; but were actually testing their moral sense. Their subjects, students, had been divided into groups with differing opportunities to cheat and different levels of moral reinforcement.[5] In the first series of experiments, participants were rewarded with the possibility of receiving a cash prize; subsequent experiments involved the use of tokens. Mazar *et al.* demonstrate that students who could cheat generally did, except where they had been reminded before the test of standards of morality. However, students did not engage in "maximal" cheating. That is to say, the degree of cheating was kept to a level where students did not have to update their self-image of themselves as moral individuals (see Goldstone and Chin 1993 in this context). Mazar *et al.* also demonstrate cheating was significantly greater where the rewards were tokens rather than money. That is, the level of cheating increased as "categorisation malleability" increased.

Taken together, these findings indicate humans form an over-arching decision or meta-preference which constrains their daily actions. This is based, in part, on their perception of their level of altruism and how they like to see themselves. When reminded of this "standing decision", students in Mazar *et al.*'s experiment were more inclined to conform to social mores, even where (so far as they perceived) there was no chance of their being found out.

In sum, humans may be motivated by altruism; this will be true for offenders and potential offenders as much as for others members of the communities within which they live. Sadly, not all intrinsic rewards will be motivated by high ideals. On the other hand, there is equal evidence that human beings may also be motivated by spite – that is, they may choose to penalise another for perceived injustice, even if there are extrinsic costs imposed by such revenge (De Quervain *et al.* 2004). This is important as it implies that some may commit criminal acts, not because of monetary or property gain, but by way of revenge or spite. If this hypothesis is valid, it implies that, where individuals feel unfairly excluded from the benefits of society, they may engage in crimes against property (for example vandalism) or against the person even where there is no material gain from such.[6]

At first sight, this evidence of a range of motivations for action poses a threat to the Rational Choice theory on which Becker and Erlich's model draws. However, that individuals might be motivated by egoism or by altruism is not, in and of itself, a threat to the model; it merely means we must consider a broader range of motivating factors. Regardless of on what an individual's particular preferences are based, Rational Choice theory assumes that self-interest will lead the individual to pursue them consistently. Thus, Hollis says of the altruist and the egoist that:

> Both are moved to seek whatever rewards are important to them. If the martyr's faith is important enough to him, he will go to the stake for it; and the theory of rational choice is set no problem in assigning his utilities accordingly.
>
> (Hollis 1994: 62)

The point, then, is that although different individuals have different preferences, they all have the same underlying disposition, which is to pursue these according to their self-interest. "In this sense saints are as self-interested as sinners and the theory of Rational Choice is not committed to any view about how saintly or sinful we are" (Hollis 1994: 118).

In sum, Rational Choice theory implies that individuals' actions must be rational to them, whether or not such actions appear rational to us. Such a view of rationality is, however, both tautological and eviscerated as a guide to policy. It does not explain at all how individuals come to hold the set of preferences which motivates them, nor does it allow for human shortcomings and mis-judgements. Further, although Rational Choice theory may not be "committed to any view about how saintly or sinful we are", society clearly will find some actions, whether rational or not, to be conducive to the smooth running of the state, and other actions to be inimical to its smooth running.

Conflicts between rationality at the individual and group level

At the heart of Rational Choice theory is the instrumentally rational individual who pursues their own self-interest. However, irrespective of how self-interested we are, we live in societies. These societies are filled with others, like ourselves, all seeking their self-interest. As others pursue their self-interest, it is clear they will often, knowingly or unknowingly, pursue actions which might be opposed to our pursuit of our own interest. In the limit, unmitigated pursuit of self-interest will make social activity and intercourse impossible:

> "Where is the railway station?" he asks me. "There," I say, pointing at the post office, "and would you please post this letter for me on the way?" "Yes," he says, determined to open the envelope and check whether it contains something valuable.
>
> (Sen 1977: 332)

If Rational Choice theory is to form the basis of a successful social theory, its claim, that everything in the social world can be explained as the sum of instrumentally rational actions, must be justified. However, when we consider complex social institutions, clearly part of a fully rounded theory of JR, this claim starts to look vulnerable. If we assume that individuals have a mutual interest in coordinating their rational choices so as to avoid conflict, then a theory of consensual social contracts can explain the existence of social institutions. "There is no puzzle about the emergence of a society which improves on the state of nature for everyone. Furthermore, conventions which benefit everyone need no enforcing among rational agents" (Hollis 1994: 123). However, this overlooks the fact that there are many conventions of benefit to all in aggregate, which are of benefit to none at the level of the individual. Consider, for example, courtesy. Obviously everyone will benefit if all are courteous, but any individual will benefit even more if they are not courteous, while everyone else is. It is indeed in no individual's interest to respect social mores. Where there is no legal sanction, it is in every person's interest to ignore others' claims of ownership, while maintaining their right to hold property for themselves. Put simply, it benefits the thief if all others are honest.

Similarly, Hobbes (1943) suggested that each individual tries to advance their own interests at the expense of everyone else. But, if everyone does this, a perpetual state of war is the result and man's life is "solitary, poor, nasty, brutish and short". Hobbes introduced a different understanding of the social contract to remedy this situation. Individuals place themselves voluntarily under an all-powerful, self-perpetuating sovereign: the Leviathan. This, then, is a social contract premised on attempts to limit futile conflict.

The implication of the Hobbesian view of the world is that "We are good when it pays be good; and it pays only when we are sure of the punishment for being bad" (Hollis 1994: 134). As Beccaria puts it:

> Laws are the conditions by which independent and isolated men, tired of living in a constant state of war and enjoying a freedom made useless by the uncertainty of keeping it, unite in society. They sacrifice a portion of this liberty in order to enjoy the remainder in security and tranquillity.
>
> (Beccaria 1764: 7)

Thus the conflict between what is good for society and what is good for the individual can apparently be resolved by the creation of a system of incentives and punishments – a criminal justice system – which makes it in each individual's self-interest to respect the social contract.

This view of society forms the basis for the models of Becker and Ehrlich discussed above. However, it doesn't seem to fit particularly well with our experience of society. Casual observation makes it clear most members of society will continue to obey social mores, even where there is little or no likelihood of enforcement. Tyler's (2006) study of *Why People Obey the Law* finds that they do so because they believe it is legitimate, not because they fear punishment. Thus he concludes:

> [N]ormative issues matter. People obey the law because they believe that is proper to do so, they react to their experiences by evaluating their justice or injustice, and in evaluating the justice of their experiences they consider factors unrelated to outcome, such as whether they have had a chance to state their case and been treated with dignity and respect. On all these levels people's normative attitudes matter. *The image of the person resulting from these findings is one of a person whose attitudes and behavior are influenced to an important degree by social values about what is right and proper. This image differs strikingly from that of the self-interest models which dominate current thinking* [emphasis added].
>
> (Tyler 2006: 178)

Theorising norms and mores

The Hobbesian view of the world struggles to explain social norms, but even the consensus model of social contract struggles ultimately to explain conventions which give rise to social norms. Hollis demonstrates this using the convention of driving on the left (in the UK):

> Jack is rational to keep left if he expects Jill to keep left and *vice versa*. Yes; but he is also rational to keep right if he expects Jill to keep right and *vice*

> *versa*. Both pairs of expectations are mutually self-reinforcing. How and why exactly does an established habit of keeping left (in Britain) give Jack sufficient reason to keep left next time? To reply that left has become salient begs the question and, surprisingly, nothing [in Rational Choice theory] offers more. Left is Jack's rational choice only if he expects that Jill expects … (that he expects that she expects …) that he will choose left. Equally, right is his rational choice only if he expects that she expects … (that he expects that she expects …) that he will choose right. Each of these infinite hypotheticals is a tautology and nothing shows why previous behaviour renders one categorical and the other irrelevant.
>
> (Hollis 1994: 137)

This echoes the finding of Arrow (1951), whose "Impossibility Theorem" shows there is no method for constructing societal preferences out of arbitrary individual preferences. The solution to this seeming paradox is to allow social norms into our analysis.

Meta-preferences

In the first instance, we might recognise that individuals are as often in conflict with themselves just as they are with others, as anyone who has tried to give up smoking will know. Hollis suggests that "[R]ational agents who were more reflective and distanced from their own preferences might each do better for themselves" (Hollis 1994: 136). Sen (1977) suggests that such conflicts arise because we have more than one set of potentially mutually exclusive preferences. He considers that the traditional version of Rational Choice theory provides too limited an understanding of individual choice.

> The purely economic man is indeed close to being a social moron. Economic theory has been much preoccupied with this rational fool decked in the glory of his one all-purpose preference ordering. To make room for the different concepts related to his behavior, we need a more elaborate structure.
>
> (Sen 1977: 336)

Building on Harsanyi's (1955) discussion of "ethical preferences" and "subjective preferences", Sen postulates that decisions are made in several steps. Thus he distinguishes between what a rational individual would choose to prefer, and what they do prefer. This ranking of preference sets is made on the basis of what Sen calls a meta-preference. That is to say, an individual might decide, for example "I would really like a beer; however, given that I committed to being teetotal, I prefer tea to coffee".

Such a meta-ranking of preferences is a required response to such rational paradoxes as the "Tyranny of Small Decisions" (Kahn 1966). This paradox arises in situations where a number of cumulatively small decisions result in an outcome which is neither intended nor desired. Kahn's original analysis considered economic issues such as public good provision and market failure; however, the need to look beyond the immediate return and cost of an action is widely applicable, albeit less widely applied. In the context of individual's preferences, the daily decision, that we will begin to exercise and diet *tomorrow*, adds up, in the long run, to a decision never to exercise and diet. The process of forming a meta-ranking of preferences, in effect creating a "standing decision", is one which the rational individual may use to reconcile the demands of long-term planning and short-term preferences; to see, in other words, "the big picture".

This approach may be used to resolve the paradox, noted by behavioural economists such as Thaler and Shefrin (1981), of the two-self model. They postulate that each individual is engaged in reconciling the desires of two "selves", one a myopic "doer", the other a "planner". Each wants to maximise their respective utilities. The planner is interested only in short-term goals; however, the "doer" is the self who chooses the actions ultimately carried out. By deciding rationally between short-term actions, constrained by a long-term plan, a more rational decision is possible.[7] Thus, the individual who wishes to maximise long-term satisfaction must begin by making a "standing decision" regarding what type of person they are and/or hope to become.

However, such a subtle analysis will still not be sufficient to explain in full the existence of social norms and trust between individuals (Hollis 1987). Fundamentally, even where there are tiers of preferences which allow individuals more room for manoeuvre, these preferences will still lead, eventually, to sub-optimal choices. For example:

> Consider the dilemma facing a woman who has hitherto been a contented mother and home-maker but has begun to wonder whether she has, in effect, been conned in a vicarious life of self-denial. Shall she settle for her existing preferences, presumably second- as well as first-order, or shall she radically reorder them? Answers call for judgement at a yet higher order, where there is surely more to it than adjusting a pair of mental scales so as to give a more satisfying balance of utilities.
>
> (Hollis 1994: 193)

Beyond deterrence and punishment with Adam Smith

To recap then, we started looking for a theory of JR which is based on economic theory. JR implies a degree of reciprocity between offenders and other people in the communities where they live. It also implies that community and wider social institutions will have a role in managing crime and offending. However, Rational Choice theory does not seem to allow us sufficient room for manoeuvre to describe how such institutions would develop or why individuals might choose to engage in such reciprocity. Neither does Rational Choice theory, in its simplest form, explain social mores or the decision by individuals to engage in apparently selfless action. A theory of altruism is required.

We need a different understanding of rationality, one in which virtue is rewarded, and this implies a society in which a simple model of criminal justice based on deterrence and punishment will not be sufficient. Irrespective of whether modern Rational Choice theory is committed to a theory of virtue, classical economic thought was certainly committed. This is made clear in Adam Smith's writing. Thus:

> Human society, when we contemplate it in a certain abstract and philosophical light, appears like a great, an immense machine, whose regular and harmonious movements produce a thousand agreeable effects. As in any other beautiful and noble machine that was the production of human art, whatever tended to render its movements more smooth and easy, would derive a beauty from this effect, and, on the contrary, whatever tended to obstruct them would displease upon that account: so virtue, which is, as it were, the fine polish to the wheels of society, necessarily pleases; while vice, like the vile rust, which makes them jar and grate upon one another, is as necessarily offensive.
>
> Smith (1759: VII:III:I).

These virtues, Smith summarises into three: "The man who acts according to the rules of perfect prudence, of strict justice, and of proper benevolence, may be said to be perfectly virtuous" (1759: VI:III:Introduction). The first of these, prudence, refers to "The care of the health, of the fortune, of the rank and reputation of the individual, the objects upon which his comfort and happiness in this life are supposed principally to depend" (VI:I). According to Smith it is, then, a virtue to care for our own self-interest; the other two virtues put limits on this care.

Smith's second virtue:

> Justice … is the main pillar that upholds the whole edifice. If it is removed, the great, the immense fabric of human society, that fabric which to raise and support seems in this world, if I may say so, to have been the peculiar and darling care of Nature, must in a moment crumble into atoms.
>
> (II:II:III)

Justice, Smith argues, is the most important of the societal virtues and we should expect no less. However:

> The rules of justice may be compared to the rules of grammar; the rules of the other virtues, to the rules which critics lay down for the attainment of what is sublime and elegant in composition. The one, are precise, accurate, and indispensable. The other, are loose, vague, and indeterminate, and present us rather with a general idea of the perfection we ought to aim at, than afford us any certain and infallible directions for acquiring it.
>
> (III:VI:II)

Smith's ultimate virtue is indefinable and, indeed, cannot be legislated: "Even the most ordinary degree of kindness or beneficence, however, cannot, among equals, be extorted by force" (II:II:I), and it is for this reason that

> Though the mere want of beneficence seems to merit no punishment from equals, the greater exertions of that virtue appear to deserve the highest reward. By being productive of the greatest good, they are the natural and approved objects of the liveliest gratitude.
>
> (ibid.)

Further to illustrate the distinction, consider Figure 8.2. The vertical axis represents the good to society as a whole; generally higher is better, and below the origin (where the axes cross) society is made worse off by the individual's actions. The horizontal axis represents the good to the individual. The further to the right the better; to the left of the origin, the individual is made worse off by their actions. The provinces of three virtues are indicated. Clearly those acts which are to the advantage of society and the individual will be carried out through prudence; those acts which are of value to the individual, but which reduce societal well-being, are proscribed by criminal justice; those acts which disadvantage the individual and society we disregard;[8] and those acts which cost the individual but which benefit society may be carried out if the individual has sufficient beneficence (kindness). It will be noted that the state's criminal justice policy, seeking to punish infringements, seeks to move the respect for criminal justice into the sphere of prudence. That is to say, it is in the individual's best interests to abide by the law. However, Smith's "virtue" does not require this. Individuals may be motivated to behave in a just fashion merely because they acknowledge that it is "right" to do so.

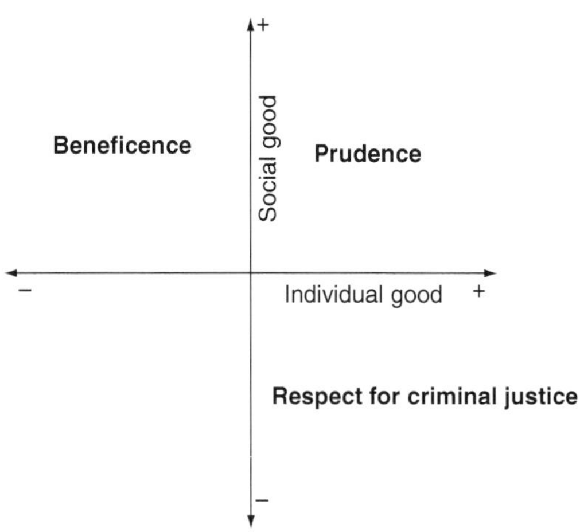

Figure 8.2 The impact of individual choice on society (adapted from Albertson and Fox 2012: 34).

In sum, of Smith's three virtues, the first we may leave to self-interest, the second to legislation and the criminal justice system; the last (the one "productive of the greatest good") is up to the individual, but Rational Choice theory does not give us a sufficiently "rounded" view of human nature to construct it.

A different concept of rationality

Substantive rationality and the common good

Standard Rational Choice theory, based on the concept of instrumental rationality, does not allow for the rationality of the individual's choice of needs or ends to be judged, because to do so would involve making a moral judgement. Strict adherents of the Rational Choice model might comment that a murder was "inefficient" but could not claim that it was "wrong". To suggest individuals would do better to consider their course of action subject to constraints of objective and universal human needs is to employ a different concept of rationality to the standard. However, if the original vision of JR is to have any theoretical support, it must be that individuals recognise that they have common needs and interests; and that these are best served by establishing social institutions which are able to promote and protect these. We assume, therefore, that there is an objective foundation to normative judgement; there are, in other words, inalienable rights which humans enjoy.

To suggest that the individual must rationally choose their ends and means bearing in mind normative constraints is to invoke the concept of "substantive (materielle) rationality" (Weber 1968: 85, 657). The substantively rational individual is one who allows constraints based on normative values such as ethics, utilitarian rules, or social or political maxims. In other words, they will not always pursue unregulated self-interest, but will recognise the necessity of subsuming this to the pursuit of objective and universal human needs. For the substantively rational individual a social solution is a necessary facet of rationality. It is assumed that individuals must cooperate within a social context. Thus, viewed from the perspective of the substantively rational individual, some social institutions and rules would themselves be rational and others irrational.

A theory based on substantive rationality will differ significantly from standard Rational Choice theory. One difference is that, in assuming that human needs can be objective and universal, the substantively rational individual makes a judgement about the type of society in which they want to live. This is because making a judgement about which needs or ends it is most rational to pursue requires us to elaborate what is in the common good and hence which social institutions are necessary to support this good. This is therefore a theory in which political or value judgements about the form that society should take – and the way in which individuals should behave – are unavoidable.

The shape of such a society is sketched out by Hollis (1998) through an exploration of trust: the "glue" that holds society together. He first establishes that the egoism that characterises agents described by Rational Choice theory does not give a basis for impersonal trust or reciprocity. What is needed instead is a "liberal society ... where trust is secured by mutual respect and generalised reciprocity among reasonable persons. Such a normative approach makes it possible to distinguish the genuinely civic virtues from those which are merely functional" (Hollis 1998: 159). This is a society based on "reciprocity", where active engagement in social life provides the basis for strong communities where different versions of a Good Life are possible. This provides a very different basis for both obedience to the law and the wider criminal justice system, as summed up by Clear and Karp:

> Ideally, obedience to the law derives from motives other than self-interest or fear of sanctions. People obey the law because they believe it is morally valid and thus they see enforcement as legitimate. This ideal, voluntary cooperation, refers to the cultivation of socially astute, emotionally intelligent citizens who are as concerned with and engaged in the life of the community as they are with their own lives. Concern for the collective good becomes the motivating force in obeying the law.
>
> (Clear and Karp 2000: 22)

Being reasonable and being rational

We have seen that a simple model of self-interested rationality will be insufficient to describe completely the human condition; we suggest that the consideration of constraints imposed by social norms and mores will give a more complete picture. This much of rationality remains, though: that individuals, subject to value judgements, always act rationally. There is a good deal of evidence from behaviour economics and psychology that even this approach is incomplete. In the introduction to their book *Nudge*, Thaler and Sunstein (2008) draw a distinction between beings motivated by rationality and "real species"; they somewhat whimsically label these "econs" and "humans". Thaler and Sunstein hold that "econs" follow the rules of formal rationality, while "humans" rely more on instinct:

> If you look at economics textbooks, you will learn that homo economicus can think like Albert Einstein, store as much memory as IBM's Big Blue, and exercise the willpower of Mahatma Ghandi. Really. But the folks that we know are not like that.
>
> (Thaler and Sunstein 2008: 7)

The essence of Thaler and Sunstein's argument is that human beings are not so rational as we think we are. This is the theme which forms the background to Kahneman (2011)'s contention that human intuition is made up of two processes: system 1, which is quick and intuitive, but often incorrect; and system 2, which is more thoughtful and rational. Human actions are a result of the complex interplay between these two systems. Kahneman's description of the human condition is echoed by Haidt's (2007, 2012) metaphor of the "rider on the elephant".

The "rider", the rational part of the individual, may quite often know the path they wish to take, but if the "elephant", the intuitive side of the individual, wishes to go a different way, there is little which will influence it in the short term. And where the "elephant goes", the "rider" will also travel. In the longer term, Haidt suggests, the rider can train the elephant so that the whole individual becomes more rational. Such a process of decision-making can be described as procedural rationality (see Simon 1976, 1986). Procedural rationality "is viewed in terms of the processes it employs" (Simon 1986: S210):

> The rational person of neoclassical economics always reaches the decision that is objectively, or substantively, best in terms of the given utility function. The rational person of cognitive psychology goes about making his or her decisions in a way that is procedurally reasonable in the light of the available knowledge and means of computation.
>
> (Simon 1986: S211)

In summary, it is clear that decisions undertaken by humans can be rational, but rationality is a broader concept than suggested by the traditional economic model. As Kahneman (2011: 441) puts it, there is a distinction between being rational and being reasonable – "econs" are rational, "humans" are reasonable. This will clearly have implications for how society manages its criminal and social justice.

Criminological research

Before we continue, a word about methodology in the social sciences. In Chapter 7 we explored some of the implications of adopting different research and evaluation paradigms when generating the evidence that might underpin practical approaches to JR. What does the discussion in this chapter add to that debate?

Part of the attraction of Rational Choice theory is it combines the possibility of hermeneutic and interpretive enquiry with objectivity (Albertson and Fox 2012, Chapter 4 and references therein). However, as we have suggested above, this position is ultimately untenable given the resources at the disposal of Rational Choice theory. The substantive rationalist approach provides a solution to the problem of how to contextualise knowledge claims and how to contextualise moral claims. The solution to these problems, from a substantive rationalist point of view, is to reflect upon the essential qualities of human existence and show the universal necessity of rational thought, individual autonomy and determination of purpose. Substantive rationalism shows that the principles so derived are necessarily true in the sense that to deny them involves contradiction on the part of the person denying them (see Hollis 1977).

Thus rationalism provides a solution to the epistemological problem of grounding knowledge (Toddington 1993: 4). Toddington argues that if we attempt to describe the social world, we cannot avoid making judgements about how the social world should ideally be.

> To individuate aspects of social action, whether in respect of individuals or of institutions, is first to assume the existence of discrete ends, and secondly to identify the essential features of these ends. To select these essential features from the immensely complex and densely interwoven flux of normative phenomena is to force our capacity for abstraction to the very boundaries of intelligibility. It is to imagine an ideally rational world. It is the immediate consequence of the assumption of the possibility of social science that we are deprived of the hope of finding our idealisations instantiated in actuality. It is at this point that we lose our innocence in employing the term "description". For, in the attempt to merely describe the social world we arrogate to ourselves the competence to judge what is practically rational and what is not.
>
> (Toddington 1993: 13)

However, at an epistemological level (that is, when we consider the study of knowledge itself), to recognise that human behaviour is purposive and has a moral dimension is not to give up all claims to objective knowledge. Rationalism claims that we have at least one thing that we must accept as true: namely, that we have the capacity for rational thought (see Hollis 1977, Gewirth 1978). Toddington explains the substantive rationalist strategy thus:

> We may say that assertorically, fundamental claims concerning the constitution of the natural or social world or even mathematics and logic cannot be substantiated by any procedures available to us. However, dialectically, from the basis of claims which, as presuppositions of our experience, must be made, we can at least identify certain epistemological principles which must be accepted on pain of contradiction – especially by those who seek to deny them.
>
> (Toddington 1993: 4–5)

Rational Choice theory assumes that individuals behave predictably and, sitting as it does within the positivist tradition, can draw upon a unified scientific method and "take a spectator's or outsider's view of the workings of nature. Explanation naturally takes the form of finding causes for effects, which are systematically linked by causal laws" (Hollis 1987: 5). This is an approach which sits comfortably with experimental criminologists and Systematic Reviewers. The position we have outlined above, resting as it does on substantive and procedural rationality, does not reject the use of experimental research designs or Systematic Reviews. Taking a hermeneutic and interpretative position and recognising the life within (Hollis 1987), our position, in methodological terms, suggests that experiments and quantitative studies will not provide us with a complete picture.

At the level of methodology a more encompassing approach is likely to be one in which quantitative studies of cohorts is *set alongside* in-depth qualitative studies. In our case, theses will comprise studies which seek to understand crime and interventions which seek to tackle crime from the perspectives of professionals, offenders and community members involved in the resettlement process. Understanding "theories of change" (see, e.g., Weiss 1995) and the development of mid-level theory thus becomes a more important and an ongoing process. This approach is neatly summed up by Hough (2010), focussing particularly on the evidence base for interventions which reduce re-offending. He is concerned that "traditional" Systematic Reviews fail to recognise that "work with offenders is a highly reflexive process in the sense that the meanings attributed to the process by those involved in it will affect the outcomes" (Hough 2010: 14). Systematic Reviews that look for "'clinching evidence' based on Randomised Control Trials (RCTs) and similar evaluative methods can result in an accumulation of generalisable hard knowledge about what works in reducing reoffending" (ibid.) but may fail to recognise that the effectiveness of interventions will be highly context-specific. Thus, "What is missing from systematic reviews in this field – as currently practised – is the development of 'middle level theories' to explain why some things work and others don't" (ibid.).

Reconstructing an economic model of Justice Reinvestment

It has been suggested, that, while economics has something to offer in developing a theory of JR, an approach based on Rational Choice theory is not adequate. We consider the implications of adopting a substantive concept of rationality for a theory of JR.

The rational criminal

As we have seen, most economists who consider crime and criminal justice adopt the micro-economic view of agents as individually rational actors who weigh their actions and decide, given the prevailing criminal justice framework, which actions are in their own best interests. However, the substantive rationalist approach we have sketched out allows us to also explore how the individual responds to social norms and the extent to which they accept the prevailing morality. This allows us to move beyond the limitations of *homo economicus*, who is a very mechanical individual, "a mere throughput between given preferences and an automatically computed rational choice" (Hollis 1994: 186) and towards *homo sociologicus*, whether they be an intelligent rule-follower (Hollis 1994) or a social actor rationally playing roles (Hollis 1987). This does not mean that we discard all the insights afforded by Rational Choice theorists; rather we build on them.

As discussed above, Becker (1968) and Erlich (1973, 1996) consider that all individuals are likely to commit crime if they benefit from it – either extrinsically or intrinsically; in other words, every individual is constantly on the lookout for criminal opportunities. In contrast to the analysis of Becker and Ehrlich, Cornish and Clarke (1986), who develop a more "sociological" version of Rational Choice theory as applied to crime and criminal justice, suggest that the decision to become involved in crime differs from the decision over which crimes to commit. Individuals, it is suggested, must first decide *what kind of person they are*, before deciding, conditional on the former decision, what that means for their day-to-day choices.

Such a two-stage decision process is clearly in line with Sen's (1977) concept of meta-preferences. A rational (potential) criminal will decide, prior to engaging in criminal activities, whether it is in their best interest to make a "standing decision" to consider criminal opportunities. If they do decide that they will commit crime, they then consider, conditional on the first choice, which crimes to commit. According to Cornish and Clarke (1986), focussing on property crime, the decision to become a criminal is based on a combination of: background psychological and demographic factors; previous experience and learning; needs; available solutions; and reactions to chance events. However, we should also be aware that criminals may be drawn into crime all unawares, simply because of shortcomings in their procedural rationality. By their choosing the wrong part of the city in which to live, a circle of friends with a divergent moral code, and a series of other seemingly disparate choices, the triggers which influence a person to criminality may be reinforced (compare Kahn's 1966 Tyranny of Small Decisions).

There is a similar choice to be made by the criminal regarding whether to desist from criminality. A decision to turn away from crime does not mean that desistance is instantly achieved. Rather, it is a process, as Cornish and Clarke emphasise by the ongoing balance between temptations (for example money problems and criminal peers) and constraining factors (for example spouse and job). There are, then, three stages in a (potential) offender's life-story when intervention may be fruitful:

1 At the point of the decision to become a criminal. We may intervene in individuals' lives and their communities so as to reduce the incentive to make the standing decision to become a criminal. In one sense, this is the most sensible time to intervene. Successful intervention at this time will prevent more than crime; indeed, it will prevent a criminal career. However, this begs the question of how we might best recognise those most at risk of falling into crime. It is not sufficient merely to postulate that relative poverty may lead to crime, as there are many of the relatively poor who remain law-abiding citizens. It cannot be guaranteed that this is the most efficient approach on its own, as interventions may be employed to divert from crime those who would have remained honest anyway.
2 After the individual has taken a standing decision to commit criminal acts. The purpose of the intervention here is to reduce, perhaps remove, the incentive to continue with a criminal life. To demonstrate the attractions of desistance and influence the choice to turn from crime is to invite the individual to take a new standing decision. From the societal point of view, any such intervention must take place after crime has been committed, and thus there will be more harm involved than persuading the individual not to

become criminal in the first place. Also it will be costly on an individual basis to change a standing decision once taken. These disadvantages may be offset by the fact that the offender has self-identified as being at risk of committing (further) crime. An example of an intervention here would be drug rehabilitation. The change in outlook which follows successful rehabilitation may lead to improved self-esteem and the possibility, in the offender's own estimation, of a different life-course.

3 After the individual has chosen to turn from crime. Where an offender has indicated that they wish to take the decision to become a desistor, they will require support to prevent their falling back due to, for example, work or social circumstances, peers, and visceral factors. Interventions at this time would include, for example, help in finding legitimate work, housing, and education.

However, for the same reasons discussed above, Cornish and Clarke's theory, based on Rational Choice theory, is also flawed. What the substantive rationalist perspective adds to this understanding is, first, a stronger account of the interface between individual decisions and the social context in which decisions are made. *Homo sociologicus* does not mechanically follow preferences or meta-preferences, but has a role in constructing their version of a Good Life through interaction with social norms and the adoption of different roles. The implication for preventing offending and reducing re-offending is that the efficient criminal justice system will engage with individuals' wider goals rather than simply focussing on their criminogenic needs. Second, because this is a normative explanation, we can also introduce a discussion of the offender's rights and obligations in relation to their community and wider society.

Parallels with the Good Lives model of offender rehabilitation

This new theory of JR has some parallels with the Good Lives model of offender rehabilitation. Our model suggests an individual offender who has the ability to make choices, albeit constrained ones, and who has both rights and responsibilities in relation to the society or community within which they live. Similarly, the Good Lives model of offender rehabilitation has, at its heart, the concept of an individual who has agency (Maguire and Raynor 2006), and whereas offending-focussed approaches concentrate on targeting offender deficits, desistance-focussed approaches promote offender strengths or assets, for example, strong social bonds, pro-social involvements and social capital (Ward and Maruna 2007, Farrall 2004):

> Emerging out of the science of positive psychology … strengths-based approaches shift the focus away from criminogenic needs and other deficits and instead ask what the individual can contribute to his or her family, community and society. How can their life become useful and purposeful.…
>
> (Ward and Maruna 2007: 23)

Our model is normative and considers the offender's rights and obligations in relation to their community and wider society. Similarly, the Good Lives model rests on the assumption that interventions should aim to promote an individual's goods and recognise individual strengths, as well as to manage or reduce risk (McNeill 2009). From this, a discussion of what a good life *should* be must follow:

> Strength-based approaches such as the Good Lives Model (GLM) of offender rehabilitation: (a) focus on the utilization of an individual offender's primary goods or values in the design of intervention programs and (b) aim to equip him with the capabilities necessary to implement a better life plan founded on these values. The GLM is an approach based on the pursuit of a better life, ways of living that are constructed around core values, and concrete means of realizing their goals in certain environments.
>
> (Ward and Maruna 2007: 24)

Similarly, the suggestion in our model that meta-preferences are not mechanically chosen, but are constructed by a socially literate individual, has parallels with the understanding of self-narratives central to the theory of desistance on which the Good Lives model draws. Thus, the Good Lives model of offender rehabilitation draws on an understanding of desistance that is grounded in psychology. In particular, the individual's self-narrative is a dynamic element of personality that is key to the process of desistance (Ward and Maruna 2007). Based on the work of McAdam, Ward and Maruna (2007) describe how

> modern adults create an internalized life-story – or personal myth – in order to provide their lives with unity, purpose and meaning. The construction and reconstruction of this narrative, integrating one's perceived past, present and anticipated future, is itself the process of identity development in adulthood. Essentially, this is a reflective understanding of an individual's life that captures what is of importance to him or her, and how these commitments evolve over time in response to his or her personal circumstances and the various people he or she is acquainted with. In other words, self-identity is a story with characters, a set of themes, and a plot . . . Essentially, people construct stories to account for what they do and why they did it.
>
> (Ward and Maruna 2007: 85)

Maruna (2001) describes the importance of offenders' internal "narratives" in supporting either continued offending or desistance. In his research with ex-offenders he found that individuals needed to establish an alternative, coherent and pro-social identity in order to justify and maintain their desistance from crime (Ward and Maruna 2007). Thus, desisting offenders appeared to live according to a redemption script where negative past experiences were reinterpreted as providing a pathway or conduit to the forging of a new identity. In the framework of Sen (1977), we might say that individuals are in the process of forming and justifying a new meta-preference set.

It is beyond the scope of this book, but we suggest that there would be mileage in exploring the extent to which the Good Lives model of offender rehabilitation might sit comfortably within a broader theory of JR, explaining how effective offender rehabilitation *should* proceed as part of the delivery of a broader theory of JR that delivers social justice.

Reducing offending and re-offending

One implication of Cornish and Clarke's approach is that it is clearly in society's interest to prevent the individual from making the initial decision to become a criminal, hence the importance of increasing the opportunity cost associated with crime by investment in education, growth and effective welfare. This is, of course, in addition to the fact that once a person commits a crime and is convicted, they are much less likely to find work, and thus the opportunity cost of crime is reduced – leading to the increased likelihood of further criminality. Our model goes a step further, because it can present a fully "social" understanding of crime and criminal justice in the sense there is scope to explore the individual's rationality in the context of their response to social norms and prevailing morality. It therefore accords much better with the principles of JR, which indicate that we should not only be concerned with management of the individual's criminogenic needs, but also with their place in their environment – in the locale and the society they keep – and with their broader aspirations for a Good Life.

Therefore, we must consider that criminal justice and the law in general enjoy a symbiotic relationship with society. This means making judgements about what a Good Life consists of, and developing services that help offenders to live it.

The role of the market in delivering criminal justice

Discussion of the role of society in reducing offending and re-offending takes us neatly to a discussion of the role of markets. For the neo-liberal economic paradigm, "society" is a problematic concept; the paradigm prefers a concept of the market, which emphasises an individual's freedoms and the single-minded pursuit of self-interest. We mean here the market in its most narrow sense, a place where goods and services are traded – usually for monetary tokens. Our model, while allowing some role for the market, does not present it as a panacea, and in this section we explain why.

The theoretical justification for self-interest as a foundation for (replacement of) civilised society has been summarised thus by Adam Smith:

> It is not from the benevolence of the butcher, the brewer or the baker, that we expect our dinner, but from their regard to their own self interest. We address ourselves, not to their humanity but to their self-love, and never talk to them of our own necessities but of their advantages.
>
> (Smith 1776: I.2.2)

Smith also argues the "invisible hand" of market mechanisms acting through self-interest will lead individuals to provide for the good of others:

> The rich … are led by an invisible hand to make nearly the same distribution of the necessaries of life, which would have been made, had the earth been divided into equal portions among all its inhabitants, and thus without intending it, without knowing it, advance the interest of the society.
>
> (Smith 1759: IV:I:10)

The main policy implications arising (at first sight) from Adam Smith's observations have been summarised by George (1999):

> the market should be allowed to make major social and political decisions; … the State should voluntarily reduce its role in the economy, … corporations should be given total freedom, … trade unions should be curbed and citizens given much less rather than more social protection.
>
> George (1999: unnumbered)

However, this is based on only a partial reading of Smith; Adam Smith considered that the "invisible hand" of self-interest (prudence) must be tempered with both criminal justice and beneficence, as we have seen. Notwithstanding, over the last three decades, the so-called neo-liberal economic paradigm of market fundamentalism has gained ground in western economies.

In 1987, Margaret Thatcher gave one of her most famous and (we would argue) least understood quotes in an interview with *Women's Own* magazine (Thatcher 1987). In response to her own rhetorical question – "who is society?" – she continued "There is no such thing! There are individual men and women". On the face of it, Thatcher is dismissing society. However, we suggest that Thatcher has been (perhaps wilfully) misunderstood. The context in which she makes this statement is that of individuals "casting their problems on society" (Thatcher 1987) and, by implication, abdicating their individual responsibility for themselves.

Summing up Smith's three virtues (see above), Thatcher goes on: "the quality of our lives will depend upon how much each of us is prepared to take responsibility for ourselves and each of us prepared to turn round and help by our own efforts those who are unfortunate" (ibid.). It need hardly be said that Thatcher is appealing to interactions above and beyond the trade of goods and services when she talks of the quality of our lives; we need hardly "take responsibility" for actions which will be of benefit to us.

Thatcher's preferred metaphor for society, the "living tapestry of men and women and people" (ibid.), will not spontaneously come into existence, yet she suggests that it is by the strength and vitality of this tapestry that we might evaluate the effectiveness of our nation; it is to the strength of this tapestry that we can contribute as we may, and on which we can draw as we need. Clearly this living tapestry includes, and encompasses the trading for, goods and services which we generally refer to as the market. However, we have argued that not all trade is for monetary tokens and extrinsic rewards. The strength of an economy may also be measured in the level of its intrinsic wealth – the extent to which individuals are motivated out of altruism. As intrinsic rewards cannot be traded in the goods and services market, a mixed economy is needed, comprising the state, the private sector and not-for-profit organisations. Such is the idea of Tucker and Cadora (2003), who argue that reductions in criminality can and will follow from investment in communities as well as in individuals. Tucker and Cadora suggest that the cycle of offending and re-offending can be broken by a concerted effort from national government, state government, NGOs, the private sector, the individual at risk from criminality, and their family, working together to improve education, health, job training and (especially pertinent given the recent rise in youth unemployment worldwide, and particularly in the western democracies) job creation. All of this will need a strong community focus.

Conclusion

The adoption of the assumption of instrumental rationality and an extrinsic reward structure has limited the scope of criminal justice interventions in the UK and the USA. By assuming that individuals' preferences are set, and subsequent decisions instrumentally rational, the state has limited its choice of interventions to an emphasis on punishment and reaction to crime. In effect, the criminal justice system has misdiagnosed the problem. Human beings do, at times, make decisions which are in accord with the theory of instrumental rationality as described in Rational Choice theory, but this is far from a universal explanation of human behaviour and of societal responses to behaviours that we deem criminal. We need to recognise aspects of substantive and procedural rationality if we are to construct a fully social theory of justice. The response to criminality must therefore be far more nuanced, and the choice of intervention more wide, than narrower versions of JR would suggest. An over-emphasis on criminal justice and the extrinsic rewards of crime has led to an under-emphasis on beneficence and the intrinsic rewards of building social capacity and tapping into community resources to prevent offending and re-offending.

We have argued that criminality in the individual must be considered in the context of their own rationality and self-interest; of substantive rationality, which considers social norms and mores; and of procedural rationality, in which decisions are made, in part, according to their context. Taken together, these concepts indicate that it is not possible to consider criminality in an efficient manner without considering the society which has given rise to it. A society with a high level of social capital and with strong social norms and mores has the potential to be a society with a low level of marginalisation and exclusion. Such a strong society will only result where individuals are prepared to contribute to it and enter into reciprocal relationships even where their immediate self-interest is not served. Adam Smith's and Thatcher's analyses makes clear that it will not be brought about either by market forces or by criminal justice alone.

Ultimately, therefore, it must be the role of society to encourage adherence to approved codes of conduct as well to discourage crime and anti-social conduct. As Adam Smith notes:

> It is thus that man, who can subsist only in society, was fitted by nature to that situation for which he was made. All the members of human society stand in need of each other's assistance, and are likewise exposed to mutual injuries.
>
> (Smith 1759: II, II, III)

Economists would generally tend not to try to model our affinity for our fellows, conditioning on the presence of such feeling and including it merely as part of our preference set. But in our revised model, a rational society will seek to educate its members with the concept of what is "right", meaning what will in general benefit the society, and what is "wrong", meaning those actions which will in general undermine the society. Further, as we have seen, the intrinsic penalties of criminal activity may weigh as heavily as or more heavily than the extrinsic penalties. That is, if, in addition to any sanction society might impose in response to crime, a potential criminal is aware that they will feel negative emotions – remorse and guilt – as a consequence of their actions, they may refrain in the hope of avoiding those negative sensations. In our model, individuals are not in a social vacuum. They have links to families and communities. It is the strength of these links and the influence of these links which determines their behaviour towards society at large.

Tony Fabelo, executive director of the Texas Criminal Justice Policy Council from 1991 to 2003, defines JR as "reweaving the fabric of society"[9] so as to promote criminal justice through social justice. There is compelling evidence the one follows the other. The challenges, both political and social, are great. Budgets are tight, and short-term solutions seem more politically suitable. However, appropriate economic analysis can make a compelling and forceful case for those interventions which are less expensive than neglect.

In summary, we suggest the following ten observations might inform our efficient response to criminal justice policy:

1 Any fully formed justice policy must foster Adam Smith's three virtues: Prudence, self-reliance; Justice, obeying the law; Beneficence, goodwill and kindness.
2 Mores and norms matter. Human rationality is conditioned by, and conditions, what is socially acceptable.
3 Immediate social circles matter as much as or more than the norms of wider society.
4 The context of any decision matters.
5 People act in accordance with their "view of self".
6 Emotional involvement is as important as (or maybe more important than) intellectual consideration in decision-making.

7 Often short-term influences and short-term considerations can override fully rational consideration.
8 People respond to intrinsic motives. They are psychologically programmed to reward themselves for their altruism and, somewhat more darkly, to punish those who have contravened (their perception of) social mores.
9 Perceptions of fairness and social justice are important.
10 People respond to extrinsic motives – "playing by the rules" must ultimately be of benefit.

As Labour MP Frank Field puts it. "Laws are short-term solutions. We need to go back to the way Greeks saw government. For them, the first and most important question was: 'What sort of citizens should I and my fellow human beings be' " (*The Guardian* 2006).

9 Applications of a new theory of Justice Reinvestment

In Chapter 8 we argued that human motivation is inadequately modelled by instrumental rationality. Human behaviour needs to be understood as social action in which reciprocal rights are central to explaining how rational actions may be constrained by social norms. It follows that effective interventions favouring criminal justice and social justice are primarily those which are focussed at the level of the community. Even where interventions are directed towards individuals, the effect of immediate and national community will need to be taken into account.

Here we discuss a broad framework for community-focussed interventions which are likely to have both a prehabilitative effect and a rehabilitative effect. In general, such interventions must engage with the communities from which offenders come and, in the case of prisoners, to which they will return. There will, of course, be some individuals for whom no amount of prehabilitation will deter crime. We argue that, for these individuals, community-based sentences should be imposed where possible.

Finally, we discuss the delivery of Justice Reinvestment. In the UK the government's currently favoured approach to commissioning criminal justice is to rely on greater use of markets and, in particular, Payment by Results. We summarise and critique this approach and suggest promising alternatives which might also allow for Justice Reinvestment to be promoted.

Introduction

Having outlined a new theory of Justice Reinvestment (JR), we are left with the questions of in what way and with whom to intervene, and how to provide effective interventions. In this chapter we describe first the approach to intervention and the kinds of interventions which are most consistent with JR as envisaged in Chapter 8. Second, we consider how such interventions might be provided, with particular reference to a range of innovative commissioning strategies currently being developed in England and Wales.

Which interventions are most consistent with Justice Reinvestment?

The criminal justice system has roles both in preventing offending and in reducing re-offending, but clearly, it alone can neither prevent crime or reduce re-offending. In essence, before an offence occurs, the criminal justice system's influence on an individual has traditionally been limited to general deterrence. One of the innovations of JR is to draw attention to the potential for earlier intervention and to draw clear links with the wider process for community safety. The theory of JR that was developed in the previous chapter sketched out a version of JR sufficiently broad to justify a range of social and criminal justice interventions. Notwithstanding the broadness of the approach, there are several strands we may tease out.

A strong community focus

Justice Reinvestment does not involve a quick-fix, one-size-fits-all approach, but instead "public safety must be locally tailored and locally determined" (Tucker and Cadora 2003: 4). As Allen (2007: 7) suggests, "Inherent in the concept of JR is a greater emphasis on local ownership of those in trouble with the law and the development of local solutions". First, it is clear the need for intervention in communities involves the identification of which communities are most at risk of criminality. Justice mapping (described above) can help here in identifying communities where there are significant numbers of criminals either coming from or being released into those communities. However it is clear this can only follow after there is a degree of criminality extant. Therefore, to some extent, when we consider community and social interventions, JR is reactive. This is not to say, of course, that interventions which create, for example, employment in a relatively deprived area may not also benefit the wider community, irrespective of the fact that the need for such might be highlighted by a high level of criminal involvement.

What is a community?

Before we go on to discuss community and highlight its central role in JR, it is worth being precise about the concept. On the face of it, the communitarianism of writers such as Etzioni (1995, 1997) seems broadly to fit the interpretation JR places on it. Thus Etzioni (1995: ix) argues: "Communitarians call to restore civic virtues, for people to live up to their responsibilities and not to merely focus on their entitlements and to shore up the moral foundations of society". He also suggests that the communitarian position is "deeply concerned with the balance between individual rights and social responsibilities, individuality and community, and autonomy and social order" (Etzioni 1997: 5). Etzioni is certainly concerned with the same issues which have been discussed above: the relationship between individuals and the state, the centrality of community, and the moral foundations of society. Furthermore, his explanation of the individual's relationship to society seems similarly to fit the model described above. Thus, Etzioni recognises the importance of individual autonomy in a healthy society (ibid.: 18–23), and he emphasises the social context of individualism:

> not only are human beings social by nature but also ... their sociability enhances their human and moral potential. Social thinking has to cease viewing communal attachments as cannonballs chained to inmates' legs, needed to maintain their stability but "encumbering". *The social fabric sustains, nourishes, and enables individuality rather than diminishes it* ... communal attachments and individuality go hand-in-hand, enrich one another, and are not antagonistic [emphasis added].
>
> (Etzioni 1997: 26–27)

However, despite this, Etzioni's brand of communitarianism does not meet our requirements. Hughes (1998) outlines a number of reasons why Etzioni's version of communitarianism "may be termed moral authoritarian or conservative communitarianism" (Hughes 1998: 109). These include its "emphasis on one moral community at the expense of a recognition of the plurality and diversity of identities in late modernity"; "neglect of power structures in human societies or at least a naturalization of hierarchical relations"; "glorification of past solidaristic communities together with a failure to conceptualise the crucial importance of struggles versus oppression in the creation of collectivist communities"; and a "political and moral rallying call for a return to the 'traditional' family as the means to prevent social ills, including crime" (ibid.). Hughes summarises these criticisms thus:

> All in all, within this popular variant of communitarianism, there is a vision of a unitary, homogeneous community sustained by strongly-held moral certainties, celebrating in turn monoculturalism and setting, albeit at times implicitly, a morally prescriptive agenda for the social exclusion of marginalized and "deviant" categories of people.
>
> (Hughes 1998: 110)

At a more technical level, the reason why Etzioni cannot comprehensively repudiate these claims comes from his understanding of the way in which society as a whole functions, his precise conception of individual autonomy and his explanation of the basis of morality. Briefly, Etzioni's theory is based upon a functionalist conception of society (Etzioni 1997: 6). This provides a fundamentally different starting point from the rationalist position described above. For Etzioni, morality is based upon societal needs, rather than individual needs. A conception of needs which are universal to society rather than attributed to individuals leads to an emphasis on the needs of the moral majority, a failure to recognise the needs of minority groups, and a social structure which has difficulty adapting to the diverse and changing nature of society.

While communities are traditionally thought of in terms of geography, in many modern societies geography is only one of a range of characteristics by which a community may define itself or be defined by others. Communities have also been conceived in terms of organisations (e.g. factories, professions); however, traditional organisational forms have been replaced with the "network". It would seem, therefore, in many modern (western) economies, that communities of interest are as important as communities of geography. While it is important within JR to sustain and build communities able to prevent offending and reduce re-offending, it is also important that those communities are ones which allow and have room to accommodate different conceptions of "a Good Life".

The impact of the Big Society and the role of the voluntary sector

Politicians have long hoped to reconcile the dynamism of free-market capitalism with the social concern of a liberal democracy. An attempt at such a fusion formed the basis of President Clinton's "Third Way" (Klein 2002). Klein recounts how the three strands of the Third Way – opportunity, responsibility and community – were first championed by the moderate Democratic Leadership Council from 1991 onwards when Clinton became the chairman. The concept was used by Bill Clinton, Tony Blair and George W. Bush to win elections in the USA and the UK.

The latest interpretation of the Third Way can be seen in the UK Coalition government's concept of the "Big Society". According to David Cameron, the Big Society has three strands:

> First, social action … the daily decisions of millions of people – on them giving their time, effort, even money, to causes around them …
>
> Second, public service reform. We've got to get rid of the centralised bureaucracy that wastes money and undermines morale …
>
> And third, community empowerment. We need to create communities with oomph – neighbourhoods who are in charge of their own destiny, who feel if they club together and get involved they can shape the world around them.
>
> … You can call it liberalism. You can call it empowerment. You can call it freedom. You can call it responsibility. I call it the Big Society.
>
> (Cameron 2010)

In particular, the "Big Society" is placed firmly at the heart of public service delivery, with voluntary and community sector (VCS) agencies and ordinary citizens playing critical roles in this. The implications, insofar as criminal justice is concerned, involve:

> opening up public services to new and independent providers; increasing social action so that people give time, effort and money; and empowering

> citizens and communities to hold local agencies to account and share responsibility for making their neighbourhoods safer.
>
> (Ministry of Justice 2010c: 83)

It is clear that, in general, the role of communities is critical to the notion of JR: communities as the most appropriate location for rehabilitation and resettlement services (in preference to prison); communities as the owners and drivers of a localised criminal justice policy that is more likely to favour rehabilitation over punishment – if only the options are clearly explained to and understood by them; and ultimately communities as the locations where offenders offend and will desist (at some point) from offending. However, as noted by Wong (forthcoming), it is not clear that the Big Society can deliver strong communities. Indeed, the very notion of a Big Society depends on the existing strength of communities.

In terms of delivering JR in a period of public-finance austerity, the Big Society offers a supposed, but as yet largely untested, solution to the delivery of criminal justice and other public services across related areas of social policy. The Coalition government appears to be proffering as a policy that public services can be delivered by the VCS and by ordinary citizens. However, it is by no means clear the VCS and the public are ready and willing to play an equal role in public service delivery. Over the past few decades, the narrative of VCS delivery of public services is one of contradictory and overlapping messages, any of which are likely to be true.

On the face of it, it might be argued that successful and experienced VCS agencies have a better understanding of the needs of vulnerable individuals and communities than might a civil servant. Also, it is worth considering that the VCS might deliver public services better and at a lower cost than public and private sector agencies because they are not burdened with the overheads of public sector agencies nor the need to make a profit as in private sector agencies. Also, VCS agencies are potentially better able to provide niche services to vulnerable individuals in ways that public and private sector agencies are not. This is because of the scale of delivery, i.e. the costs of setting up and delivering services for which there is limited demand. It has been suggested the VCS are able to respond more quickly because they do not have justify their actions to shareholders or ministers. Against this, we might consider that VCS agencies are small organisations run by volunteers and/or less experienced staff (compared to public and private sector agencies). In general, the VCS has limited capacity and capability to bid for and deliver public services. The bidding process itself is likely to eat into their scarce resources. As noted by Wong (forthcoming), the range in capabilities of the VCS varies widely and reflects the diversity of a sector which encompasses large organisations, with annual turnover in excess of £5 million and with many paid staff, as well as small organisations with annual turnover of less than £10,000, principally run by volunteers.

A grant programme funded by the Home Office to test out ways to enhance VCS involvement (in particular of small VCS agencies) in Integrated Offender

Management uncovered some of the challenges of VCS involvement in criminal justice service delivery. Wong *et al.* (2012b) found that these included:

- the need for local VCS infrastructure organisations to act in a brokerage role, between the VCS (which had previously had limited involvement in the criminal justice system) and statutory criminal justice agencies;
- the need for resources and funding incentives to build capacity to increase the involvement of the VCS in delivering services to offenders, including the use of volunteers;
- the resistance of front-line staff from statutory public sector agencies to using VCS services, as such staff may perceive the VCS as being fragile and not to be relied upon to be available in the medium and long term;
- the potential that VCS agencies might ultimately operate in direct competition with public sector agencies in the delivery of services for offenders, which would clearly reduce the incentive to work collaboratively in the short term.

We have argued earlier in this book about the need for a mixed market in delivering JR. This will involve public, private and VCS agencies. If the "Big Society" as a concept is to facilitate VCS participation in JR, there must be a more nuanced and realistic assessment of the capacity and capability of communities than that which currently exists (Wong, forthcoming). As we discuss below, Payment by Results, the government's preferred model of empowering the Big Society, may well undermine such capacity.

Interventions which concentrate on individual thinking and behaviour

In the preceding chapter we rejected the sole use of the traditional model of Rational Choice theory and emphasised the social and community aspects of offender interventions. This should not be taken to imply that we also reject interventions which focus on the individual and their thought processes. The model of rationality that we advanced, while recognising the social dimension to human action, nevertheless leaves space for individuals to make choices and to reflect on the kind of person they are and the kind of life they want to lead.

In recent years, the Risk-Need-Responsivity model of offender rehabilitation has promoted the use of cognitive behavioural interventions. Our model sees clear opportunities for such interventions, alongside wider social and economic ones. For example, experience would suggest a powerful motivator for violent crimes may well be anger or spite, rather than gain. Similarly, we might consider the impact of other short-term but powerful emotions or disinhibitors, such as drugs or drink. That criminality and desistance may result from chance events and supposedly irrational factors, such as intoxication, would seem at first sight to undermine the supposed rationality of the criminal's choice. However, as Loewenstein (2000) discusses, there may well be different forms of rationality which an individual follows depending on their state of mind.

Loewenstein considers rationality in the context of "visceral factors" which include such negative emotions as anger, lust, greed, as well as impairment of an individual's critical faculties by alcohol. Adopting the approach of behavioural economics, Loewenstein posits that agents may be in one of two states: a "cold" state, that is, not under the influence of such visceral factors, and a "hot" state, where visceral factors have altered a short-term alternative set of preferences in the light of which the agent acts. Sadly, the individual, when cold or calm, may underestimate the degree to which their preferences will be altered when they are hot or disturbed. As Adam Smith puts it: "The great source of both the misery and disorders of human life, seems to arise from over-rating the difference between one permanent situation and another" (Smith 1759: III.I.73). Thus, decisions taken when under such influences may appear inexplicable both to society and to the individual when they are calm.

> When his passion is gratified, and he begins coolly to reflect on his past conduct, he can enter into none of the motives which influenced it. They appear now as detestable to him as they did always to other people.
>
> (ibid. II.II.13)

Notwithstanding the degree to which the calm individual can or cannot predict how they will respond under such visceral factors, Loewenstein (2000) contends the individual may predict under which conditions they may become "hot" and takes steps to avoid such situations or put into place checks and balances. This may involve the choice of friends; it may involve so-called pre-commitment. In other words, individuals voluntarily choose to impose physical, legal or other constraints on future actions. On a small scale, anyone who has placed their alarm clock on the other side of the room, so that they cannot turn it off without getting out of bed, is operating under similar principles.

The use of cognitive behavioural techniques have an important role in helping the individual to find more appropriate ways to respond to such visceral factors. It is also worth noting that it is in this context that many of the precepts of Situational Crime Prevention work. By reducing the level of visceral factors, society is, to all intents and purposes, reducing the likelihood of an "impulsive" crime (which is to say, a crime committed while the individual is under short-term influences). Clarke (2005) gives a list of such, which include reducing temptation (for example, gun controls) and controlling disinhibitors (such as drugs and/or alcohol, television violence, and propaganda/stereotyping).

The inter-relationship between individual interventions and social norms

One of the advantages of the model we propose is that it is far easier to explain how interventions which concentrate on individual thinking and behaviour interact with broader moral tenets within communities and across society. In brief, the norms and expectations of society – and more specifically the communities within which (potential) offenders live – will play a role in shaping behaviour.

First, individuals are unlikely in one step to change their standing decision to abide by laws and social mores to a standing decision to engage in serious crime. They may be drawn incrementally into such a decision.[1] This gives many opportunities to those closest to the individual for informal social control (see Sampson *et al.* 1997). Second, there is evidence that, in a neighbourhood where it is clear that social mores have been put aside, the potential perpetrator may feel there is less pressure on them to conform to an over-arching (national) moral code (Wilson and Kelling 1982). For example, Keizer *et al.* (2008) conducted a series of experiments where, by leaving advertising fliers attached to bicyclists' handlebars, they measured the proclivity to litter. It was observed, in a situation where social mores had already been set aside – for example an area with graffiti on a nearby wall in defiance of a sign requesting "No Graffiti!" – 69 per cent of cyclists littered, compared to only 33 per cent in an identical situation, but without graffiti. Similarly, an envelope half out of a mailbox and obviously containing a €5 note was more likely to be posted where the mailbox was clean rather than when it was surrounded by litter or covered in graffiti. Thus it is clear that an agent's decision whether to commit a crime was influenced by their perception of whether such an action was an acceptable practice in the locale of the incident. In a similar study, Stapel and Lindenberg (2011) show that people were generally less trusting of those from a different ethnic background where the physical environment was disorderly. The implications are clear: investment in social environs can help reduce asocial behaviour.

Constant reminders of social norms are important to prevent agents' altering, over a period of time, their conception of what is acceptable to fit in with what they feel is in their own interests. As Haidt (2012) puts it, we all possess an inner self which seeks to excuse our actions:

> each individual reasoner is really good at one thing: finding evidence to support the position he or she already holds, usually for intuitive reasons. We should not expect individuals to produce good, open-minded, truth-seeking reasoning, particularly when self-interest or reputation concerns are in play.
>
> (Haidt 2012: 90)

However, "if you put individuals together in the right way ... you can create a group that ends up producing good reasoning as an emergent property of the social system" (ibid.). For example, if an agent (let us suppose they are unaware of Loewenstein 2000) commits an offence while under a visceral influence, they will shortly come to perceive they have acted outside of their "cool" state preference set. In other words, they will come to realise they have not acted in accord with their standing decision that they will not, in fact, commit such acts. At this point, the agent may seek to rationalise their behaviour through an unconscious process of reducing this cognitive dissonance (Festinger 1957). To resolve the paradox of their recent actions and their contention that they themselves would not commit a criminal act, the individual may conclude that what they did was "not so bad", or that "everyone does it". In essence, they are, albeit unconsciously, deciding they are, in fact, the person who will commit such offences.

In this way, partly through accident, partly through ignorance of the changing nature of their life trajectory, partly through unawareness of the tenets of behavioural economics, an individual may come to revise their standing decision that they will not commit such acts. In sum, a series of momentary weaknesses may lead to the beginning of a criminal lifestyle as a result of the individual's attempt to reduce cognitive dissonance. As Mazar and Ariely (2006) and Mazar *et al.* (2008) point out, a reminder of a moral code makes dissonance reduction more difficult; thus Clarke's (2005) suggestion that society should set rules, post instructions, and alert the conscience. More informally, where social capacity is high, the (potential) offender's family and community will play a part in reinforcing social mores (see Sampson *et al.* 1997, Office for National Statistics 2001, Smith and Kulynych 2002).

This is not to say, as Clarke (2005) makes clear, that we should blame the victim for failing to set boundaries. However, somewhere in between placing the blame solely on the perpetrator (implying that society may abdicate responsibility), and placing the blame solely on the victim (implying the perpetrator may abdicate responsibility), there is the line of reasonable preventative measures.[2]

Irrespective of whether the general physical state of society can influence social norms, it is well established that an individual's norms are formed, in part, by those with whom they associate. This, indeed, forms the premise of the business principle of self-made millionaire Jim Rhon, the "farm boy who made it to Beverly Hills", which is summarised thus: "you are the average of the five people you spend the most time with". In the context of social and criminal justice, peer group pressure and self-reinforcing behaviour may lead to a sub-set of social norms which are outside the mores of society at large (see for instance Farrington 2007 and Smith 2007). As Adam Smith notes:

> Every individual is naturally more attached to his own particular order or society, than to any other. His own interest, his own vanity, the interest and vanity of many of his friends and companions, are commonly a good deal connected with it. He is ambitious to extend its privileges and immunities. He is zealous to defend them against the encroachments of every other order or society.
>
> (Smith (1759: VI, II, II))

This is, of course, all well and good where the individual's society shares its mores with society at large. Where it does not, it may well be the case that, in encouraging individuals to adopt a more pro-social lifestyle life, we are asking them to turn away from the comfort of the life with which they are familiar, from their friendship circle, often even from the area in which they live. This also suggests the importance of policing, particularly neighbourhood policing, in the mix of interventions which should be supported within a JR strategy.

In closing this section on communities, we have implicitly assumed that wider societal norms are pro-social. However, where affluent communities and individuals behave in flagrantly self-interested fashion – setting aside Adam Smith's virtues of respect for the law and beneficence – it will become increasingly unrealistic to expect marginalised communities to adhere to pro-social norms. Therefore, increasing social capacity is required in all strata of our society. If those who can afford to invest in social capital refuse to do so, how can we expect the marginalised to invest?

The importance of education and employment

A key area for intervention in effective JR strategies will be around employment for those at risk of offending, and offenders being resettled into communities.

Referring to refraining from resumption of criminal activities on release from prison as "successful re-entry", Tucker and Cadora (2003: 4) argue: "The likelihood of successful re-entry – without decent jobs in their communities, counselling to identify opportunities and childcare – will be minimal". There is plenty of empirical support for this observation in the literature. Empirical support substantiating the link between offender employment deficits and recidivism was provided in a meta-analytic review of the literature by Gendreau *et al.* (1996). In the UK, *Surveying Prisoner Crime Reduction*, a longitudinal cohort study of 1,457 adult prisoners sentenced to between one month and four years in custody in 2005–2006, found only around a third of prisoners (32 per cent) reported being in paid employment in the four weeks prior to custody, and 51 per cent reported being in paid employment during the 12 months prior to custody (Ministry of Justice 2010b). Both of these figures are considerably lower than the UK general employment rate, which was 75 per cent in 2006 for those of working age (Ministry of Justice 2010b, reporting on data from the Office for National Statistics). Many prisoners reported needing help to find a job on release (48 per cent), help with education (41 per cent) and help to improve work-related skills (40 per cent), and agreed that having a job would help them stop re-offending (68 per cent) (Hopkins 2012). Those offenders in employment in the year before custody were less likely to be re-convicted (40 per cent) compared with those who had not been in employment (65 per cent) (Ministry of Justice 2010b).

Similarly, there is theoretical and empirical work to support the supposition that employment will be a factor in offending (as opposed to re-offending on re-entry to the community). Based on the work of Ehrlich (1973, 1996, described in Chapter 8) it is clear that we would expect improvements in the labour market to lead to an increase in the opportunity cost of crime – where well-paid employment is relatively easy to come by, individuals must choose to give up on the prospect of such for the period of time they engage in illicit activities. Therefore, as employment becomes less well paid or less readily available or both, Ehrlich's model would suggest that crime rates will increase. In addition, there has been an increasing move to part-time work in the UK. Again, the Ehrlich (1973, 1996) model would suggest this would give rise to increasing opportunities to commit crime. Flexible employment hours give an individual more flexibility to engage in other activities, whether legal or illegal.

Thus, as the workforce in the USA, and to some extent in the UK, move to a situation where the return from work is, at best, static, and employment is increasingly part-time and flexible, we would expect criminality to increase. This would also have an impact on other aspects of life for the less well-off. For example, as Edin and Reed (2005) show, the romantic aspirations of the least well-off of USA men are less likely now to be realised than in the 1960s. Despite the fact that the desire to form long-lasting romantic attachments, for example marriage, has remained unchanged over the last 40 years, "poor men and women are only about half as likely to be married as those with incomes at three or more times the poverty level" (ibid.: 118). This provides a double blow to young men: not only will they be less likely to be in a double-income household, but it has been shown that the establishing of a long-term attachment, particularly marriage, provides an incentive to refrain from illicit activity (Laub *et al.* 1998).

There is also evidence that labour markets worldwide are turning against youth generally. According to data presented at the World Economic Forum 2012, 37.5 per cent of all unemployed are in the 16–24 age range (BBC 2012). In 2011, the global youth unemployment rate, according to the International Labour Organisation (International Labour Office 2011), was 12.6 per cent; in the so-called developed world the rate was 18.2 per cent. According to the Organisation for Economic Co-operation and Development (OECD)[3] the figure for the UK as at March 2012 was 21.9 per cent (up from 13.6 per cent in December 2007) and for the USA, 16.4 per cent.[4] A further 6.4 per cent of the youth population of the UK is economically inactive. Under these circumstances, Ehrlich's model would predict an increase in criminal behaviour by youth.

As the labour market has turned against youth, so too has the willingness of society to provide compensating welfare. As LSE economist Tim Leunig writes, "For the past 100 years we have generally tolerated the feckless to protect the unlucky. This government has decided to do the opposite".[5]

Less use of prison and more use of community sentences

Our discussion has focussed so far on strengthening communities and the individual in a broadly prehabilitative framework. Of course, all these approaches and considerations will play a part in rehabilitation also. It remains for us briefly to recap our earlier discussion of how the community may also play a role in the formal punishment of offenders.

We have seen economic and behavioural economic theories suggest, in general, that more criminal activity will result from weaker intrinsic inhibition to commit criminal activity; a less effective education system; less rewarding legitimate work; less easily available legitimate work; and more exclusion from the benefits of engagement with society. Partly as a result of the neo-liberal economic policies pursued by successive UK governments, and partly through global factors – including the so-called global financial crisis – all these effects are in play in the UK economy at present.

The state may respond by increasingly punitive action, and this has indeed been the response of the UK government in recent years, to the point where, in 2007, the UK government spent approximately 2.5 per cent of GDP on public order and safety (Duffy *et al.* 2007).

However, the disincentive effect of prison is limited, especially as life outside becomes increasingly hostile because of austerity and prevailing economic conditions. During the last decade, crime rates on both sides of the Atlantic have been falling while prison numbers have been rising. As discussed in Chapter 2, there is only limited evidence that the increase in the use of prison has impacted on crime (see, for instance, Carter 2003). If we look more generally at published research studies which seek to establish the impact of imprisonment on criminality (i.e. the general deterrent effect of imprisonment) the evidence suggests that prison has, at most, a small impact on overall crime rates (see for instance Liedka *et al.* 2006, Marvell and Moody 1994, Witt and Witte 1996, and Levitt 1996 – all discussed in more detail in Chapter 2).

In economic terms, an efficient criminal justice system will be one in which the state's expenditure leads to the maximal level of social good (or, in the case of criminal justice, minimises social harm). Striking this balance is at the heart of the JR approach. If there are interventions which will lead to a reduction in criminality and an increase in justice and social justice which are cheaper than prison, it makes good economic sense to invest in these. Many of the interventions discussed in Chapter 4, including alternatives to custody and measures to divert offenders away from the criminal justice system or minimise their contact with it, will feature in an efficient strategy.

How should interventions be commissioned in a Justice Reinvestment approach?

Tucker and Cadora (2003) suggest that the cycle of offending and re-offending can be broken by a concerted effort from national government; state government; NGOs; the private sector; the individual at risk of criminality; and their family. These work together to improve education, health, job training and (especially pertinent given the recent rise in youth unemployment worldwide, particularly in the western democracies) job creation. All of this will need a strong community focus. We find theoretical support for this proposition in the model we have developed, which emphasises that JR needs a strong community and social focus on a range of outcomes which allow individuals to live a Good Life. This implies both broad coalitions of services to support offenders, and a mixed economy of provision in order for relevant services in the public, private and not-for-profit sectors to collaborate together. For reasons discussed above, purely market-driven solutions are unlikely to be effective.

In this section we look at recent developments in the commissioning of justice provision in England and Wales which might lead to the development of a more mixed economy of provision. However, we also identify potential barriers to this being achieved. We devote most space to Payment by Results, for the reason that this is the process by which the UK government hopes to implement their vision of JR. However, we must conclude that this approach is too limited. There are other innovative funding approaches which might also be harnessed to help deliver an effective, mixed economy of JR provision.

Payment by Results and Social Impact Bonds

In the *Coalition Agreement* published by the UK government elected in 2010, the Conservative/Liberal Democrat administration set out a new approach to commissioning criminal justice provision: "We will introduce a 'rehabilitation revolution' that will pay independent providers to reduce reoffending, paid for by the savings this new approach will generate within the criminal justice system" (Her Majesty's Government 2010: unnumbered). Key to the "rehabilitation revolution" was to be Payment by Results (PbR) which "will link payment to the outcomes achieved, rather than the inputs, outputs or processes of a service" (Cabinet Office 2011: 9). The idea of paying for specified outcomes, which will, it is hoped, reduce government costs, is particularly attractive at the moment because of the current state of public sector funding in the UK.

Social Impact Bonds

As Fox and Albertson (2011) note, because payment arises after outcomes are known, which might involve substantial time delays, a key challenge to the delivery of PbR models of service delivery is the challenge of raising working capital (Mulgan *et al.* 2010). A related policy innovation, Social Impact Bonds (SIBs), will allow the government, in theory, to privatise the up-front costs of social innovations and the associated risks, thus reducing taxpayer expenditure in the short term and eliminating the risk of government money being spent on interventions which do not deliver the desired outcomes. A social investor might be, for example, an individual philanthropist or a charitable trust. Mulgan *et al.* (2010) suggest that a philanthropic Social Impact Bond will see funds raised from philanthropic sources invested through a special-purpose "vehicle" (organisation) which would sub-contract with non-governmental organisations to deliver services to achieve the desired outcomes. Thus the SIB arises from the desire to facilitate the private (non-government) sector to become involved in the delivery of social services.

Potential advantages of Payment by Results

A system focussed on the delivery of outcomes might look very different from the current system of government provision. It is suggested that there will be a wider range of service providers, more variation in models of service delivery, and a much reduced role for "national standards" which have been key to the delivery of criminal justice provision, particularly by the Probation Service, over recent years. As Fox and Albertson (2011) discuss, proponents of PbR and SIBs argue that they will drive greater efficiency, innovation and impact in tackling social problems while also reducing risk for government. So, for example, by focussing reward on outcomes, and providing minimal prescription as to how these outcomes should be achieved, PbR models (including the SIB) will drive greater efficiency in tackling social problems. This aim, if realised, could be extremely helpful in delivering the JR approach. Proponents of PbR also argue that freeing up providers to deliver services in different ways will encourage greater innovation: again, potentially helpful in delivering JR. The focus on outcomes which is a part of the PbR initiative, and the associated reduced focus on commissioners micro-managing the processes put in place to achieve those outcomes, seems to be a rejection of the prevailing New Public Management approach which has dominated the public sector[6] and, increasingly, voluntary sector services over recent years in the UK.

Implicit in the concept of PbR, though not a necessary requirement of it, is the possibility of promoting more market testing of public services and encouraging new market entrants, particularly from the private and voluntary sectors. Promoting a more mixed economy of provision, allowing for a wider range of providers with expertise in delivering a wider range of relevant social outcomes, might be a mechanism which would promote the adoption of a JR approach; indeed, the Coalition government in the UK has a commitment to ensure that proportions of specific public services should be delivered by independent providers, including civil society organisations; by which is meant mutuals, cooperatives, charities and social enterprises.

To date, the evidence for the success of civil society organisations in the criminal justice sector is mixed. The first PbR experiments developed in the criminal justice system utilised the Social Impact Bond model of PbR and were dominated by not-for-profit organisations, both in terms of service delivery and financial backers.

As Fox and Albertson (2011) describe, the Social Impact Bond initiative recently begun at HMP Peterborough is the first pilot of models of this kind in the English and Welsh criminal justice system. The Ministry of Justice has signed a contract with Social Finance (2010) to attempt to reduce the re-offending of a cohort of 3,000 adult males discharged from HMP Peterborough having served sentences of less than 12 months in custody. The outcome measurement framework is supposedly designed to reduce the likelihood of "cherry-picking" whereby the service provider concentrates on clients more amenable to change. Thus outcomes are measured for all offenders discharged from the prison, rather than just those who engage with SIB-funded services, and frequency of re-conviction is measured, rather than a binary measure of whether offenders were re-convicted or not (Disley *et al.* 2011: iv). There is evidence that the Peterborough SIB has introduced some new funding into the delivery of criminal justice services, thus transferring risk away from government to non-governmental investors.[7] Disley *et al.* (2011) report that investors[8] have put £5 million in social impact bonds to fund the rehabilitation work, and they could earn a return of up to £8 million from the government and the Big Lottery Fund if re-offending among three cohorts, each of a thousand offenders, falls by 10 per cent or if the rate of re-offending for all 3,000 offenders falls by at least 7.5 per cent. If a reduction in re-offending beyond 7.5 per cent is delivered, investors receive an increasing return capped at 13 per cent over an eight-year period (Social Finance 2011: 3). The government might realise substantial savings if the scheme pays off. Conversely, if offending does not fall, the government has little down-side risk, while investors potentially lose all their money.

Subsequently, further pilots have been established within other parts of the Criminal Justice Sector including in other prison settings, both public and private.[9] At the time of writing, a competition is also underway to deliver rehabilitation services within a PbR context, as part of the Innovation pilot programme.[10] The Ministry of Justice reports the "innovation pilot" work stream is expected to result in one large or two medium-sized pilots with a high throughput of offenders. Bids have been submitted by voluntary, charitable and private sector organisations.[11]

Challenges posed by Payment by Results

Fox and Albertson (2011) combine analysis of the underlying concepts behind PbR together with early experiences from approaches being piloted in the UK to suggest a number of challenges which must be faced if PbR mechanisms are to work effectively.

The first challenge is "gaming". A problem of all performance management systems is that they encourage service providers to concentrate on achieving those outputs and/or outcomes which are included in the system. In doing so, service providers might ignore or neglect other measures, even though they know these are also important (Hoverstadt 2011). The aim of government in replacing specific targets with more generalised outcome measures is to avoid this problem (ibid.). However, it is not clear this will have the desired effect, as Hoverstadt (2011: 1), arguing from a systems thinking perspective, explains: "merely shifting the level of abstraction of what is being measured upwards from activities to 'outcomes', doesn't alter the systemic structure and the same unfortunate consequences are likely to ensue". In this sense, PBR is no different from any other performance management system, and while outcome measures may be appropriate at a governmental level, the challenge comes when they are implemented and providers assume that they are the only measures which count (ibid.). In this scenario, "gaming" is likely, in particular "cherry-picking" whereby providers might select "easy" cases to work with and ignore "hard" cases, thereby maximising their returns without accepting fully the transfer of risk envisaged by the public sector commissioner (Battye and Sunderland 2011). This issue can, in part, be ameliorated by giving providers higher payments to work with more challenging cases (ibid.).

Second, the challenge of measuring outcomes is a substantial one, particularly in sectors where outcomes are difficult to define and evaluate. Early findings from the Peterborough SIB suggest that "The development of a methodologically robust outcome measure, which had the confidence of all stakeholders, was a time-consuming and analytically complex process" (Disley *et al.* 2011: iii). Fox and Albertson (2011) discuss this challenge at length and consider three main issues: defining outcomes; scale of change; and evaluation methodology.

- Key to PbR models is a clear definition of the outcome which is being purchased. Using the example of criminal justice, in the English and Welsh criminal justice sector this is not straightforward. Consider, for example, the seemingly straightforward result of reducing re-offending: re-offending will generally be measured via the proxy of re-convictions (i.e. "proven re-offending"). Thus, it would appear to matter little to the PbR model whether offenders cease to offend, or merely become less easy to catch. Further, even this proxy can be defined differently. As noted in the recent Ministry of Justice (2010d) consultation on offender statistics, at present, there are six different measures of re-offending. If outcomes are difficult to define and measure, the result is likely to be that PbR models in the criminal justice system will tend to concentrate on the narrow set of outcomes which is easiest to define and measure.
- Standard economic theory suggests that a provider signing up to PbR will want a return on investment which reflects the increased level of risk assigned to them, and the investor in a SIB will wish to be further compensated for their taking on a risk which is arguably higher than that available in the regular bond market. Mulgan *et al.* (2010) argue that prudent impacts for programmes seeking reductions in re-offending would be in the range of 10 to 20 per cent. However, evidence from criminal justice evaluations indicates that even well-executed projects and programmes often bring about only relatively small changes, a point made by Berman and Fox (2010) in their thought-provoking examination of success and failure in criminal justice policy reform. If only small changes to outcomes are possible, this potentially creates problems for investors looking for a decent return.
- Important to PbR is the ability of a commissioner to be confident not only that the desired outcome has been achieved, but also that it was achieved because of the actions of the service provider which has been commissioned. Thus evaluation designs with high levels of internal validity (experiments and quasi-experiments) will be preferred to those with lower levels of internal validity. If we adopt this approach to the evaluation of PbR models, the result, as Mulgan *et al.* (2010) suggest, will be the widespread use of evaluations which make use of comparator groups, and this will raise the overhead costs of PbR substantially,[12] particularly when we consider that detecting small changes in outcomes measures will require large intervention cohorts in order to show statistically significant results (Mulgan *et al.* 2010). This will limit the range of interventions offered, and the number of organisations able to become involved.

The third methodological challenge comes when we consider how fiscal benefits to public agencies might be identified and allocated. The UK government argues that PbR, as part of a broader approach to changing the way public services are commissioned and to promote localism, must be based on a "full understanding of the value of the potential results" (Cabinet Office 2011: 18). By this they mean that "Understandings of value should be driven by citizens and communities, wherever appropriate. This will enable commissioners to focus services on the social, environmental and economic priorities of the people they serve" (Cabinet Office 2011: 18). In economic terms, this would imply that the viewpoint to adopt when valuing outcomes in a PbR contract should be a broad one in which the full social value is considered. But this is also one the main paradoxes of the PbR approach. If PbR models are to become widespread, they will rely on the commissioning organisation being able to realise a monetary saving from which to pay for the results. This implies taking a relatively narrow view of value, one in which value is limited to the fiscal benefits realised by the commissioning organisation over the lifetime of the PbR contract.

Consider the example of a PbR contract in which the outcome is a reduction in (criminal) re-offending.

Work by economists at the UK Home Office has produced a set of valuations of crime (Home Office 2005) which could be used to place a value on a reduction in re-offending. However, half of the costs of crime identified are a mix of public (fiscal) and private sector costs. If re-offending declines, it is not clear that all these costs can be "saved". Savings in private sector costs cannot be recovered by a public sector commissioning body. The remaining cost savings are the physical and emotional impact of reduced victimisation (Home Office 2005: Chart 4.2). These are not costs which can be recovered by the commissioning body, as we cannot identify those who would have been victims had re-offending not declined. It should further be borne in mind that not all potential fiscal savings can, in practice, be converted into cash. Not all such costs are marginal – they will not decline proportionally as re-conviction rates fall. The intervention impact which might allow a whole wing of a prison to close might well be beyond the scope of a single PbR model. As Clear and Austin (2009: 315) argue, "rehabilitation programs, no matter how good, cannot by themselves truly substantially reduce incarceration rates by reducing recidivism". In any event, there is no guarantee that desistance from offending by one individual might save any resources. There might, in effect, be a waiting list for prison places in a supply-constrained equilibrium. Roman (2004) shows how it is necessary to understand whether demand for a service is finite.

In addition to these challenges, Fox and Albertson (2011) also identify a number of more "operational" or practical challenges to implementing PbR, which include:

- whether to assign payments to the results of individuals or groups – this decision has implications for monitoring and evaluation;
- how to segment offender populations;

- what approach to use in setting tariffs for payments against different segments of a client group;
- balancing the risk between commissioners and service providers, particularly where smaller private and not-for-profit organisations are involved.

Some preliminary conclusions about PbR

At the time of writing, PbR is still a concept very much in development, and so our conclusions are necessarily preliminary ones. PbR models have a place in the provision of public services. The transference of risk is attractive to government. In some parts of the public sector, where the potential client group is fairly large and homogenous and service provision is highly integrated, measurement of outcomes is straightforward and the fiscal return on achievement of outcomes is easy to establish. Here, a PbR mechanism might be attractive to commissioners, service providers, and investors looking for a return. However, as we have illustrated through a consideration of the practical challenges of delivering PbR in the criminal justice sector, where outcomes are relatively difficult to measure and value, service provision is complex, fiscal benefits are shared across a number of potential commissioners, and existing evidence on what works is still relatively patchy, PbR is unlikely to be a panacea – either as a driver of service reform, or as a means of attracting new sources of funding into the sector.

From an economic perspective, PbR has something to offer in terms of delivering JR; but whether it can do so depends in large part on the intentions of government. The theory of JR that we have outlined suggests that a mixed economy of provision is preferable and that therefore there is a place for the private sector in such provision. PbR could be a mechanism to introduce such involvement. If the real focus of PbR is on innovation and change, then private sector involvement could be valuable. Sometimes, although not always, the private sector can be a champion of change and innovation. Private sector expertise in the management of complex supply chains also provides a good opportunity to bring together a wide range of not-for-profit and for-profit providers into consortia well equipped to deliver JR. However, the constitution of those consortia will be important if the involvement of the not-for-profit sector is to be genuine, as opposed to tokenistic or exploitative.

Payment by Results in other government departments

The Payment by Results model is not only applied in the criminal justice sector. The concept is also used in the government's Work Programme. The Work Programme has elements of PbR attached to the task of finding work for the unemployed. The programme is delivered by contractors retained by the Department for Work and Pensions (Department for Work and Pensions 2011), with two large private sector "prime contractors" for each region. It was envisaged that the "primes" would sub-contract interventions in their local area, at which level charities and social entrepreneurs would be able to provide interventions to the region's unemployed. The primes might also offer interventions at a local level.

Under this PbR model, local providers would receive a start fee for each unemployed person they took on; a job outcome payment after a participant had been in work for three to six months; and sustainment payments after the participant had been in work for periods of up to two years (ibid.). There is an obvious risk for the prime contractors: if programme participants fail to find employment, contractors will receive little or no funding from the government. This risk is all the greater given the current state of the UK economy.

In his speech on the first anniversary of the Work Programme, Chris Grayling (at that time Minister of State for Work and Pensions) promised "I won't settle for second best, and nor should those relying on providers to help them get their life back on track" (Grayling 2012). The (apparent) Darwinian nature of the programme is designed to cause the least efficient of the large prime contractors to leave the market. Thus the government would be free to find another (possibly more efficient) provider of services. Grayling made this clear: "It is designed to encourage excellence in supply chain management by prime providers, to ensure fair treatment of sub-contractors" (ibid.).

It was envisaged that the large prime contractors would take on and absorb the risk from the government, leaving local providers free to innovate and improve services. However, there is evidence of sub-contractors being squeezed out by the primes passing on to the lowest level the risks associated with the contracts. In February 2012, North Devon MP Nick Harvey wrote to Chris Grayling claiming that charities in his local area were effectively subsidising the Work Programme and that the "rear end funding is not being de-risked by the prime contractors" (*The Guardian* 2012b). Harvey highlights that the small charitable sector is not geared up for the level of risk which is being passed on to them. In commenting on Harvey's concerns, *The Guardian* (2012c) opined that "the work programme is structured in a way that actively excludes charities, and punishes – to the point of bankruptcy – many social businesses that try to operate in this most unbending of markets".

At the time of our writing, evaluation of the success or otherwise of the Work Programme has not been made publicly available, and pilots of PbR in the criminal justice sector are still ongoing. Notwithstanding, the UK government has decided to push ahead with expanding PbR in criminal justice. The "success" of the Work Programme was cited by the *Telegraph* (2012) as part justification for Chris Grayling's decision increasingly to sub-contract criminal justice provision via PbR before the evaluation of the approach is complete.

Summary

If the primary interest of government is in cost saving and risk transfer – and if outcomes are defined purely in terms of reducing re-offending – PbR is likely to have little to offer the JR movement.

First: consider the investment proposition from the perspective of private investors. In general, governments can borrow money more cheaply than the private sector. Therefore, in the long run, services delivered by the private sector using PbR will cost more than state provision. This might be justified if PbR is going to deliver services which either would not otherwise have been delivered, or which are more innovative than would otherwise have been delivered, by the public sector. The additional cost resulting from PbR would be justified as the price of doing things differently and delivering real change in the criminal justice system. However, if PbR providers are simply delivering the same service but with deferred costs, this seems harder to justify.

Second: In general, private investors have a higher discounting factor than government; they expect to see their investments yield returns in the short term. However, the social return on any social investment is likely to be long-term. There are few quick fixes in criminal justice. Thus the range of interventions which may be funded by PbR is limited.

Third: by definition, reducing re-offending is not the same as reducing crime. There is no provision for "prehabilitative" work in PbR schemes; the possibility of investing in communities and individuals to address the underlying causes of criminality are not considered in current PbR models within the criminal justice system. There is limited room for social justice in narrowly constituted PbR schemes. Social justice is not a "result"! However, social justice might be delivered in more broadly conceived commissioning strategies, perhaps centred around the services delivered by local authorities. This could be delivered through PbR, but, as we discuss below, there are other options, such as Community Budgets, which might be more appropriate.

Fourth: There is an inherent inconsistency in the government's emphasising the efficiency of generating start-up funds using SIB's. Under the PbR approach, the government is limiting its downside risk, while SIB investors will lose their capital if their projects do not pay off. Therefore, only those projects likely to lead to substantial benefits will be offered – those projects where social returns are either large, certain or both. This begs the question, why does not the government invest in such projects already on behalf of the taxpayer?

Other commissioning models

Given the uncertainties surrounding the PbR implementation of JR outlined above, it is therefore worth returning to the aims of the PbR experiment and asking whether there are other innovative approaches to commissioning public services which might deliver some or all of the same aims. We suggest here two alternative approaches that might be particularly relevant in England and Wales.

Whole Place Community Budgets

As outlined in Chapter 2, in the UK there is a recognition among policy-makers and commentators that JR is hampered by the divisions between different central government funding schemes[13] of public funds within government departments and the stickiness of public funding.

One radical solution identified to "kick start" a JR revolution (Allen 2007) would be to devolve budgets for custodial sentences to local authorities. The English Commission on Prisons Today (2009) recommended that, with local authorities as lead partner, local partnerships of key delivery agencies within criminal justice, health and education should lead JR initiatives. In his evidence to the Justice Committee, Jon Gamble, Director for Adults and Lifelong Learning, National Learning and Skills Council, said of funding for preventing crime and reducing re-offending: "I would put it all in one big bag and give it to the local authority and say, 'sort it out'" (quoted in Justice Committee 2009: 109). As discussed above, this level of devolution might be too localised to be effective, and it implicitly assumes that criminals from one local authority area will not offend in the neighbouring area.[14] However, Gamble's suggestion does capture a key element of the USA experience which, to date, is missing from UK attempts to implement JR. In the USA, JR has been implemented at state and county levels, where a single body or elected official has responsibility for all the key services required to effect sustained reductions in offending and re-offending over a criminal career: from early preventative measures which target at-risk individuals, families and communities, through to interventions for persistent and prolific offenders.

The Whole Place Community Budgets approach, which is being piloted in four areas in England, may go some way towards providing this kind of solution to current complexities in commissioning. It aims to test ways in which funding from across government departments can be re-modelled and reinvested at a local and regional level to more effectively deliver better social outcomes.

Greater Manchester (with a population of 2.6 million) – one of the Ministry of Justice's Local Justice Reinvestment Pilot sites (discussed in Chapter 3) – is also a Whole Place Community Budget pilot. This has provided agencies in Greater Manchester with an opportunity to move beyond the systems-based approach to JR (referred to as Transforming Justice), focussed on points of transition within the criminal justice system, to locating criminal justice within a wider social policy context. This is illustrated in Figure 9.1, which places

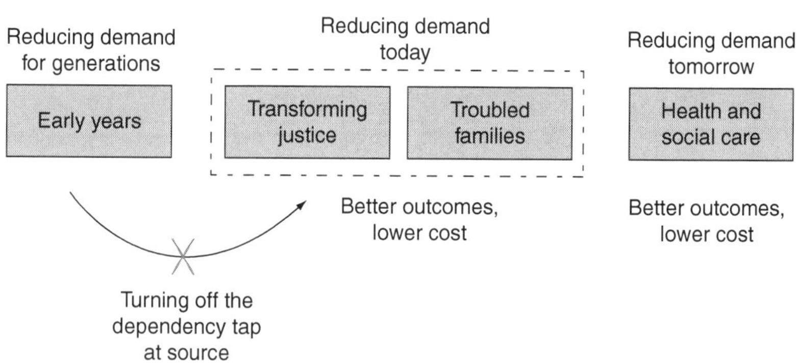

Figure 9.1 Overview of community budget organisation in Greater Manchester (source: Pleasant and Harris 2012).

Transforming Justice as part of an approach to reducing demand and dependency on public services while delivering better social outcomes.

In this more holistic approach, there remains an explicit aim to reduce re-offending. Alongside this is a recognition that other agencies – for example, health, housing and local authorities – must be involved:

> The TJ [Transforming Justice] workstream of the [Community Budget] pilot aims to reduce reoffending, and reduce demand across criminal justice agencies, health, housing and local authorities. The aim set out in the CB [Community Budget] bid to Government is to achieve a 30–40% reduction in the reoffending rates of certain groups. This will mean generating evidence-based new delivery models for point of arrest, point of sentence and point of release, building on small-scale exemplars such as intensive alternatives to custody and greater use of conditional discharge.
>
> (Greater Manchester Public Protection Commission 2012)

There is a clear aspiration that interventions which support offenders who are on the path to desistance will exploit synergy with the other socially-inclusive themes within the area: for example, help for troubled families, early years interventions, and health improvement. This provides an opportunity within Greater Manchester to locate the systems approach to JR within a more holistic social policy context. The mechanisms which are intended to underpin this work are:

- designing new delivery models which can reduce demand and improve outcomes, underpinned by clear cost-benefit modelling of the expected return on investment for different organisations;
- implementing new delivery models, and tracking actual outcomes achieved and financial benefits over time through evaluation;
- using this evidence as a basis for negotiating investment from partners to enable working examples to be scaled up;
- once the examples are scaled up, decommissioning existing services so that cashable savings may be extracted by partners. Some of the savings are recycled into joint recommissioning (for example, further scaling up, or early intervention), underpinned by an investment agreement and multi-agency investment fund.

(Report to the Greater Manchester Public Protection Commission April 2012)

Personalisation

A second possibility which draws on experience in the social care sector, but which has yet to be implemented fully in the criminal justice sector, is personalisation. The concept of (semi-) personalisation of intervention budgets has been rolled out widely in the social care sector. In a personal budget-based system, people who have been assessed (or in some cases, have self-assessed) as eligible for a service are told how much money is available to fund their service and are given the option of taking control of that money, either through taking a direct cash payment, or through co-producing a spending plan (a managed personal budget) with the council, an independent brokerage organisation, or a service provider (an Individual Service Fund) (Department of Health 2010). Personal budgets and direct payments have been transformative for a significant proportion of people using care and support services, although it is worth noting that they were only envisaged to be one element of a wider reform.

The ministerial concordat Putting People First (Department of Health 2007, but see also Crosby and Duffy 2008) set out a comprehensive vision for personalising social care, including:

- a universal offer of advice and information to help people make informed choices;
- a focus on developing inclusive and supportive communities ("social capital");
- a focus on investing in prevention;
- introducing choice and control through personal budgets and self-directed support.

Although, to date, progress on the latter three points has been slower, most service users and their carers report that taking a personal budget has had a positive impact upon their lives (In Control 2011). In addition, there are some examples of a more plural and creative market for services, including a large number of voluntary sector providers and a growing number of non-traditional approaches and enterprises (Fox 2012).

Over recent years there has been an emerging dialogue in offender rehabilitation about more individualised services. This has been evident in research and theorising around the concept of desistance (Ward and Maruna 2007) and the emergence of the Good Lives model of offender rehabilitation (McNeill 2009). Concepts such "end-to-end" management have placed more emphasis on continuity in the relationship between an "offender manager" and the offender, and on developing a package of services which are tailored to each offender's needs. Fox *et al.* (forthcoming) argue that drawing on the experience of personalisation in the social care sector would bring three important new elements to work to reduce the likelihood of an offender re-offending.

First, co-production offers new opportunities for offenders to be empowered to take "ownership" of factors which have contributed to their offending behaviour and to develop their self-reliance and personal capacity. The social care experience suggests that previously excluded people can become full citizens when they have access not only to rights, but also to responsibilities. Similar advantages might be felt by offenders. The developing literature on desistance stresses the importance of "agency" in the offender desistance process, and already some commentators are pointing to the concept of "co-production" as a potential approach to adopt in the criminal justice system (Weaver 2011).

Second, the use of personalised budgets could stimulate innovation in the criminal justice sector by putting in place opportunities for the development of new providers and new, more specialist provision in the criminal justice sector.

Third, individual support with a focus upon people's ability to form and sustain informal relationships, alongside community development work, could help offenders establish more positive and socially-included patterns of living.

Conclusion

The insights of the behavioural approach to economics stress context and community involvement in economic decisions – including the decision to become involved in criminality. We suggest that justice is best served by focussing on interventions – prehabilitative, sentencing and rehabilitative – which view the (potential) offender in the context of the community. We have argued that the success of the community in diverting potential offenders from crime relies heavily on social capacity; the state of the built environment; education; and employment opportunities which provide reasonable security and legitimate access to a reasonable quality of life.

Conversely, the UK government's favoured (and limited) vision of JR, PbR, does not consider issues of social capacity and community building at all. Focussed on intervening with the individual after they have already come into contact with the criminal justice system through committing crime, PbR schemes appear likely not only to neglect what may be the most effective way of reducing offending, but to reduce innovation and efficiency in rehabilitation. However, it is too early to say whether such schemes will produce reductions in re-offending, as evaluation is incomplete at the time of writing.

Notwithstanding, even if appropriate evaluation shows that PbR schemes may save money, they will do nothing to address community problems which give rise to offending in the first place. Ultimately, we suggest there are other approaches to funding JR which will allow a more holistic approach, and therefore produce better results. These are, at the least, worthy of consideration.

10 Conclusion

Justice Reinvestment (JR) represents a shift in criminal justice policy on both sides of the Atlantic. JR differs from the traditional approach of criminal justice, and its emphasis on incarceration. Traditional criminal justice is primarily focussed on society's response to criminality, emphasising the essential self-interest of each individual. JR forms a continuum of perspectives. At its most holistic, JR emphasises the essential and innate desire of individuals to exhibit altruism as well as self-interest. Thus JR may aim to discourage criminality at source by emphasising licit lifestyle choices and supporting those at risk of criminality. More narrowly, JR may be employed to reduce the costs of providing a given intervention.

Thus the cumulative effect of JR must be to make close links between criminal justice policy and broader policy on social justice. This was certainly an aim of much JR work in the USA, but it is less clear whether this is the case in the UK. Here, the JR narrative favoured by policy-makers has tended to have a narrower focus on reducing re-offending. We present a compelling argument for the consideration of the more holistic view of JR. In the final instance, however, the strength of JR is that it has something to say about all aspects of justice; as an encompassing approach, it provides a frame of reference in which to coach debate.

Introduction

Justice Reinvestment (JR) differs from the traditional criminal justice in three main regards. First, there is much greater emphasis on "holistic" responses to reducing crime and re-offending. Thus, JR attempts to reduce re-offending are seen in terms not just of resettlement and rehabilitation but also of addressing the underlying causes of offending and re-offending. Second, JR is based on localism and the idea that criminal justice policy needs to be tailored to local areas and communities. Third, JR suggests a greater role for communities in tackling crime. In the UK it might be seen to relate to the "big society" concept promoted by the Coalition government.

JR, we have argued, represents a continuum across which criminal justice can be considered. We conclude here by arguing that the most radical interpretation deserves to be, at the least, considered.

It's the economic paradigm, stupid

Justice Reinvestment is an approach to reducing offending and re-offending that draws on economic thinking. This is clear from the political rhetoric that surrounds it and some of the approaches to analysis that often underpin it. At the start of any discussion on crime, rehabilitation and prehabilitation, the underlying question is: "Why do people commit crime?" According to David D. Friedman's entry on "Crime" in the *Concise Encyclopaedia of Economics*:

> Economists approach the analysis of crime with one simple assumption – that criminals are rational. A mugger is a mugger for the same reason I am an economist – because it is the most attractive alternative available to him. The decision to commit a crime, like any other economic decision, can be analyzed as a choice among alternative combinations of costs and benefits.
>
> (Friedman 2008: unnumbered)

Friedman goes on to suggest that "To stop someone from doing something that injures you, whether robbing your house or polluting your air, it is not necessary to make it impossible for him to do it – merely unprofitable" (ibid.). Thus society must answer "the question of how to choose the best combination of probability of apprehension and amount of punishment" (ibid.). We would not argue that Friedman's analysis is incorrect; it is simply incomplete. In his brief entry, Friedman mentions "punishment" 11 times, but does not mention once the possibility of making crime less attractive by improving the lot of those who abide by the law. Similarly, Becker (1968) (whom Friedman cites) focusses, as we have seen, on the response of society to criminality, without considering whether society may influence the (potential) offender in a more subtle fashion.

It is clear from Friedman's discussion that the basic paradigm behind his analysis, and indeed that of Becker and the majority of quantitative analyses of the study of crime and deterrence, is that of the instrumentally rational individual making decisions on the basis of maximising their utility over the range of all possible alternatives. However, as we have outlined, the theory of instrumental rationality falls short when we come to explain how social institutions (including justice) develop and endure.

A brief recent history of inequality

The interpretation of human behaviour favoured by Friedman is not only used in the analysis of crime, of course, but also forms the foundation of the political and economic paradigm which the UK and the USA have adopted since the 1980s. The rise of the neo-liberal paradigm in the UK began in earnest in 1979 when Margaret Thatcher became prime minister and emphasised the market and individual self-interest as the central features of economic, political and social policy for the nation. The means by which this would supposedly lead to an efficient society is through competition. It was recognised at the time that this approach would lead to increasing inequality; as Thatcher herself suggested, "It is our job to glory in inequality and see that talents and abilities are given vent and expression for the benefit of us all" (Thatcher 1996). However, it was suggested that inequality would merely lead to increased competition and therefore increased efficiency. Thatcher insisted, despite the inequality in which she gloried, that "everyone in the nation has benefited from increased prosperity – everyone" (Thatcher 1988).

However, there is evidence that the increasing inequality promoted by her policies arguably held back growth, with critics ranging from, among others, Michael Bruno, chief economist of the World Bank, to (of all things) *The Economist* (13 October 2012). In Bruno's opinion, reported in the *Independent on Sunday* (21 July 1996), "Reducing inequality not only benefits the poor immediately, but will benefit all through higher growth". Similarly, *The Economist* notes "inequality has reached a stage where it can be inefficient and bad for growth". Even leaving aside the drag on the economy which it is suggested arises from inequality, market-led macro-economic policies have led to a far from efficient allocation of resources, a phenomenon which is now being witnessed globally (see Martins 2011).

A brief recent history of social justice

In December 2006, the Centre for Social Justice published its ground-breaking report, *Breakdown Britain* (Social Justice Policy Group 2006). At a time when many in the world's capitalist economies were congratulating themselves on what appeared to be the longest period of sustained economic growth in recent history – and nine months before the bursting of the economic bubble in August–September 2007 – the Social Justice Policy Group were concerned that Britain was "breaking".

The report describes the breakdown in social capital which the UK has witnessed while seemingly enjoying sustained growth. The Centre's research documented five pathways to poverty: family breakdown; economic dependency and worklessness; educational failure; addiction; and personal indebtedness (Social Justice Policy Group 2006).

Many of these factors might lead to poverty, but they also derive from poverty. Take family breakdown, for example. In the USA, Edin and Reed (2005) find that, while in the 1960s marriage rates were similar across income groups, in 2005, "poor men and women are only about half as likely to be married as those with incomes at three or more times the poverty level" (Edin and Reed 2005: 118). This is despite the fact that marital expectations are high among Americans of all social classes. It need hardly be pointed out that economic dependency, worklessness, and indebtedness go hand in hand with poverty, and there is also evidence that educational outcomes are connected to poverty. As Friedman (2005) puts it:

> It is distressing to realize that more than 50 percent of the game is over on the first day that the child walks into kindergarten. Nobody can think that this is because of lack of effort of the child. If somebody graduates from high school not knowing how to read or write, you can say, "Well, that's the student's fault". If it comes down to the first day of kindergarten, who could ever think that this is the child's fault?
>
> (Friedman 2005: unnumbered)

And the gap in educational outcomes is growing. The difference in test scores between rich and poor American children is 30 to 40 per cent greater than it was 25 years ago (*The Economist* 2012). Thus we see that poverty can become (indeed, probably always is) a vicious circle.

A brief recent history of criminal justice

And so, we come at last to the canary down the mine-shaft, criminal justice. Poverty and social marginalisation have increased while, for many, opportunities to achieve reasonable aspirations in the legitimate economy have declined. It is against this backdrop that the instrumentally rational model of criminal justice emphasises detection and incarceration. Indeed, as inequality increases, "the easier it becomes for the well-off to advocate greater pain for the less fortunate" (Mauer 2001: 9). However, the law-abiding feel no safer, partly because there is little evidence that prison does, in fact, deter crime, and partly because the economic climate is conspiring further against the socially marginalised (Duffy *et al.* 2007).

Further, because under the instrumentally rational paradigm we assume that the law-breaker has decided rationally that crime is their preferred way of life (while we have rationally decided not to engage in criminal activities), we see the "growth of a social and cultural divide between 'us' and 'them'" leading to "new levels of fear and insecurity" and in consequence "the emergence of a more repressive state power" (Garland, 2001: 182). It is, therefore, no surprise that those nations which adhere most to the instrumentally rational, self-interested, individual view of their citizens adopt both neo-liberal economic policies and justice systems based on incarceration (Beckett and Western 2001, Cavadino and Dignan 2006).

However, the assumption that an offender rationally chose a life of crime over the life of an economist (as Friedman 2008 suggests) seems a little hard to defend. Where life outcomes have been limited by birth, neighbourhood and the wealth of one's parents, perhaps the choice was not so instrumentally rational as we might theorise. Indeed:

> The separation of crime from its wider social context, and the belief that problems of crime can be solved by criminal justice measures taken in isolation, have always been unrealistic, as the Home Office came to acknowledge 30 years ago.
>
> (Faulkner 2010: 8)

Faulkner notes that public attitudes may generally reflect a negative view of human nature; this leads to an emphasis on "conformity and control" and an "appeal to self-interest" (ibid.: 26). Alternatively, we may view human nature in a more positive light, holding that people can change for the better and that improvement is possible. This leads to an emphasis on "recognition and reward", "initiative and innovation" and, for offenders, "compassion, repentance and forgiveness" (ibid.: 26).

The instrumentally rational approach to homo sociologus

It would appear that both UK and USA governments have misjudged their approach to criminality. Our analysis throughout this book, but particularly in Chapters 9 and 10, indicates that policy-makers should not assume that crime and the criminal justice system can be explained by starting with a model of humans as instrumentally rational.

Although it would not be correct to assume that there are no instrumentally rational people in the economy (there are, for example, many economists; see Frank *et al.* 1993), neither is it is clear that all (potential) offenders behave in the way that instrumental rationality suggests (Thaler and Sunstein 2008; Haidt 2007, 2012; Kahneman 2011). Similarly, the decision to become involved in crime may be taken in stages or unawares (Cornish and Clarke 1986). Further, there is good behavioural evidence that humans are biologically programmed to respond positively to altruism (O'Doherty 2004, De Quervain *et al.* 2004, Rilling *et al.* 2002, 2004) or to revenge themselves on a person or a system that they feel has let them down. At a theoretical level, we have outlined a theory of rationality that explains why people will come together to form communities and societies based on "reciprocity", where active engagement in social life provides the basis for strong communities where different versions of a Good Life are possible.

Once we move beyond the restrictive assumptions of instrumentally rational, self-interested individuals, we must consider their decisions in the context of their human and social capital and that of the society in which they live; therefore a portfolio of interventions is required. Individuals and societies, like justice, exist along a continuum. JR provides the framework in which this portfolio may be justified and evaluated.

A brief recent history of Justice Reinvestment

It's still the economy

During the time that it has taken us to complete this book, the criminal justice policy landscape in the both the UK and the USA has changed considerably. Much, if not all, of the policy changes and the quickened pace of change result from the state of the economy and the reduced and further reducing levels of public sector expenditure on both criminal justice and social policy more widely. As mentioned in Chapter 2, it is the economy that has the most significant impact on shaping the implementation of JR and the types of JR approaches being adopted on both sides of the Atlantic.

A continuum of justice

The ambitions for JR in the UK contained in the Justice Committee (2010) Report appear somewhat lofty at the time of writing (hindsight is a wonderful thing). JR in the UK is progressing along a different route – superficially, one focussed on criminal justice system redesign rather than on the social justice approach advocated by the Justice Committee. The centre-right, Conservative-led Coalition government in the UK appears committed to localism (the transfer of responsibility for public services from central government to local agencies) and to Payment by Results as a preferred commissioning model – transferring risk in the delivery of public services from the government to the private and not-for-profit sector.

However, at a more local level, a narrative focussed on social justice survives, promoted by middle managers and strategic managers responsible for the implementation, oversight and leadership of JR pilots. This narrative is designed to win over a number of stakeholders: first and foremost the managers themselves – they buy into this, because it's about "doing the right thing";[1] front line staff – the system changes are about providing a better service to offenders and their families; the public and sentencers – the changes are designed to provide better protection for the public by delivering more effective interventions and thereby reducing the likelihood of re-offending by offenders.

For example, as discussed in Chapter 9, the Greater Manchester Transforming Justice Programme, a Local Justice Reinvestment Pilot, has (through its incorporation as a key component of the Whole Place Community Budgets pilot) morphed into a public service redesign programme with the aim of protecting public services (in the face of significant cuts) by redesigning them to make them more cost-effective, and in so doing delivering public services (by public, private or not-for-profit sectors) which promote resilience and less reliance on public services by offenders and their families.

Meantime, as discussed in Chapters 3 and 4, the social justice approach to JR favoured by Tucker and Cadora (2003) in the USA and by Allen (2007, 2008a) in the UK appears to have given way, in the USA at least, to a more limited criminal justice system redesign project. This model is, perhaps, best exemplified by the JR implementation guidance to county and city authorities in the USA produced by La Vigne *et al.* (2010). However, as detailed in Chapter 4, when we examine the interventions which constitute JR in the USA (based on the guidance by La Vigne *et al.* 2010), each of them blends what may appear to be a straight criminal justice intervention – such as diverting an individual from arrest through conditional cautioning – with social welfare support.

It is this real-life (and real-time) implementation of JR which has led us to conceptualise JR as a continuum, driven by a criminal justice redesign approach at one end and a social justice approach at the other end. We have categorised these as "more efficient on crime; more efficient on the causes of crime". Applied interventions which blend these two aims locate themselves anywhere along the continuum.

But it's also the data

As noted in previous chapters, the development of JR approaches in the USA and the UK has seen the increasingly sophisticated use of data to inform decision-making.

Justice Investment and Reinvestment relies on appropriate data, from the approach advocated by the Council of States – which includes justice mapping and the use of evidence to determine which interventions are efficient – to the economic modelling of Aos and colleagues (detailed in Chapter 6). JR includes a commitment to the analysis of data, the analysis of costs, the use of evidence, and the development of Cost Benefit Analysis models to facilitate the redesign of services. All of these approaches, implemented by policy-makers and practitioners, have marked out the distinctiveness of JR in relation to reforming the criminal justice system and more wider social policy as it relates to crime, offenders and re-offending.

Arguably, some of the economic principles underpinning this use of analysis have altered the language and, perhaps as a consequence, the aspiration of public service commissioning. Policy-makers, commissioners and (to a lesser degree) practitioners are conversing in terms of investment and particularly cost-effective investment in services. While this may be a way of spinning a negative story about how and why funding cuts need to be made, it nevertheless contributes to a culture of scrutiny about using public funding more effectively. Also it enables informed choices to be made.

At the WSIPP, Aos *et al.* (2006) offer up so-called aggressive and less aggressive portfolios in their modelling of cost-effective interventions. Similarly, JR, in its implementation of a portfolio of interventions, allows for a blended approach to deploying interventions with differing degrees of evidential rigour and differing levels of cost. In the same way that investment portfolios are constructed mixing high and low risk, so JR portfolios can also be deployed in which a mix of interventions carry higher and lower levels of evidential rigour. It is of critical importance that this is understood in the portfolio development and commissioning process. The portfolio approach also allows for an additional dimension to be addressed: that of political acceptability across the multiple stakeholders, policy-makers, practitioners and public. With JR's rigour and logic comes a greater likelihood of consensus and cross-party support.

Conclusion

In an interview with the authors in 2011, Rob Allen, an early UK proponent of JR and Special Advisor to the House of Commons Justice Committee when it produced its influential report *Cutting Crime: The Case for Justice Reinvestment*

(Home Office 2010), expressed dismay and frustration about the development of JR in the UK. While he welcomed the interest in JR from national and local policy-makers, including civil servants and politicians from across the political spectrum, he observed that JR was like "motherhood and apple pie". No-one is going to disagree with it, but if you ask individuals what they mean by JR, this is a different matter.

Allen posited that conceptualisations of JR varied considerably – "Three or four people will give you five or six definitions of what it is". This disparity may be seen by comparing Home Office Minister Nick Herbert's pronouncements (Herbert 2010) about the equivalence of JR with Payment by Results – according to Allen, the "bastard child" of JR – to Allen's own view of JR as a progressive way of linking together three critical elements: reducing imprisonment; local responsibility for organising and resourcing offender rehabilitation and reintegration; and a focus on effective use of resources.

A meta-rational approach!

Justice Reinvestment is not a criminal justice intervention; it is more a way of framing the issues under consideration. At its core it seeks to answer the question society has – indeed all societies have – to address: is there a better way to deliver justice? The strength of the approach is that it allows policy-makers access to a portfolio of interventions through both criminal justice and social justice; a process of evaluation; and a way of lifting the policy debate above short-term, ideological and political ends. There is no optimal intervention, but there is an optimal approach.

In the same way that Sen (1977) postulates that the rational individual will prefer one preference ranking to another, thereby forming a meta-preference set, governments require a rational way of choosing between rationally appealing interventions; this is what JR provides. Therefore the consideration of many social interventions should begin by their being considered in a Justice Investment and Reinvestment context.

The process of building a truly just and free society is less a matter of force and more a matter of focus.

Appendix

Interviewees

The authors are grateful to the following, who were all interviewed during the preparation of this book.

Rob Allen (May 2011), writer and commentator on criminal justice policy and former special advisor to the House of Commons Justice Select Committee
Steve Aos (September 2011), Director of the Washington State Institute for Public Policy
Marshall Clement (August 2011), Director of the Justice Reinvestment project at the Council of State Governments Justice Center
Julian Cox (June 2011), economist in the New Economy (Association of Greater Manchester Authorities) and part of the Transforming Justice project in Greater Manchester
Tony Fabelo (August 2011), former Executive Director of the Texas Criminal Justice Policy Council (1991–2003); in charge of designing, developing and implementing a research agenda for the Council of State Governments Justice Center
Sarah Henry (June 2011) Head of Research and Intelligence at Manchester City Council and part of the Transforming Justice project in Greater Manchester
Jennet Peters (July 2011) [at time of interview] strategic adviser to the Transforming Justice project in Greater Manchester, on secondment at Greater Manchester Probation Trust

Notes

1 Introduction

1 It should be noted that we do not subscribe to Civitas's call for the greater use of incarceration as a response to crime. There is little evidence that incarceration reduces criminality, as we shall discuss.

2 Current challenges for criminal justice policy

1 This was used in an article written by Tony Blair for the *New Statesman* (Blair 1993), which was widely regarded as repositioning the Labour Party's traditional libertarian approaches to criminal justice policy.
2 A term used to describe the policy-making, information management and funding in one sector as separate from other, related sectors.
3 MAPPA provided assessment and management of the most serious sexual and violent offenders.
4 International Centre for Prison Studies, London, "World Prison Brief" data, downloaded January 2008. Available at www.prisonstudies.org/info/worldbrief/wpb_stats.php?area=all&category=wb_poprate.
5 Some crimes do take place in prison, and there are also examples of criminals in organised crime networks continuing to coordinate criminal activity while in prison.
6 http://en.wikipedia.org/wiki/It's_the_economy,_stupid [accessed 26 April 2011].
7 The authors would recommend "Progress vs. more of the same; subject to a positive benefit to cost evaluation". We recognise that this lacks some of the punch of the original.
8 http://news.bbc.co.uk/1/hi/business/7073131.stm [accessed 26 April 2011].
9 www.treasurydirect.gov/govt/reports/pd/pd_debtposactrpt_1103.pdf [accessed 2 November 2012].
10 http://cdn.hm-treasury.gov.uk/sr2010_departmentalexpenditure.pdf [accessed 26 April 2011].

3 What is Justice Reinvestment?

1 The opportunity cost of any project is defined as the maximum benefit which might have been received from an alternative use of the project resource.

4 Theorising Justice Reinvestment

1 Psychometrically robust measures are those that yield observations which we may be confident of applying to individuals not necessarily involved in the initial study.
2 From the Greek aitia (αιτία), "cause".

3 For example, Hope (2009) contrasts a "realist" conception of crime statistics with a "constructivist" one. Many justice mapping projects seem, implicitly, to adopt the realist perspective on crime statistics.
4 They are therefore better referred to as measures of "proven re-offending" (Ministry of Justice 2011) and are likely to underestimate "true" levels of re-offending.
5 A foundation assumption of the positivist paradigm is that the object studied and the study itself are independent of the researcher. In comparison, the constructivist paradigm assumes that researchers interact with the object studied. Constructivists hold that there is no objective reality, while the realist paradigm would hold that there is objective reality, but no objective way of establishing what it is. See Krauss (2005) and references therein.
6 The categories of comparison between 2000 and 2011 were: keeping money found in the street; lying; smoking cannabis; damaging someone's car and not paying for repairs; being unfaithful in marriage; engaging in sex under age; buying stolen goods; dropping litter; claiming benefits fraudulently; and driving while under the influence of alcohol. The only category where participants demonstrated more integrity in 2011 than 2000 was in their condemnation of people claiming benefits fraudulently. This might, of course, be symptomatic of their being less willing to help out the less fortunate.
7 Serious or persistent offenders were defined as those who had committed at least three offences in the last year of any type, and/or one or more serious offence (assault, threatening or hurting someone with a weapon, burglary, car or motorbike theft, pick-pocketing or snatch theft).
8 While this was not a statistically significant result, it was approaching the 0.1 level traditionally used as a guide.
9 Online guidance on the Scottish Government website: *Arrest Referral: A Guide to Principles and Practice*. Available at www.scotland.gov.uk/Publications/2002/05/14526/2751 [accessed 25 July 2012].
10 An independent public body set up to "protect the public purse", helping public bodies manage their finances by providing unbiased, evidence-based analysis and advice.

5 Data analysis and justice mapping

1 These measures were further reiterated and emphasised in the Police and Justice Act 2006 and the Crime and Disorder (Overview and Scrutiny) Regulations 2009 (Chainey 2010).
2 In the UK, the website of the Office for National Statistics, and in particular its website for neighbourhood statistics (www.neighbourhood.statistics.gov.uk/dissemination/), contain much relevant data on demographic, social and economic variables. In the US, similar types of data can be accessed from local research institutions or the US Census (La Vigne and Cowan 2005).
3 They suggest that any figure below 80 per cent should be viewed sceptically.
4 Data for the justice mapping came from a number of sources and related to the years 1998 to 2000.
5 Undertaken in July 2011.

6 Economic methods

1 Economists would generally hold, philosophically, that nothing is "free" – someone, somewhere, is paying. In this case we mean that the good or service is not paid for out of the intervention budget.
2 Generally known in the USA as "offender re-entry".

3 Mathematically, if the annual interest rate is denoted r, and we wish to discount an amount, A, from t years in the future to the present, we may write $PV = \frac{A}{(1+r)^t}$.
4 Indeed, from the economic point of view, one should continue to collect data until the marginal cost of collecting more data exceeds the marginal benefit expected from having that data.
5 In practice, unless all the interventions have been assessed in the same CBA study, comparing the results of different CBA studies is far from straightforward (Roman 2004).
6 Following MacLeod in Home Office (2003), let us write the probability of re-conviction in the first year after release from prison using the symbol p.
7 Denoted as p.
8 Modelled by Ministry of Justice (2008) as p^2.
9 Unsurprisingly, p^3.
10 Note that, following MacLeod, where an offender is re-convicted, their probability of being convicted of future offences is "reset" to p on their subsequent release.
11 Mathematically, the probability of being re-convicted in year j after completing a sentence is $p^j \prod_{k=1}^{j} \left(1 - p^k\right)$. The parameter p is determined by considering the re-conviction rate of cohorts of offenders in the first year after their release from prison.
12 Levitt suggests it is reasonable to consider the effects of the local economy and other factors on both budgets and crime. For example, a cash-strapped local government might reduce fire and police budgets and other social services. It is the change in the latter which might influence crime rates. He controls for this by considering local economic variables.
13 In some cases the confidence interval is so narrow, it is hidden by the point which represents the centre of the range. The expression "ln (police per capita) t-1" refers to the natural log of the number of police per capita in the previous time period; we are looking at how the relative size of the police force in the previous time period impacts on crime. IV refers to instrumental variables, a method of estimation similar to ordinary least squares (OLS). "Year dummies" refers to a series of binary variables (taking the value 0 or 1) which capture the effects of "unusual" events which have occurred in particular years; dummy variables refer to qualitative rather than quantitative data.
14 We discuss meta-analyses in more detail in Chapter 7.

7 Using evidence and negotiating politics

1 Aos and colleagues do not describe the project in Washington State of which they are a part as a "Justice Reinvestment" project. Indeed, Aos prefers not to use this term (interview with Aos undertaken by the authors).
2 www.cabinetoffice.gov.uk/content/about-cabinet-office [accessed 7 September 2012].
3 Sherman (2009) notes that the far smaller number of experiments and Systematic Reviews undertaken in criminology, compared to health care, does not reflect the difference in the number of questions to be answered. Rather it reflects the relative resources invested in research. Sherman cites figures from the US suggesting that the US National Institutes of Health spend about $28 billion a year on new evidence, whereas the comparable amount given to the US National Institute of Justice is about $28 million.
4 Information taken from the Cochrane Collaboration website: www.cochrane.org [accessed 25 July 2012].
5 This project is ongoing. The figures quoted here are taken from the project's website: www.colorado.edu/cspv/blueprints/index.html [accessed 8 July 2010].

6 www.campbellcollaboration.org/reviews_crime_justice/index.php [accessed 23 October 2012].
7 Prison Me No Way website at: www.pmnw.co.uk/?page_id=3 [accessed 2 September 2012].
8 In the intervening period, responsibility for criminal justice policy was split by the New Labour Government between the Home Office, with responsibility for policing and community safety, and the Ministry of Justice, responsible for prisons, probation, courts and judiciary.
9 According to Thorpe and Hall (2009) the proportion of people thinking that the level of crime has increased in their local area has generally been between 15 and 20 per cent lower than those thinking that crime rates are increasing nationally. However, these trends have diverged, with a lower proportion of people thinking that crime has increased in their local area.
10 While it is recognised the term "positivism" means different things to different people, the aim here is to provide a very basic outline of the positivist position, and no attempt is made to distinguish different philosophical or theoretical positions that exist within the broad church of the positivist approach.
11 Known variously as the hypothetic-deductive method or the logico-deductive method.

8 Towards a new theory of Justice Reinvestment: the economic dimension

1 A way of representing the relationship between an output and two inputs.
2 HM Government (2002), *Proceeds of Crime Act 2002*, available at www.legislation.gov.uk/ukpga/2002/29/contents (accessed 23 January 2012).
3 See Clarke (2005) Table 3.3 techniques 1–8 for further examples.
4 Compare Kahneman's "system 1" and "system 2" thinking (Kahneman 2011).
5 For example, some students had been asked to write the ten commandments, while others had been asked to write the titles of ten books they had read at high school.
6 We might speculate, therefore, that as the world's labour markets turn against the youth, it is surely foolish to reduce the level of state support they receive.
7 It should be borne in mind, of course, as Thaler and Shefrin (1981) note, that the "doer" may be so myopic as to renege on the constraining decision.
8 For the sake of argument, let us define those acts which benefit society as "good", and those acts which are anti-social, "bad". While an individual might choose to do "good" (even if it is to their disadvantage) just because it is "good", we assume no rational individual will choose to do "bad", even if it is to their disadvantage, just because it is "bad". People choose "bad" because it is to their advantage.
9 Private conversation, 4 August 2011.

9 Applications of a new theory of Justice Reinvestment

1 As Juvenal puts it "Nemo repente fuit turpissimus" (Satire II line 83, available at www.fordham.edu/halsall/ancient/juv-sat2lat.asp).
2 Of course, out of decency, we should not tempt people beyond their capacity to resist. One should no more leave valuables on display in a parked car than one should offer a smoke to someone trying to give up cigarettes.
3 OECD (2012) G20 Labour Ministers must focus on young jobseekers, 15 May. Available at www.oecd.org/document/39/0,3746,en_21571361_44315115_50323559_1_1_1_1,00.html.
4 The figures for Spain and Greece were 51.1 per cent and 51.2 per cent respectively.
5 *Prospect* (2012) Winning the welfare war, 22 February. Available at www.prospect-magazine.co.uk/magazine/winning-the-welfare-war/.

6 See 6 and Peck (2004) for a summary of New Labour's approach to public management.
7 Interesting questions are raised about the sources of charitable funding, with some investors using their grant-giving mechanisms, but others investing their endowment capital on the basis that the SIB is a financial instrument which offers a return on investment as well as meeting an organisation's charitable mission (Disley *et al.* 2011).
8 Our reading of Disley *et al.* (2011) is that none are from the private sector.
9 See www.justice.gov.uk/offenders/payment-by-results/programme-overview [accessed 24 August 2012].
10 See www.justice.gov.uk/offenders/payment-by-results/innovation-pilots [accessed 24 August 12].
11 See www.justice.gov.uk/offenders/payment-by-results/programme-overview [accessed 24 August 12].
12 Disley *et al.* (2011: 8) also point out that outcome measurements relying on comparison with a control group cannot be rolled out nationally because, for example: "If every short-sentenced prisoner in England and Wales could be part of a SIB, there would be no control group with which to compare".
13 So-called funding "silos".
14 Although the distances most offenders travel to commit crime are modest (Wiles and Costello 2000), some cross-border offending is inevitable.

10 Conclusion

1 This is the phrase that summed up the ethos of the Local Justice Reinvestment Pilot in Greater Manchester.

Bibliography

6, P. and Peck, E. (2004) "Modernisation": The ten commitments of New Labour's approach to public management? *International Public Management Journal*, vol. 7(1), 1–18.

Albertson, K. and Fox C. (2012) *Crime and Economics: An Introduction*, Oxford: Routledge.

Allen, G. (2011) *Early Intervention: The Next Steps*, London: Cabinet Office.

Allen, R. (2007) From restorative prisons to justice reinvestment, in Allen, R. and Stern, V. (eds.) *Justice Reinvestment: A New Approach to Crime and Justice*, London: International Centre for Prison Studies.

Allen, R. (2008a) Justice reinvestment: Making sense of the costs of imprisonment, *Criminal Justice Matters*, vol. 71(1), 41–42.

Allen, R. (2008b) *LCJB Neighbourhood Pathways Project – Potential Interventions*, London: London Criminal Justice Board.

Allen, R., Jallab, K. and Snaith, E. (2007) Justice reinvestment in Gateshead – The story so far, in Allen, R. and Stern, V. (eds) *Justice Reinvestment: A New Approach to Crime and Justice*, London: International Centre for Prison Studies.

Andrews, D. A. and Bonta, J. (2006) *The Psychology of Criminal Conduct*, Newark, NJ: Lexis/Nexis.

Andrews, D. A. and Bonta, J. (2007) *Risk-Need-Responsivity Model for Offender Assessment and Rehabilitation 2007–06*, Ottowa: Public Safety Canada.

Andrews, D. A., Bonta, J. and Hoge, R. D. (1990) Classification for effective rehabilitation: Rediscovering psychology, *Criminal Justice and Behavior*, vol. 17, 19–52.

Aos, S. and Drake, E. (2010) *WSIPP's Benefit-Cost Tool for States: Examining Policy Options in Sentencing and Corrections*, Olympia, WA: Washington State Institute for Public Policy, Document No. 10–08–1201.

Aos, S., Miller, M. and Drake, E. (2006) *Evidence-Based Public Policy Options to Reduce Future Prison Construction, Criminal Justice Costs, and Crime Rates*, Olympia, WA: Washington State Institute for Public Policy.

Aos, S., Phipps, P., Barnoski, R. and Lieb, R. (2001) *The Comparative Costs and Benefits of Programs to Reduce Crime*, Olympia, WA: Washington State Institute for Public Policy.

Arrow, K. (1951) *Social Choice and Individual Values*, New York: John Wiley & Sons.

Audit Commission (1996) *Misspent Youth*, London: Audit Commission. Available at www.audit-commission.gov.uk/SiteCollectionDocuments/AuditCommissionReports/NationalStudies/misspentyouthyoungpeopleandcrime.pdf [accessed 24 October 2012].

Audit Commission (2004) *Youth Justice 2004: A Review of the Reformed Youth Justice*

System, London: The Audit Commission. Available at www.audit-commission.gov.uk/SiteCollectionDocuments/AuditCommissionReports/NationalStudies/Youth Justice_report_web.pdf [accessed 24 October 2012].

Babcock, J. C., Green, C. E. and Robie, C. (2004) Does batterers' treatment work? A meta-analytic review of domestic violence treatment, *Clinical Psychology Review*, vol. 23(8), 1023–1053.

Bandyopadhyay, S. (2012) *Acquisitive Crime: Imprisonment, Detection and Social Factors*, London: Civitas. Available at www.civitas.org.uk/crime/crimeanalysis2012.pdf.

Barnett-Page, E. and Thomas, J. (2009) Methods for the synthesis of qualitative research: A critical review, *BMC Medical Research Methodology*, vol. 9(59).

Barrett, R. (2010) Disadvantaged groups in the labour market, *Economic and Labour Market Review*, vol. 4(6), 18–24.

Battye, F. and Sunderland, J. (2011) *Thinking About … Payment by Results*, London: GHK.

BBC (2005) Byers to face rail "lies" inquiry, 19 October. Available at http://news.bbc.co.uk/1/hi/uk_politics/4353956.stm [accessed 2 November 2012].

BBC (2010a) Justice Secretary plans "radical" prison policy change, 30 June. Available at www.bbc.co.uk/news/10457112 [accessed 2 November 2012].

BBC (2010b) George Osborne outlines detail of £6.2bn spending cuts, 24 May. Available at http://news.bbc.co.uk/1/hi/uk_politics/8699522.stm [accessed 2 November 2012].

BBC (2012) Davos 2012: Youth unemployment "disaster", 28 January. Available at www.bbc.co.uk/news/business-16774301 [accessed 2 November 2012].

Beccaria, C. (1764) *On Crimes and Punishments*, translation, Indianapolis: Hackett Publishing Company, 1986.

Becker, G. (1968) Crime and punishment: An economic approach, *Journal of Political Economy*, vol. 76, 169–217.

Beckett, K. and Western, B. (2001) Governing social marginality: Welfare, incarceration and the transformation of state policy, *Punishment and Society*, vol. 3, 43–59.

Belfield, C. R., Nores, M., Barnett, W. S. and Schweinhart, L. J. (2006) The HighScope Perry Preschool Program: Cost-benefit analysis using data from the age-40 follow-up, *The Journal of Human Resources*, vol. 41(1), 162–190.

Berman, G. and Fox, A. (2010) *Trial and Error in Criminal Justice Reform: Learning from Failure*, Washington, DC: The Urban Institute Press.

Bernburg, J. and Krohn, M. D. (2003) Labeling, life chances, and adult crime: The direct and indirect effects of official intervention in adolescence on crime in early adulthood, *Criminology*, vol. 41(4), 1287–1318.

Blair, T. (1993) Why crime is a socialist issue, *New Statesman and Society*, 29 January, 27–28.

Boden, R. and Epstein, D. (2006) Managing the research imagination? Globalisation and research in higher education, *Globalisation, Societies and Education*, vol. 4(2), 223–236.

Boba, R. (2001) *Introductory Guide to Crime Analysis and Mapping*, Washington, DC: US Department of Justice.

Brand, S. and Price, P. (2000) The economic and social costs of crime, *Home Office Research Study 217*, London: The Home Office.

Brantingham, P. and Brantingham, P. (1990) *Environmental Criminology*, Long Grove, IL: Waveland Press.

Brewer, M., Goodman, A., Muriel, A. and Sibieta, L. (2007) *Poverty and Inequality in the UK: 2007*, Institute for Fiscal Studies Briefing no. 73, London: Institute for Fiscal Studies.

Bureau of Justice Statistics (1999) *Prison and Jail Inmates at Midyear 1998*. Available at https://www.ncjrs.gov/App/Publications/abstract.aspx?ID=173414 [accessed 2 November 2012].

Burtless, G. (1999) Effects of growing wage disparities and changing family composition on the US income distribution, *European Economic Review*, vol. 43, 853–865.

Cabinet Office (1999) *Professional Policy Making for the Twenty-first Century*, London: Cabinet Office.

Cabinet Office (2011) *Modernising Commissioning: Increasing the Role of Charities, Social Enterprises, Mutuals and Cooperatives in Public Service Delivery*, London: Cabinet Office.

Cadora, E. (2007) Justice reinvestment in the US, in Allen, R. and Stern, V. (eds) *Justice Reinvestment: A New Approach to Crime and Justice*, London: International Centre for Prison Studies.

Cadora, E., Gordon, M. and Swartz, C. (2002) *Criminal Justice and Health and Human Services: An Exploration of Overlapping Needs, Resources, and Interests in Brooklyn Neighborhoods*, Washington, DC: Urban Institute.

Cadora, E., Swartz, C. and Stoe, D. (2000) Corrections mapping and community justice, abstract of paper presented at the American Society of Criminology Conference, 14–18 November, Los Angeles.

Cameron, D. (2010) Speech on the Big Society, 19 July. Available at www.number10.gov.uk/news/big-society/speech [accessed 8 November 2012].

Campbell, S. and Harrington, V. (2000) *Youth Crime: Findings From The 1998/99 Youth Lifestyles Survey*, Research Findings No. 126, London: Home Office.

Cappelli, P. (1993) Are skill requirements rising? Evidence from production and clerical jobs, *Industrial and Labor Relations Review*, vol. 46, 515–530.

Carter, P. (2003) *Managing Offenders, Reducing Crime: A New Approach*, London: Home Office.

Cavadino, M. and Dignan, J. (2006) Penal policy and political economy, *Criminology and Criminal Justice*, vol. 6(4), 435–456.

Centre for Social Justice (2006) *Breakdown Britain*, London: The Centre for Social Justice. Available at www.centreforsocialjustice.org.uk/default.asp?pageRef=180 [accessed 2 November 2012].

Centre for Social Justice (2009) *Locked Up Potential: A Strategy for Reforming Prisons and Rehabilitating Prisoners*, London: The Centre for Social Justice. Available at www.centreforsocialjustice.org.uk/client/downloads/CSJLockedUpPotentialFULLrE-PORT.pdf [accessed 2 November 2012].

Chainey, S. (2010) *Information Sharing for Community Safety: Guidance and Practice Advice*, London: Home Office.

Chambers, M., Ullmann, B. and Waller, I. (2009) *Less Crime, Lower Costs: Implementing Effective Early Crime Reduction Programmes in England and Wales*, London: Policy Exchange.

Chandler, R. (1953) *The Long Goodbye*, Boston: Houghton Mifflin.

Civitas (2010) *Latest International Comparison of Crime in OECD Countries*. Available at www.civitas.org.uk/wordpress/2010/08/05/latest-international-comparison-of-crime-in-oecd-countries/ [accessed 2 November 2012].

Clarke, J. and Newman, J. (1997) *The Managerial State*, London: Sage.

Clarke, K. (2010) *Public Services from First Principles*, speech given by Justice Secretary

Kenneth Clarke to the Centre for Crime and Justice Studies, 30 June. Available at www.poauk.org.uk/index.php?political-debate-1&newsdetail=20100630–84_justice-secretary-ken-clarke-makes-speech-at-the-centre-for-crime-and-justice-studies [accessed 2 November 2012].

Clarke, R. V. (2005) Seven misconceptions of situational crime prevention, in Tilley, N. (ed.) *Handbook of Crime Prevention and Community Safety*, Devon, UK: Willan Press.

Clear, T. and Austin, J. (2009) Reducing mass incarceration: Implications of the iron law of prison populations, *Harvard Law and Policy Review*, vol. 3, 307–324.

Clear, T. and Karp, D. R. (2000), Toward the ideal of community justice, *National Institute of Justice [NIJ] Journal*, October, 20–28. Available at https://www.ncjrs.gov/pdffiles1/jr000245f.pdf [accessed 2 November 2012].

Cohen, M. A. (2000) Measuring the costs and benefits of crime and justice, in *Criminal Justice 2000*, vol. 4: *Measurement and Analysis of Crime and Justice*, Washington, DC: National Institute of Justice, NCJ.

Cohen, M. A. (2007) *Valuing Crime Control Benefits using Stated Preference Approaches*, paper prepared for a workshop on Cost-Benefit Analysis and Crime Control, 20 November 2006, Washington, DC: Urban Institute.

Commission on English Prisons Today (2009) *Do Better, Do Less: The Report of the Commission on English Prisons Today*, London: The Howard League for Penal Reform. Available at www.howardleague.org/fileadmin/howard_league/user/online_publications/Do_Better_Do_Less_low_res.pdf [accessed 2 November 2012].

Conservative Party (2009) *Prisons with a Purpose: Our Sentencing and Rehabilitation Revolution to Break the Cycle of Crime*, London: The Conservative Party. Available at www.conservatives.com/~/media/Files/Green%20Papers/Prisons_Policy_Paper.ashx [accessed 2 November 2012].

Cook, D., Burton, M. and Robinson, A. (2004) Enhancing "safety and justice": The role of specialist domestic violence courts in England and Wales, *British Society of Criminology*, vol. 7. Available at www.britsoccrim.org/volume7/008.pdf [accessed 27 July 2012].

Cook, T. and Campbell, D. (1979) *Quasi-experimental Design and Analysis Issues for Field Settings*, Boston: Houghton Mifflin Company.

Corman, H. and Mocan, H. N. (2000) A time-series analysis of crime, deterrence and drug abuse in New York City, *American Economic Review*, vol. 90, 584–604.

Cornish, D. and Clarke, R. (eds.) (1986) *The Reasoning Criminal*, New York: Springer-Verlag.

Council of State Governments (undated) *Justice Reinvestment*, briefing paper downloaded from www.justicereinvestment.org [accessed 1 June 2010].

Council of State Governments Justice Center (2010) *Justice Reinvestment Overview*. Available at www.justicereinvestment.org/files/JR_overview_2010_rev.pdf [accessed 2 November 2012].

Coyle, A. (2007) Making prisons locally accountable, in Allen, R. and Stern, V. (eds.) *Justice Reinvestment: A New Approach to Crime and Justice*, London: International Centre for Prison Studies.

Crosby, N. and Duffy, S. (2008) *A Whole-life Approach to Personalisation: Self-directed Support for Every Child and Young Person*, Birmingham: In Control.

Dalrymple, T. (2005) In the asylum, *City Journal*, Summer, reprinted in Dalrymple, T. (2008) *Not With a Bang But a Whimper: The Politics & Culture of Decline*, Cheltenham, UK: Monday Books.

Davies, P. (1999) What is evidence-based education?, *British Journal of Educational Studies*, vol. 47(2), 108–121.

Davies, P. (2004) *Is Evidence-Based Government Possible?* Jerry Lee Lecture presented at the Fourth Annual Campbell Collaboration Colloquium, Washington, DC, 19 February.

Davis, G., Boucherat, J. and Watson, D. (1988) Reparation in the service of diversion: The subordination of a good idea, *Howard Journal*, 27(2), 127–134.

De Quervain, D., Fischbacher, U., Treyer, V., Schellhammer, M., Schnyder, U., Buck, A. and Fehr, E. (2004) The neural basis of altruistic punishment, *Science*, vol. 305, 1254–1258.

Department for Work and Pensions (2011) *The Work Programme*, London: Department for Work and Pensions. Available at www.dwp.gov.uk/docs/the-work-programme.pdf [accessed 2 November 2012].

Department of Health (2007) *Putting People First: A Shared Vision and Commitment to the Transformation of Adult Social Care*, London: Department of Health.

Dhiri, S. and Brand, S. (1999) Analysis of costs and benefits: Guidance for evaluators, *Crime Reduction Programme – Guidance Note 1*, London: Home Office.

Disley, E., Rubin, J., Scraggs, E., Burrowes, N., Culley, D. and RAND Europe (2011) *Lessons Learned from the Planning and early Implementation of the Social Impact Bond at HMP Peterborough*, London: Ministry of Justice.

Dodge, C. R. (1979) *A World Without Prisons: Alternatives to Incarceration Throughout the World*, Lexington, MA: Lexington Books.

Dolan, P. and Peasgood, T. (2007) Estimating the economic and social costs of the fear of crime, *The British Journal of Criminology*, vol. 47, 121–132.

Dolan, P., Loomes, G., Peasgood, T. and Tsuchiya, A. (2005) Estimating the intangible victim costs of violent crime, *The British Journal of Criminology*, vol. 45, 958–976.

Downey, A., Kirkby, P. and Sherlock, N. (2010) *Payment for Success: How to Shift Power from Whitehall to Public Service Customers*, KPMG LLP (UK). Available at www.kpmg.co.uk/pubs/204000%20Payment%20For%20Success%20Access.pdf [accessed 2 November 2012].

Drummond, M., Sculpher, M., Torrance, G., O'Brien, B. and Stoddart, G. (2005) *Methods for the Economic Evaluation of Health Care Programmes*, third edition, Oxford: Oxford University Press.

Duffy, B., Wake, R., Burrows, T. and Bremner, P. (2007) *Closing the Gaps – Crime and Public Perceptions*, London: Ipsos Mori. Available at www.ipsos-mori.com/DownloadPublication/11_sri_crime_closing_the_gaps_012008.pdf [accessed 2 November 2012].

Edin, K. and Reed, J. M. (2005) Why don't they just get married? Barriers to marriage among the disadvantaged, *The Future of Children*, vol. 15, 117–137.

Eide, E. (1999) The economics of criminal behaviour, in Bouckaert, B. and De Geest, G. (eds.) *Encyclopedia of Law and Economics*, vol. 5: *The Economics of Crime and Litigation*, Cheltenham, UK: Edward Elgar.

Ehrlich, I. (1973) Participation in illegitimate activities: A theoretical and empirical investigation, *The Journal of Political Economy*, vol. 81(3), 521–565.

Ehrlich, I. (1996) Crime, punishment, and the market for offenses, *The Journal of Economic Perspectives*, vol. 10(1), 43–67.

Etzioni, A. (1995) *The Spirit of Community*, London: Fantana.

Etzioni, A. (1997) *The New Golden Rule: Community and Morality in a Democratic State*, London: Profile Books.

Farrall, S. (2004) Social capital and offender reintegration: Making probation desistance focussed, in Maruna, S. and Immarigeon, R. (eds.) *After Crime and Punishment: Pathways to Offender Reintegration*, Cullompton, UK: Willan.

Farrell, G., Tilley, N., Tseloni, A. and Mailley, J. (2010) Explaining and sustaining the crime drop: Clarifying the role of opportunity-related theories, *Crime, Prevention and Community Safety*, vol. 12, 24–41.

Farrington, D. P. (1983) Randomized experiments on crime and justice, in Tonry, M. and Morris, N. (eds.) *Crime and Justice*, vol. 4, Chicago: University of Chicago Press, 257–308.

Farrington, D. P. (2003) Methodological quality standards for evaluation research, *The Annals of the American Academy of Political and Social Science*, vol. 587(1), 49–68.

Farrington, D. P. (2007) Childhood risk factors and risk-focussed prevention, in Maguire, M., Morgan, R. and Reiner, R. (eds.) *The Oxford Handbook of Criminology*, fourth edition, Oxford: Oxford University Press.

Farrington, D. P. and Jolliffe, D. (2002) A feasibility study into using a randomised controlled trial to evaluate treatment pilots at HMP Whitemoor, Home Office Online Report, 14/02, London: Home Office.

Farrington, D. P. and Welsh, B. C. (2005) Randomised experiments in criminology: What have we learned in the last two decades, *Journal of Experimental Criminology*, vol. 1(1), 9–38.

Faulkner, D. (2010) *Criminal Justice and Government at a Time of Austerity*, London: Criminal Justice Alliance. Available at www.criminaljusticealliance.org/cjausterity3.pdf [accessed 2 November 2012].

Festinger, L. (1957) *A Theory of Cognitive Dissonance*, Stanford, CA: Stanford University Press.

Fox, A. (2012) *Personalisation: Lessons from Social Care*, London: Royal Society of Arts.

Fox, A., Fox, C. and Marsh, C. (forthcoming), Could personalisation reduce re-offending? *Criminal Justice Matters*, vol. 90.

Fox, C. (2010) Developing an offender problem profile, *Safer Communities*, vol. 9(3), 17–27.

Fox, C. and Albertson, K. (2011) Payment by results and social impact bonds in the criminal justice sector: New challenges for the concept of evidence-based policy? *Criminology & Criminal Justice*, vol. 11(5), 395–413.

Fox, C., Williams, P., Albertson, K., Provan, A. and Woods, A. (2010) *Interim Findings from the Evaluation of Choose Change*, Manchester: Manchester Metropolitan University.

Frank, R. H., Gilovich, T. and Regan, D. T. (1993) Does studying economics inhibit cooperation? *The Journal of Economic Perspectives*, 7(2), 159–171.

Friedman, B. M. (2005) *The Moral Consequences of Economic Growth*, Carnegie Council for Ethics in International Affairs, 27 October. Available at www.cceia.org/resources/transcripts/5278.html [accessed 2 November 2012].

Friedman, D. D. (2008) Crime, *The Concise Encyclopedia of Economics*, Library of Economics and Liberty. Available at www.econlib.org/library/Enc/Crime.html. [accessed 2 November 2012].

Garland, D. (2001) *The Culture of Control: Crime and Social Order in Contemporary Society*, Oxford: Oxford University Press.

Gateshead Housing Company (2005), *Justice Reinvestment*, Report to the Board of the Interim Assistant Chief Executive, 8 September.

Gendreau, P., Little, T. and Goggin, C. (1996) A meta-analysis of the predictors of adult offender recidivism: What works! *Criminology*, vol. 34(4), 575–607.

George, S. (1999) *A Short History of Neo-liberalism*, Conference on Economic Sovereignty in a Globalising World, Bangkok, 24–26 March. Available at www.globalexchange.org/print/11854 [accessed 2 November 2012].

Gerwith, A. (1978) *Reason and Morality*, Chicago: University of Chicago Press.

Goldblatt, P. and Lewis, C. (eds.) (1998) *Reducing Offending: An Assessment of Research Evidence on Ways of Dealing with Offending Behaviour*, Home Office Research Study 187, London: Home Office.

Goldstone, R. L. and Chin, C. (1993), Dishonesty in self-report of copies made: Moral relativity and the copy machine, *Basic and Applied Social Psychology*, vol. 14 (1), 19–32.

Government Social Research Unit (2007a) Background paper 7: Why do social experiments? Experiments and quasi-experiments for evaluating government policies and programmes, London: Cabinet Office.

Government Social Research Unit (2007b) Background paper 2: What do we already know? Harnessing existing research, London: Cabinet Office.

Granger, C. W. J. (1980) Testing for causality: A personal viewpoint, *Journal of Economic Dynamic Control*, vol. 2, 329–352.

Grayling, C. (2012) The Work Programme a year on – a revolution is under way, speech to the Institute of Economic Affairs, 30 May, London. Available at www.dwp.gov.uk/newsroom/ministers-speeches/2012/30–05–12.shtml [accessed 2 November 2012].

Greater Manchester Public Protection Commission (2012) *Community Budget Pilot Progress Report*, 19 April. Available at www.agma.gov.uk/cms_media/files/i5_ppc_community_budgets.pdf?static=1 [accessed 9 August 2012].

Grogger, J. (1998) Market wages and youth crime, *Journal of Labour Economics*, vol. 16, 756–791.

Haidt, J. (2007) *The Happiness Hypothesis*, London: Random House.

Haidt, J. (2012) *The Righteous Mind: Why Good People are Divided by Politics and Religion*, London: Pantheon.

Hale, C. (2009) Economic marginalisation, social exclusion, and crime, in Hale, C., Hayward, K., Wahidin, A. and Wincup, E. (eds.) *Criminology*, second edition, Oxford: Oxford University Press.

Hansen, K. and Machin, S. (2002) Spatial crime patterns and the introduction of the UK minimum wage, *Oxford Bulletin of Economics and Statistics*, vol. 64, 677–698.

Hansard (1910) vol. 19, cc1344, 20 July. Available at http://hansard.millbanksystems.com/commons/1910/jul/20/class-iii [accessed 2 November 2012].

Hansbury, S. (2011) *Evaluation of the Alternatives to Custody Pilots*, Research Summary 3/11, London: Ministry of Justice.

Hargreaves Heap, S., Hollis, M., Lyons, B., Sugden, R. and Weale, A. (1992) *The Theory of Rational Choice: A Critical Guide*, Oxford: Blackwell.

Harper, G. and Chitty, C. (eds.) (2005) *The Impact of Corrections on Re-offending: A Review of "What Works"*, Home Office Research Study 291, London: Home Office. Available at www.homeoffice.gov.uk/rds/pdfs04/hors291.pdf [accessed 25 March 2010].

Harsanyi, J. (1955) Cardinal welfare, individualistic ethics, and interpersonal comparisons of utility, *Journal of Political Economy*, vol. 63, 309–321.

Haynes, L., Service, O., Goldacre, B. and Torgerson, D. (2012) *Test, Learn, Adapt: Developing Public Policy with Randomised Controlled Trials*, London: Cabinet Office.

Heckman, J. J. and Smith, J. A. (1995) Assessing the case for social experiments, *The Journal of Economic Perspectives*, vol. 9(2), 85–110.

Hedderman, C. (2008) *Building on Sand: Why Expanding the Prison Estate is Not the Way to Secure the Future*, London: Centre for Crime and Justice Studies.

Henrich, J., Boyd, R., Bowles, S., Camerer, C., Fehr, E., Gintis, H. and McElreath, R.

(2001), In search of homo economicus: Behavioral experiments in 15 small-scale societies, *American Economic Review*, vol. 91(2), 73–78.

Henrichson, C. and Delaney, R. (2012). *The Price of Prisons: What Incarceration Costs Taxpayers*, New York: Vera Institute of Justice. Available at www.vera.org/download?file=3476/the-price-of-prisons-updated.pdf.

Herbert, N. (2010) *Howard League for Penal Reform's Annual Parmoor Lecture*. Available at www.nickherbert.com/media_centre.php/386/Parmoor%20Lecture [accessed 2 November 2012].

Her Majesty's Government (2010) *The Coalition: Our Programme for Government*, London: Cabinet Office. Available at www.cabinetoffice.gov.uk/sites/default/files/resources/coalition_programme_for_government.pdf.

Her Majesty's Prison Service (2001) Resettlement: Prison Service Order 2300, date of initial issue 23 October 2001, amended 5 January 2004, 1 March 2005, 29 November 2005.

Her Majesty's Treasury (undated) *The Green Book: Appraisal and Evaluation in Central Government*, London: The Stationery Office.

HEUNI (2010) *International Statistics on Crime and Justice*, European Institute for Crime Prevention and Control, affiliated with the United Nations (HEUNI), Helsinki: HEUNI. Available at www.heuni.fi/Etusivu/Publications/1266333832841 [accessed 2 November 2012].

Hickey, A. (2011) North Wales Police issue highest number of Asbos in Wales, *Daily Post*, 27 January. Available at http://www.dailypost.co.uk/news/north-wales-news/2011/01/27/north-wales-police-issue-highest-number-of-asbos-in-wales-55578-28063265/ [accessed 9 August 2012].

Hicks, J. and Allen, G. (1999) *A Century of Change: Trends in UK Statistics since 1900*, Research paper 99/111, 21 December, Social and General Statistics Section, House of Commons Library. Available at www.parliament.uk/documents/commons/lib/research/rp99/rp99–111.pdf [accessed 2 November 2012].

Hoare, J. (2009) Extent and trends, in Walker, A., Flatley, J., Kershaw, C. and Moon D. (eds.) *Crime in England and Wales 2008/09*, vol. 1: *Findings from the British Crime Survey and Police Recorded Crime*, Home Office Statistical Bulletin, London: Home Office. Available at http://news.bbc.co.uk/1/shared/bsp/hi/pdfs/16_07_09_bcs.pdf [accessed 2 November 2012].

Hobbes, T. (1943) *Leviathan*, London: Everyman.

Hollin, C. (2008) Evaluating offending behaviour programmes: Does only a randomization glister? *Criminology and Criminal Justice*, vol. 8(1), 89–106.

Hollis, M. (1977) *Models of Man*, Cambridge: Cambridge University Press.

Hollis, M. (1987) *The Cunning of Reason*, Cambridge: Cambridge University Press.

Hollis, M. (1994) *The Philosophy of the Social Sciences: An Introduction*, Cambridge; Cambridge University Press.

Hollis, M. (1998) *Trust within Reason*, Cambridge: Cambridge University Press.

Homel, R. (2005) Developmental crime prevention, in Tilley, N. (ed.) *Handbook of Crime Prevention and Community Safety*, Cullompton, UK: Willan Publishing.

Home Office (2003) *Modelling Crime and Offending: Recent Developments in England and Wales*, Home Office Occasional Paper 80, London: Home Office.

Home Office (2005) *The Economic and Social Costs of Crime against Individuals and Households 2003/04*, Home Office Online Report 30/05, London: Home Office.

Home Office (2010) *Integrated Offender Management: Key Principles*, London: Ministry of Justice.

Hope, T. (2009) What do crime statistics tell us? in Hale, C., Hayward, K., Wahidin, A. and Wincup, E. (eds.) *Criminology*, Oxford: Oxford University Press.

Hopkins, K. (2012) *The Pre-custody Employment, Training and Education Status of Newly Sentenced Prisoners: Results from the Surveying Prisoner Crime Reduction (SPCR) Longitudinal Cohort Study of Prisoners*, London: Ministry of Justice.

Houchin, R. (2005) *Social Exclusion and Imprisonment in Scotland – A Report*, Glasgow: Glasgow Caledonian University.

Hough, M. (2010) Gold standard or fool's gold? The pursuit of certainty in experimental criminology, *Criminology and Criminal Justice*, vol. 10(1), 11–22.

Hough, M. and Roberts, J. (1998) *Attitudes to Punishment: Findings from the British Crime Survey*, Home Office Research Study 179, London: Home Office. Available at http://webarchive.nationalarchives.gov.uk/20110218135832/rds.homeoffice.gov.uk/rds/pdfs/hors179.pdf [accessed 2 November 2012].

Hough, M., Roberts J., Jacobson, J., Moon, N. and Steel, N. (2009) *Public Attitudes to the Principles of Sentencing*, Sentencing Advisory Panel – Research Report 6, London: Sentencing Advisory Panel.

House of Commons (2011) *Written Evidence from Rebecca Clarke (Greater Manchester Probation Trust) (PB 73)*. Available at www.publications.parliament.uk/pa/cm201012/cmselect/cmjust/519/519vw56.htm [accessed 2 November 2012].

House of Commons Science and Technology Committee (2006) *Scientific Advice, Risk and Evidence Based Policy Making*, Seventh Report of Session 2005–6, vol. 1, London: House of Commons.

Hoverstadt, P. (2011) *A Systemic View of Payment by Outcomes*, Lymm, UK: Fractal Consulting.

Hughes, G. (1998) *Understanding Crime Prevention: Social Control, Risk and Late Modernity*, Buckingham, UK: Open University Press.

In Control (2011) *The National Personal Budget Survey: Think Local, Act Personal*, Birmingham: In Control.

International Labour Office (2011) *Global Employment Trends 2011: The Challenge of a Jobs Recovery*, Geneva: International Labour Office. Available at www.ilo.org/wcmsp5/groups/public/—dgreports/—dcomm/—publ/documents/publication/wcms_150440.pdf [accessed 2 November 2012].

IRISS [Institute for Research and Innovation in Social Services] (2010) *Intensive Supervision, Surveillance and Monitoring of Young People*, Insights no. 9, Glasgow: Institute for Research and Innovation in Social Services. Available at www.iriss.org.uk/sites/default/files/iriss-insight-9.pdf [accessed 4 November 2012].

Johnson, W. (2012) New challenge for "jackal" Chris Grayling as he replaces Ken Clarke as Justice Secretary, *The Independent*, 4 September. Available at www.independent.co.uk/news/uk/politics/new-challenge-for-jackal-chris-grayling-as-he-replaces-ken-clarke-as-justice-secretary-8104444.html [accessed 2 November 2012].

Justice Committee (2010) *Cutting Crime: The Case for Justice Reinvestment*, London: The Stationery Office. Available at www.publications.parliament.uk/pa/cm200910/cmselect/cmjust/94/94i.pdf [accessed 2 November 2012].

Kahn, A. E. (1966) The tyranny of small decisions: Market failures, imperfections and the limits of economics, *Kyklos*, vol. 19, 23–47.

Kahneman, D. (2011) *Thinking, Fast and Slow*, London: Allen Lane.

Karuppannan, J. (2005) Mapping and corrections: Management of offenders with geographic information systems, *Corrections Compendium*, vol. 30(1), 1–11.

Keizer, K., Lindenberg, S. and Steg, L. (2008) The spreading of disorder, *Science*, vol. 322, 1681–1685.

Kerr, K., Thomkins, C., Wojtek, T., Dickens, S., Grimshaw, R., Wright, N. and Barnard, M. (2011) *The Dedicated Drugs Court Pilot Evaluation Process Study*, London: Ministry of Justice.

Kessler, D. and Levitt, S. (1999) Using sentence enhancements to distinguish between deterrence and incapacitation, *Journal of Law and Economics*, vol. 42, 343–363.

Klein, J. (2002) *The Natural: The Misunderstood Presidency of Bill Clinton*, London: Hodder and Stoughton.

Krauss, S. E. (2005) Research paradigms and meaning making: A primer, *The Qualitative Report*, vol. 10(4), 758–770.

Labour Party (1997) *Manifesto*. Available at www.labour-party.org.uk/manifestos/1997/1997-labour-manifesto.shtml [accessed 2 November 2012].

Lanning, T., Loader, I. and Muir, R. (2011) *Redesigning Justice: Reducing Crime through Justice Reinvestment*, London: IPPR.

Larimer, M. E., Malone, D. K., Garner, M. D., Atkins, D. C., Burlingham, B., Lonczak, H. S., Tanzer, K., Ginzler, J., Clifasefi, S. L., Hobson, W. G. and Marlatt, G. A. (2009) Health care and public service use and costs before and after provision of housing for chronically homeless persons with severe alcohol problems, *The Journal of the American Medical Association*, vol. 301(13), 1349–1357.

Laub, J. H. and Sampson, R. J. (2003) *Shared Beginnings, Divergent Lives: Delinquent Boys to age 70*, Boston: Harvard University Press.

Laub, J. H., Nagin, D. S. and Sampson, R. J. (1998) Trajectories of change in criminal offending: Good marriages and the desistance process, *American Sociological Review*, vol. 63, 225–238.

La Vigne, N. (2007) *Mapping for Community-based Prisoner Reentry Efforts: A Guide Book for Law Enforcement Agencies and Their Partners*, Washington, DC: Police Foundation.

La Vigne, N. G. and Cowan, J. (2005) *Mapping Prisoner Reentry: An Action Research Guidebook*, Washington, DC: Urban Institute, Justice Policy Center.

La Vigne, N. G., Elderbroom, B. and Brazzell, D. (2008) *Charting a New Direction: Exploring the Future of Justice Mapping*, Washington, DC: Urban Institute.

La Vigne, N. G., Neusteter, R. S., Lachman, P., Dwyer, A. and Nadeau, C. A. (2010) *Justice Reinvestment at the Local Level, Planning and Implementation Guide*, Washington, DC: Urban Institute, Justice Policy Center. Available at www.urban.org/UploadedPDF/412233-Justice-Reinvestment.pdf [accessed 2 November 2012].

Leeson, C. (2004) Tough talk fuels public ignorance, *Safer Society*, no. 22, 26–27.

Levitt, S. D. (1996) The effect of prison population size on crime rates: Evidence from prison overcrowding litigation, *Quarterly Journal of Economics*, vol. 111, 319–351.

Levitt, S. D. (1997) Using electoral cycles in police hiring to estimate the effect of police on crime, *American Economic Review*, vol. 87, 270–290.

Levitt, S. D. (2001) Alternative strategies for identifying the link between unemployment and crime, *Journal of Quantitative Criminology*, vol. 17, 377–390.

Levitt, S. D. (2002) Using electoral cycles in police hiring to estimate the effects of police on crime: Reply, *American Economic Review*,vol. 92, 1244–1250.

Levitt, S. D. and Lochner, L. (2001) The determinants of juvenile crime, in Gruber, J. (ed.) *Risky Behavior among Youths: An Economic Analysis*, Chicago: University of Chicago Press.

Lewis, S., Vennard, J., Maguire, M., Raynor, P., Vanstone, M., Raybould, S. and Rix, A.

(2003) *The Resettlement of Short-term Prisoners: An Evaluation of Seven Pathfinders*, RDS Occasional Paper no. 83, London: Home Office.

Liedka, R. V., Piehl, A. M. and Useem, B. (2006) The crime-control effect of incarceration: Does scale matter? *Criminology & Public Policy*, 5(2), 245–276.

Lipsey, M. W. (1992) Juvenile delinquency treatment: A meta-analytic inquiry into the variability of effects, in Cook, T. D., Cooper, H., Cordray, D.S., Hartmann, H., Hedges, L.V., Light, R.J., Louis, T.A. and Mosteller, F. (eds.) *Meta-analysis for Explanation: A Casebook*, New York: Russell Sage Foundation, 83–127.

Lipsey, M. W. and Cullen, F. T. (2007) The effectiveness of correctional rehabilitation: A review of systematic reviews, *Annual Review of Law and Social Science*, vol. 3, 297–320.

Lipsey, M. W. and Wilson, D. (2001) *Practical Meta-Analysis*, Thousand Oaks, CA: Sage.

Lipsey, M. W. and Wilson, D. B. (1993) The efficacy of psychological, educational, and behavioral treatment, *American Psychologist*, vol. 48(12), 1181–1209.

Lipsey, M. W., Chapman, G. and Landenberger, N. A. (2001) Cognitive-behavioural programs for offenders, *Annals of the American Academy of Political and Social Science*, vol. 576, 144–157.

Lloyd, K. and Foster, J. (2009) *Citizen Focus and Community Engagement: A Review of the Literature*, London: The Police Foundation.

Local Government Information Unit (2008) *Getting to the Heart of Local Accountability*, consultation paper in response to Community Empowerment White Paper, London: Local Government Information Unit.

Lochner, L. (2004) Education, work, and crime: A human capital approach, *International Economic Review*, vol. 45, 811–843.

Lochner, L. and Moretti, E. (2004) The effect of education on crime: Evidence from prison inmates, arrests, and self-reports, *The American Economic Review*, vol. 94(1), 155–189.

Losel, F. and Schmucker, M. (2005) The effectiveness of treatment for sexual offenders: A comprehensive meta-analysis, *Journal of Experimental Criminology*, vol. 1(1), 117–146.

Loewenstein, G. (2000) Emotions in economic theory and economic behavior, *The American Economic Review*, vol. 90, 426–443.

Lum, C. and Yang, S. M. (2005) Why do evaluation researchers in crime and justice choose non-experimental methods? *Journal of Experimental Criminology*, vol. 1, 191–213.

Machin, S. and Meghir, C. (2004) Crime and economic incentives, *Journal of Human Resources*, 39(4), 958–979.

MacKenzie, D. L. (2001) Evidence-based corrections: Identifying what works, *Crime and Delinquency*, vol. 4(4), 457–471.

MacKenzie, D. L., Wilson, D. B. and Kider, S. B. (2001) Effects of correctional boot camps on offending, *Annals of the American Academy of Political and Social Sciences*, vol. 578, 126–143.

Maguire, M. and Raynor, P. (2006) How the resettlement of prisoners promotes desistance from crime: Or does it? *Criminology and Criminal Justice*, vol. 6(1), 19–38.

Marsh, K. and Fox, C. (2008) The benefit and cost of prison in the UK: The results of a model of lifetime re-offending, *The Journal of Experimental Criminology*, 4(4), 403–423.

Marsh, K. and Fox, C. (forthcoming) The influence of research design on measures of effect: Evidence from studies of sentencing options.

Marsh, K., Chalfin, A. and Roman, J. (2008) What does economic analysis add to decision making? Evidence from the criminal justice literature, *Journal of Experimental Criminology*, vol. 4(2), 117–135.

Marsh, K., Fox, C. and Hedderman, C. (2009) Do you get what you pay for? Assessing the use of prison from an economic perspective. *Howard Journal of Criminal Justice*, vol. 48(2), 144–157.

Martins, N. (2011) Globalisation, inequality and the economic crisis, *New Political Economy*, vol. 16(1), 1–18.

Maruna, S. (2001) *Making Good*, Washington, DC: American Psychological Association.

Marvell, T. and Moody, C. (1994) Prison population and crime reduction, *Journal of Quantitative Criminology*, vol. 10, 109–139.

Mason, T., de Silva, N., Sharma, N., Brown, D. and Harper, G. (2007) *Local Variation in Sentencing in England and Wales*, London: Ministry of Justice. Available at www.justice.gov.uk/downloads/statistics/mojstats/local-variation-sentencing-1207.pdf [accessed 2 November 2012].

Mauer, M. (2001) Causes and consequences of prison growth in the United States, in Garland, D. (ed.) *Mass Imprisonment: Social Causes and Consequences*, London: Sage.

Mazar, N. and Ariely, D. (2006) Dishonesty in everyday life and its policy implications, *Journal of Public Policy and Marketing*, vol. 25, 1–21.

Mazar, N., Amir, O. and Ariely, D. (2008) The dishonesty of honest people: A theory of self-concept maintenance, *Journal of Marketing Research*, vol. 45(6), 633–644.

McCracken, K., McMurran, M., Winlow, S., Sassi, F. and McCarthy, K. (2012) *Evaluation of Alcohol Arrest Referral Pilot Schemes (Phase 2)*, Occasional Paper 102, London: Home Office.

McNeill, F. (2009) *Towards Effective Practice in Offender Supervision*, Glasgow: Scottish Centre for Crime and Justice Research.

Meadows, L., Albertson, K., Ellingworth, D. and Senior, P. (2012) *Evaluation of the South Yorkshire Restorative Justice Programme, Final Report*, Sheffield: Hallam Centre for Community Justice, Sheffield Hallam University.

Ministry of Justice (2007) *Penal Policy: A Background Paper*, London: Ministry of Justice.

Ministry of Justice (2008) *Appraisal of Prisoner Resettlement Projects for Short-sentence Prisoners of the United Kingdom*, unpublished.

Ministry of Justice (2009) *Story of the Prison Population 1995–2009 England and Wales*, Ministry of Justice statistics bulletin, London: Ministry of Justice. Available at www.justice.gov.uk/downloads/statistics/mojstats/story-prison-population.pdf [accessed 2 November 2012].

Ministry of Justice (2010a) *Government Response to the Justice Committee's Report: Cutting Crime: The Case for Justice Re-investment*, London: Ministry of Justice. Available at www.official-documents.gov.uk/document/cm78/7819/7819.pdf [accessed 2 November 2012].

Ministry of Justice (2010b) *Compendium of Reoffending Statistics and Analysis*, London: Ministry of Justice. Available at www.justice.gov.uk/downloads/statistics/mojstats/compendium-of-reoffending-statistics-and-analysis.pdf [accessed 2 November 2012].

Ministry of Justice (2010c) *Breaking the Cycle: Effective punishment, Rehabilitation and Sentencing of Offenders*, London: Home Office. Available at www.cjp.org.uk/EasysiteWeb/getresource.axd?AssetID=5080&type=full&servicetype=Attachment [accessed 2 November 2012].

Ministry of Justice (2010d) *Re-offending of Adults: Results from the 2008 Cohort England and Wales*, London: Ministry of Justice.

Ministry of Justice (2011) *Proven Re-offending Statistics Quarterly Bulletin January to December 2009, England and Wales*, London: Ministry of Justice.

Ministry of Justice (2012a) *Population and Capacity Briefing for Friday 22/06/2012*. Available at www.justice.gov.uk/statistics/prisons-and-probation/prison-population-figures [accessed 2 November 2012].

Ministry of Justice (2012b) *Swift and Sure Justice: The Government's Plans for Reform of the Criminal Justice System*, London: The Stationery Office. Available at www.justice.gov.uk/downloads/publications/policy/moj/swift-and-sure-justice.pdf [accessed 24 October 2012].

Ministry of Justice (2012c) *Community Sentences to Deliver Proper Punishment*, press release, London: Ministry of Justice. Available at www.justice.gov.uk/news/press-releases/moj/community-sentences-that-deliver-proper-punishment [accessed 2 November 2012].

Mitchell, O., Wilson, D. B. and MacKenzie, D. L. (2006) *The Effectiveness of Incarceration-Based Drug Treatment on Criminal Behaviour*, Campbell Collaboration systematic review, available at www.aic.gov.au/campbellcj/reviews/titles.html [accessed 7 September 2012].

Mitford, J. (1973) *Kind and Usual Punishment: The Prison Business*, New York: Vintage.

Mulgan, G. and Bury, F. (2006) *Double Devolution: The Renewal of Local Government*, London: the Smith Institute.

Mulgan, G., Reeder, N., Aylott, M. and Bosher, L. (2010) *Social Impact Investment: The Opportunity and Challenge of Social Impact Bonds*, London: The Young Foundation.

Nagin, D. S., Cullen, F. T. and Jonson, C. L. (2009) Imprisonment and reoffending, in Tonry, M. (ed.) *Crime and Justice: A Review of Research*, vol. 38, Chicago: University of Chicago Press.

National Association of State Budget Officers (2011) *State Expenditure Report 2010*, Washington, DC: National Association of State Budget Officers.

National Audit Office (2010) *Managing Offenders on Short Custodial Sentences*, London: The Stationery Office.

National Offender Management Service (2008) *Prison Population and Accommodation Briefing 4th April 2008*, London: Ministry of Justice.

National Offender Management Service (2011) *National Offender Management Service Business Plan 2011–12*, London: Ministry of Justice.

National Offender Management Service (2012) *National Offender Management Service Business Plan 2012–2013*, London: Ministry of Justice.

Newark, L., Rempel, M., Diffily, K. and Kane, K. M. (2001) *Specialised Felony Domestic Violence Courts: Lessons on Implementation and Impacts from the Kings County Experience*, Washington, DC: The Urban Institute Justice Policy Center.

New York Times (2003) Rethinking the key thrown away; as Ashcroft cracks down, states cut prison terms, 20 September. Available at www.nytimes.com/2003/09/28/nyregion/rethinking-the-key-thrown-away-as-ashcroft-cracks-down-states-cut-prison-terms.html?pagewanted=all&src=pm [accessed 2 November 2012].

New York Times (2011), The problems of a graying population: It's the demography, stupid, 28 July. Available at www.nytimes.com/2011/07/29/world/americas/29iht-letter29.html?_r=0 [accessed 2 November 2012].

O'Doherty, J. P. (2004) Reward representations and reward-related learning in the human brain: Insights from neuroimaging, *Current Opinion in Neurobiology*, vol. 14, 769–776.

Office for National Statistics (2001) *Social Capital: A Review of the Literature*, London: Office for National Statistics.

Office for National Statistics (2010) *Public Sector Finances March 2010*, London: Office for National Statistics. Available at www.ons.gov.uk/ons/rel/psa/public-sector-finances/march-2010/public-sector-finances--march-2010.pdf [accessed 2 November 2012].

Office for National Statistics (2012a) *Public Sector Finances March 2011*, London: Office for National Statistics. Available at www.ons.gov.uk/ons/rel/psa/public-sector-finances/march-2011/public-sector-finances--march-2011.pdf [accessed 2 November 2012].

Office for National Statistics (2012b) *Public Sector Finances March 2012*, London: Office for National Statistics. Available at www.ons.gov.uk/ons/rel/psa/public-sector-finances/public-sector-finances--march-2012/stb--march-2012.html [accessed 2 November 2012].

Page, B., Wake, R. and Ames, A. (2004) *Public Confidence in the Criminal Justice System*, London: Home Office.

Park, R. E., Burgess, E. W. and McKenzie, R. A. (1925) *The City: Suggestions for Investigation of Human Behavior in the Urban Environment*, Chicago: University of Chicago Press.

Pawson, R. (2002) Evidence-based policy: In search of a method, *Evaluation*, vol. 8(2), 157–181.

Pawson, R. and Tilley, N. (1997) *Realistic Evaluation*, London: Sage.

Persky, J. (1995) Retrospectives: The ethology of homo economicus, *The Journal of Economic Perspectives*, vol. 9(2), 221–231.

Petrosino, A., Turpin-Petrosino, C. and Finckenauer, J. O. (2000) Well meaning programs can have harmful effects! Lessons from experiments of programs such as Scared Straight, *Crime and Delinquency*, vol. 46, 354–379.

Pew Center on the States (2008) *One in 100: Behind Bars in America 2008*, Washington, DC: Pew Charitable Trusts.

Phillips, N. A. (2008) *Who Decides the Sentence?* Prisoners' Education Trust Annual Lecture, 14 October. Available at www.prisonerseducation.org.uk/index.php?id=211 [accessed 2 November 2012].

Pleasant, S. and Harris, S. (2012) *Greater Manchester Community Budget Pilot – Progress Report*, 25 May, Manchester: Greater Manchester Combined Authority. Available at http://www.agma.gov.uk/cms_media/files/7_gm_community_budget_pilot_progress_report.pdf?static=1.

politics.co.uk (2007) Split will make Home Office fit for modern world, 29 March. Available at www.politics.co.uk/news/2007/03/29/split-will-make-home-office-fit-for-modern-world [accessed 2 November 2012].

Popper, K. R. (1972) *Conjectures and Refutations: The Growth of Scientific Knowledge*, London: Routledge and Kegan Paul.

Prison Reform Trust (2009) *Bromley Briefings Prison Factfile*, London: Prison Reform Trust. Available at www.prisonreformtrust.org.uk/uploads/documents/june2009factfile.pdf [accessed 2 November 2012].

Putnam, R. (2000) *Bowling Alone: The Collapse and Revival of American Community*, New York: Simon and Schuster.

Quinton, P. (2011) *The Impact of Information about Crime and Policing on Public Perceptions: The Results of a Randomised Controlled Trial*, London: National Policing

Improvement Agency. Available at www.npia.police.uk/en/docs/Full_Report_-_Crime_and_Policing_Information.pdf [accessed 2 November 2012].

Raphael, S. and Winter-Ebmer, R. (2001) Identifying the effect of Unemployment on crime, *Journal of Law and Economics*, vol. 44, 259–283.

Reiner, R. (2005) Be tough on a crucial cause of crime – neoliberalism, *The Guardian*, 24 November. Available at www.guardian.co.uk/politics/2005/nov/24/ukcrime.uk [accessed 2 November 2012].

Ridgely, M., Engberg, J., Greenberg, M. D., Turner, S., DeMartini, C. and Dembosky, J. W. (2007) *Justice, Treatment and Cost: An Evaluation of the Fiscal Impact of Allegheny County Mental Health Court*, Santa Monica, CA: RAND Corporation.

Rilling, J. K., Gutman, D. A., Zeh, T. R., Pagnoni, G., Berns, G. S. and Kilts, C. D. (2002) A neural basis for social cooperation, *Neuron*, vol. 35, 395–405.

Rilling, J. K., Sanfey, A. G., Aronson, J. A., Nystrom, L. E. and Cohen, J. D. (2004) Opposing BOLD responses to reciprocated and unreciprocated altruism in putative reward pathways, *Neuroreport*, vol. 15, 2539–2543.

Roman, J. (2004) Can cost-benefit analysis answer criminal justice policy questions, and if so, how? *Journal of Contemporary Criminal Justice*, vol. 20, 257–275.

Sampson, R. J. (2010) Gold standard myths: Observations on the experimental turn in quantitative criminology, *Journal of Quantitative Criminology*, vol. 26(4), 489–500.

Sampson, R. J., Raudenbush, S. W. and Earls, F. (1997) Neighborhoods and violent crime: A multilevel study of collective efficacy, *Science*, 277(5328), 918–924.

Sampson, R., Raudenbush, S. W. and Earls, F. (1998) *Neighborhood Collective Efficacy – Does It Help Reduce Violence?* Washington, DC: National Institute of Justice.

Schill, R. (2011) *Beyond Scared Straight: Experts Alarmed at New Show and Impact on Kids*, Juvenile Justice Information Exchange. Available at http://jjie.org/scared-straight-story-2/8693 [accessed 2 September 2012].

Schweinhart, L. (undated) *The HighScope Perry Preschool Study Through Age 40: Summary, Conclusions, and Frequently Asked Questions*, Ypsilanti, MI: HighScope Educational Research Foundation.

Scull, A. (1977) *Decarceration: Community Treatment and the Deviant: A Radical View*, Englewood Cliffs, NJ: Prentice-Hall.

Sen, A. (1977) Rational fools: A critique of the behavioral foundations of economic theory, *Philosophy and Public Affairs*, vol. 6, 317–344.

Senior, P., Wong, K., Culshaw, A., Ellingworth, D., O'Keeffe, C. and Meadows, L. (2011) *Process Evaluation of Five Integrated Offender Management Pioneer Areas*, London: Ministry of Justice.

Shadish, R., Cook, T. and Campbell, D. (2002) *Experimental and Quasi-experimental Designs for Generalized Causal Inference*, Boston: Houghton-Mifflin.

Shadish, W. R. and Heinsman, D. T. (1997) *Experiments versus Quasi-experiments: Do they Yield the Same Answer?* NIDA Research Monograph.

Shaw, A. (ed.) (1950) *The Lincoln Encyclopaedia*, New York: Macmillan.

Shaw, C. R. and McKay, H. D. (1942) *Juvenile Delinquency and Urban Areas*, Chicago: University of Chicago Press.

Shaw, C. R. and McKay, H. D. (1969) *Juvenile Delinquency and Urban Areas: A Study of Rates of Delinquency in Relation To Differential Characteristics of Local Communities in American Cities* (revised ed.), Chicago: University of Chicago Press.

Shepherd, J. (2006) The imprisonment puzzle: Understanding how prison growth affects crime, *Criminology & Public Policy*, 5(2), 285–298.

Sherman, L. (2009) Evidence and liberty: The promise of experimental criminology, *Criminology and Criminal Justice*, 9(1), 5–28.

Sherman, L. W., Gottfredson, D., MacKenzie, D., Eck, J., Reuter, P. and Bushway, S. (1998a) *Preventing Crime: What Works, What Doesn't, What's Promising: A Report To The United States Congress*, prepared for the National Institute of Justice, University of Maryland.

Sherman, L. W., Gottfredson, D., MacKenzie, D., Eck, J., Reuter, P. and Bushway, S. (1998b) Preventing crime: What works, what doesn't, what's promising, *National Institute of Justice Research in Brief*, Washington, DC: National Institute of Justice.

Simon, H. (1956) Rational choice and the structure of the environment, *Psychological Review*, vol. 63, 129–138.

Simon, H. A. (1976) From substantive to procedural rationality, in Latsis, S. J. (ed.) *Method and Appraisal in Economics*, Cambridge: Cambridge University Press.

Simon, H. A. (1986) Rationality in psychology and economics, part 2: The behavioural foundations of economic theory, *The Journal of Business*, vol. 59(4), S209-S224.

Skolnick, A. (2011) Runaway prison costs trash state budgets, *The Fiscal Times*, 9 February. Available at www.thefiscaltimes.com/Articles/2011/02/09/Runaway-Prison-Costs-Thrash-State-Budgets.aspx#page2 [accessed 13 September 2012].

Smith, A. (1759) *The Theory of Moral Sentiments*, sixth edition (1790), London: A. Millar.

Smith, A. (1776) *An Inquiry into the Nature and Causes of the Wealth of Nations*, fifth edition (1904), London: Methuen & Co., Ltd. Available at www.econlib.org/library/Smith/smWNCover.html [accessed 2 November 2012].

Smith, D. (2007) Crime and the life course, in Maguire, M., Morgan, R. and Reiner, R. (eds.) *The Oxford Handbook of Criminology*, fourth edition, Oxford: Oxford University Press.

Smith, S. S. and Kulynych, J. (2002) It may be social but why is it capital? The social construction of social capital and the politics of language, *Politics and Society*, vol. 30(1), 149–186.

Social Finance (2010) *Social Finance Releases First Social Impact Bond*, press release, London: Social Finance. Available at www.socialfinance.org.uk/sites/default/files/SIB_March18_PR.pdf [accessed 11 March 2011].

Social Finance (2011) *Peterborough Social Impact Bond*, London: Social Finance. Available at www.socialfinance.org.uk/sites/default/files/SF_Peterborough_SIB.pdf [accessed 11 March 2011].

Social Justice Policy Group (2006) *Breakdown Britain*, London: The Centre for Social Justice. Available at www.centreforsocialjustice.org.uk/default.asp?pageRef=180 [accessed 2 November 2012].

Solomon, E. and Garside, R. (2010) *Ten Years of Labour's Youth Justice Reforms: An Independent Audit*, London: Centre for Crime and Justice Studies, Kings College.

Sommer, R. (1976) *The End of Imprisonment*, New York: Oxford University Press.

Sondhi, A., O'Shea, N. and Williams, T. (2002) *Arrest Referral: Emerging Findings from the National Monitoring and Evaluation Programme*, DPAS Briefing Paper 18, London: Home Office.

Stapel, D. A. and Lindenberg, S. (2011) Coping with chaos: How disordered contexts promote stereotyping and discrimination, *Science*, vol. 332, 251–253.

Stern, V. and Allen, R. (2007) Localism and criminal justice: Suggestions for a new balance between national and local decision-making, in Allen, R. and Stern, V. (eds.) *Justice Reinvestment: A New Approach to Crime and Justice*, London: International Centre for Prison Studies.

Stevens, A. (2011) Telling policy stories: An ethnographic study of the use of evidence in policy-making in the UK, *Journal of Social Policy*, vol. 40(2), 237–255.

Stone, D., Maxwell, S. and Keating, M. (2001) *Bridging Research and Policy*, paper for International Workshop funded by DfID, Warwick University, 16–17 July.

Tarling, R. (1993) *Analysing Offending: Data, Models and Interpretations*, London: HMSO.

Thaler, R. and Shefrin, H. (1981) An economic theory of self-control, *The Journal of Political Economy*, vol. 89, 392–406.

Thaler, R. H. and Sunstein, C. R. (2008) *Nudge: Improving Decisions about Health, Wealth and Happiness*, New Haven: Yale University Press.

Thatcher, M. (1987) interview, 23 September, as quoted in by Douglas Keay, *Woman's Own*, 31 October, 8–10. Available at www.margaretthatcher.org/document/106689 [accessed 2 November 2012].

Thatcher, M. (1988) speech to the House of Commons, *Hansard*, 17 May, col. 796.

Thatcher, M. (1996) Geographical Society presidential dinner address, *The Independent on Sunday*, 21 July, p. 52.

The American Prospect (2003) *Crime and Redemption*, 20 November. Available at http://prospect.org/cs/articles?article=crime_and_redemption [accessed 2 November 2012].

The Columbus Dispatch (2008) Governor wants prisons re-evaluated, 27 January. Available at www.dispatch.com/content/stories/local/2008/01/26/GOV_PRIZ.ART_ART_01–26–08_A1_J495THB.html [accessed 2 November 2012].

The Economist (2012) True progressivism, inequality and the world economy, 13 October.

The Guardian (2006) What the Victorians could do for us, 11 January. Available at www.guardian.co.uk/society/2006/jan/11/publicservices.guardiansocietysupplement [accessed 2 November 2012].

The Guardian (2010) Kenneth Clarke hints at prison sentencing reform with attack on "bang 'em up" culture, 30 June. Available at www.guardian.co.uk/society/2010/jun/30/kenneth-clarke-prison-sentencing-reform [accessed 2 November 2012].

The Guardian (2011), Yvette Cooper: Labour remains tough on crime, tough on the causes of crime, 10 March. Available at www.guardian.co.uk/politics/wintour-and-watt/2011/mar/10/yvette-cooper-labour [accessed 2 November 2012].

The Guardian (2012a) Chris Grayling puts "punishment backing into community sentencing", 23 October. Available at www.guardian.co.uk/politics/2012/oct/23/chris-grayling-punishment-community-sentences [accessed 2 November 2012].

The Guardian (2012b) Nick Harvey's leaked letter to Chris Grayling, 26 February. Available at www.guardian.co.uk/politics/interactive/2012/feb/26/harvey-grayling-leaked-letter.

The Guardian (2012c) Why the work programme is a bad business, 28 February. Available at www.guardian.co.uk/society/2012/feb/28/why-work-programme-bad-business.

The Independent on Sunday (1996) Not enough for us, 21 July. Available at www.independent.co.uk/news/uk/not-enough-for-us-1329728.html [accessed 2 November 2012].

The Telegraph (2012) We will "push ahead" with prisoner rehabilitation plans before pilot is finished, Grayling says, 22 October. Available at www.telegraph.co.uk/news/politics/9624955/We-will-push-ahead-with-prisoner-rehabilitation-plans-before-pilot-is-finished-Grayling-says.html [accessed 2 November 2012].

The Matrix Knowledge Group (2008) *Dedicated Drug Court Pilots: A Process Report*, London: Ministry of Justice.

Thompson, M., Osher, F. and Tomasini-Joshi, D. (2007) *Improving Responses to People with Mental Illnesses: The Essential Elements of a Mental Health Court*, New York: Council on State Governments Justice Center.

Thorpe, K. and Hall, P. (2009) Public perception, in Walker, A., Flatley, J., Kershaw, C. and Moon, D. (eds.) *Crime in England and Wales 2008/09*, vol. 1: *Findings from the British Crime Survey and Police Recorded Crime*, London: Home Office.

Toddington, S. (1993) *Rationality, Social Action and Moral Judgement*, Edinburgh: Edinburgh University Press.

Treadwell Shine, K. and Bartley, B. (2011) Whose evidence base? The dynamic effects of ownership, receptivity and values on collaborative evidence-informed policy making, *Evidence and Policy*, vol. 7(4), 511–530.

Travis, A. and Hirsch, A. (2010) Kenneth Clarke pledges to cut daily prison population, *The Guardian*, 20 October. Available at www.guardian.co.uk/politics/2010/oct/20/kenneth-clarke-pledges-cut-prison-population [accessed 8 September 2012].

Travis, J., Keegan, S., Cadora, E., Solomon, A. and Swartz, C. (2003) *A Portrait of Prisoner Reentry in New Jersey*, Washington, DC: Urban Institute.

Tucker, S. and Cadora, E. (2003) *Justice Reinvestment: To Invest in Public Safety by Reallocating Justice Dollars to Refinance Education, Housing, Healthcare, and Jobs*, monograph, *Ideas for an Open Society*, 3. Available at www.soros.org/publications/ideas-open-society-justice-reinvestment [accessed 2 November 2012].

Tyler, T. R. (2006) *Why People Obey the Law*, Princeton: Princeton University Press.

US Department of Justice (2010) *Correctional Population in the United States, 2010*. Available at http://nicic.gov/Library/025520 [accessed 2 November 2012].

US Senate Judiciary Committee (2010) S. 2772 (111th): *Criminal Justice Reinvestment Act of 2010 (Reported to the Floor, March 22, 2010)*. Available at www.gpo.gov/fdsys/pkg/BILLS-111s2772rs/pdf/BILLS-111s2772rs.pdf [accessed 2 November 2012].

Villetaz, P., Killias, M. and Zoder, I. (2006) *The Effects of Custodial vs. Non-Custodial Sentences on Re-Offending: A Systematic Review of the State of Knowledge*, report to the Campbell Collaboration Crime and Justice Group. Available at www.campbellcollaboration.org/lib/download/108/ [accessed 2 November 2012].

Von Hirsch, A., Bottoms, A., Burney, E. and Wikstrom, P. (1999) *Criminal Deterrence and Sentence Severity: An Analysis Of Recent Research*, London: Home Office.

Walker, D. (2004) Light at the end of the tunnel? Review of "After Crime and Punishment: Pathways to Offender Reintegration", edited by Shadd Maruna and Russ Immarigeon, *Safer Society*, no. 22, 40.

Ward, T. and Maruna, S. (2007) *Rehabilitation*, London: Routledge.

Watts, B. (2008) *What are Today's Social Evils?* York: Joseph Rowntree Foundation.

Weaver, B. (2011) Co-producing community justice: The transformative potential of personalisation for penal sanctions, *British Journal of Social Work*, 41(6), 1038–1057.

Weber, M. (1968) *Economy and Society*, Roth, G. and Claus Wittich, C. (ed.), New York: Bedminister. Translation of edition of *Wirtschaft und Gesellschaft*, fourth revised edition.

Weisburd, D., Lum, C. M. and Petrosino, A. (2001) Does research design affect study outcomes in criminal justice? *The Annals of the American Academy of Political and Social Science*, 578, 50–70.

Weiss, C. H. (1995) Nothing as practical as a good theory: Exploring theory-based evaluation for comprehensive community initiatives for children and families, in Connell, J. P., Kubisch, A. C., Schorr, L. B. and Weiss, C. H. (eds.) *New Approaches to Evaluating Community Initiatives: Concepts, Methods, and Contexts*, Washington, DC: Aspen Institute, 65–92.

Weiss, C. H., Murphy-Graham, E., Petrosino, A. and Gandhi, A. G. (2008) The fairy godmother and her warts: Making the dream of evidence-based policy come true, *American Journal of Evaluation*, vol. 29(1), 29–47.

Welsh, B. and Farrington, D. (2001) Assessing the economic costs and benefits of crime prevention, in Welsh, B., Farrington, D. and Sherman, L. (eds.) *Costs and Benefits of Preventing Crime*, Oxford: Westview Press.

Welsh, B. and Farrington, D. (2006) Evidence-based crime prevention, in Welsh, B. and Farrington, D. (eds.) *Preventing Crime: What Works for Children, Offenders, Victims and Places*, Dordrecht: Springer.

Whitehead, T. (2010) Spending review: Tens of thousands fewer criminals jailed to save money, *The Telegraph*, 21 October. Available at www.telegraph.co.uk/news/uknews/law-and-order/8076476/Spending-review-tens-of-thousands-fewer-criminals-jailed-to-save-money.html [accessed 2 November 2012].

Whitehouse, S. (2010) *Senate Judiciary Committee Approves Bill to Manage Costs and Reduce Prison Population Growth*, 11 March. Available at http://whitehouse.senate.gov/newsroom/press/release/?id=8F4128AB-50F4–492C-8F65–7DED8F4F9C89 [accessed 2 November 2012].

Whiteley, P. (2012) Are Britons getting more dishonest? Available at www.west-info.eu/files/Research11.pdf [accessed 2 November 2012].

Wiles, P. and Costello, A. (2000) *The Road to Nowhere: The Evidence for Travelling Criminals*, Home Office Research Study no. 207, London: Home Office.

Wilson, D. B., Bouffard, L. A. and MacKenzie, D. L. (2005) A quantitative review of structured, group-orientated, cognitive behavioural programs for offenders, *Criminal Justice and Behaviour*, vol. 32(2), 172–204.

Wilson, D. B., Mitchell, O. and Mackenzie, D. L. (2006) A systematic review of drug court effects on recidivism, *Journal of Experimental Criminology*, vol. 2, 459–487.

Wilson, J. Q. and Kelling, G. L. (1982) Broken windows, *The Atlantic Monthly*, March, 29–38.

Wilson, R. (2007) The impact of software on crime mapping, *Social Science Computer Review*, vol. 25(2), 135–142.

Witt, R. and Witte, A. (2000) Crime, prison, and female labor supply, *Journal of Quantitative Criminology*, vol. 16, 69–85.

Wolf, A. (2011) *Review of Vocational Education – The Wolf Report*, London: Department for Education. Available at https://www.education.gov.uk/publications/eOrderingDownload/Wolf-Report.pdf [accessed 2 November 2012].

Wong (forthcoming) The Emperor's new clothes: Can Big Society deliver criminal justice? in Cowburn, M., Senior, P., Robinson, A. and Duggan, M. (eds.) *Values in Criminology and Community Justice*, Bristol: Policy Press.

Wong, K., O'Keeffe, C., Ellingworth, D. and Senior, P. (2012a) *Intensive Alternatives to Custody Process Evaluation of Pilots in Five Areas*, Ministry of Justice Research Series 12/12, London: Home Office.

Wong, K., O'Keeffe, C., Meadows, L., Davidson, J., Bird, H., Wilkinson, K. and Senior, P. (2012b) *Increasing the Voluntary and Community Sector's Involvement in Integrated Offender Management*, London: Home Office.

Wong, K., Sefton, M. and Webb, S. (2011) *IOM Sussex Process Evaluation Report*, Sheffield: Hallam Centre for Community Justice, Sheffield Hallam University.

Young, S. P. (2011) Evidence of democracy? The relationship between evidence-based policy and democratic government, *Journal Of Public Administration And Policy Research*, vol. 3(1), 19–27.

Youth Justice Board (2009) *Youth Rehabilitation Order with Intensive Supervision and Surveillance Operational Guidance*, London: Youth Justice Board.

Index

Page numbers in *italics* denote tables, those in **bold** denote figures.
Throughout the index, the words Justice Reinvestment are abbreviated to 'JR'.